D0934974

For Rushdie

For Rushdie

Essays by Arab and Muslim

Writers in Defense of Free Speech

GEORGE BRAZILLER
NEW YORK

First published in the United States of America in 1994 by George Braziller, Inc.

English translation copyright © 1994 George Braziller, Inc.
Originally published in French

Copyright © 1993 by Editions la Découverte under the title
Pour Rushdie
Cent intellectuels arabes et musulmans pour la liberté d'expression

Original language texts © Copyright the authors

For imformation, write to the publisher:
George Braziller, Inc.
60 Madison Avenue
New York, NY 10010

Library of Congress Cataloging-in-Publication Data

Pour Rushdie, English.
    For Rushdie: a collection of essays by 100 Arabic & Muslim
writers/Anouar Abdallah ...[et al.].
        p. cm.
    ISBN 0-8076-1354-1 (cloth).   ISBN 0-8076-1355-X (pbk)
    1. Rushdie, Salman–Censorship. 2. Censorship–Arab countries.
3. Islam and literature. I. Abdallah, Anouar. II Title.
PR6068.U757Z8313   1994
823' 914—dc20   93-46999
                                                        CIP

Contents

Translators

Publisher's Statement

On November 3, 1993, *The New York Times* carried a story on a book, newly published in France by Editions la Decouverte, entitled *Pour Rushdie*. Assembled were 100 essays by Arab and Muslim writers expressing more than their support for Salman Rushdie's novel *The Satanic Verses*, a work considered blasphemous against Islam by Ayatollah Khomeini who, in 1989, issued a *fatwa*, or death sentence, against its author that Muslim extremists have refused to lift. The writers of *Pour Rushdie* proclaimed their active support for freedom of expression as a universal right.

The book has given us a chance to reflect on the fact that the right to freedom of expression is one that we often take for granted. For writers without such liberties, or even for their colleagues, opposition often brings about tangible suffering. Not only has the Italian translator of *The Satanic Verses* been seriously wounded, but its Japanese translator has been killed. Needless to say, Rushdie himself has lived under threat of death for the past five years. Newspapers have been filled with stories about other Muslim and Arab writers who have lived and died under similar conditions. One of Egypt's foremost intellectuals, Farag Fouda, to whom homage is paid several times in this volume, was murdered by fundamentalists in June 1992. In December, Algerian poet and teacher Youssef Sebti was found with his throat cut in his room at the National Institute for Agronomy. Saudi Arabian poet Sadiq Melallah was decapitated. Taslima Nasrin, a novelist, newspaper columnist, and poet, lives in Bangladesh under a *fatwa* as well, without knowing why. In the same situation lives Masour Farhang, a professor of politics at Bennington University. And the list continues.

The writers of this volume essentially state that "one idea can only be opposed by another idea" (Naguib Mahfouz), that to condemn any writer to death for his ideas is intolerable and constitutes a disgrace both to the nation that they love and to the tolerant religion that has collectively nourished them for centuries. In an extraordinary collective act of courage, 127 Iranian writers, arguably those most in danger, risked their safety to sign a statement of support for Salman Rushdie.

We hope that the publication of this book will forcefully convey the tremendous courage of all of the writers who contributed to it. As readers and publishers, we join their efforts to keep the essence of this book—the fundamental necessities of human rights and freedom of expression—alive.

—George Braziller

For Rushdie

Preface

One of the mysteries that surrounds Salman Rushdie could be the troubling coincidence (of which some actually had a presentiment) between his novel and the events that have followed its publication. The logic is that of a certain Borges-style humor that somehow got out of hand and turned into a real-life fundamentalist nightmare. The Rushdie affair itself could be the most demented of all the visions of Farishta, the novel's main character: described in a barbed cluster of meaningful expressions and characterized also by violence marking a pause in the delirium of a schizophrenic. At this point the story would go on, more charged than ever, turning around like a band of Moebius, and then, in a sort of sulfurous interregnum, or end-of-an-era situation in which all states become confused and values inverted, a veritable jumble of persons and qualities would come out all mixed together: the flying imam would brush up against the surrealistic supporters of Khomeini, the archangel in the vision of the crazy man would stand in contrast against all the iridescent images in the media—and all the views exchanged between East and West. Finally, the metamorphic drift of the emigrant Shamsha, brought back at the end of his journey, would then be contrasted with the current forced exile of Rushdie, alone a real person among all these specters.

A strange halo hangs over this author and his work; and the work and the author are henceforth indissolubly linked. If the prism is more or less perceived in the West, its colors are too often unknown in the East, where the prohibited book can be known only through partial and incomplete—and biased—information. Four years after the *fatwa* against him was issued, nothing originating in this part of the eastern world has come along to give any comfort to Rushdie; the governments in this part of the world have generally upheld the censorship against the book. And far from stimulating discussion and debate on the relationship between the identity and current exile of the author and the cause of it all, *The Satanic Verses* continues to create misunderstandings. Transformed into a pawn in a dangerous game of geopolitics, Rushdie, in the eyes of great masses of people, remains the exile, the outlaw, the apostate—the one who caused the whole scandal in the first place. His own mixed origins, his political leanings, his previous writings, in short, his entire uncommon destiny—all these things remain unknown in the East.

In this whole affair which pits literature against the law, very probably the mere title of his novel—a title that, by itself, includes all the deadly connotations of the affair—would have sufficed to condemn him. It would seem that for too many who are ignorant of the true historical episode concerning the Prophet Muhammad—so often deliberately concealed, though reported on here by several authors—merely to associate the devil with the sacred in any way would already indicate a sacrilegious intention. Thus, the very title of the book has been substituted for the absent book itself, becoming the proof and symbol of the whole affair. Blasphemy and death which strike or threaten as a consequence are in effect themselves clearly satanic in this particular case; so is the miserable uproar brought about by some and the furious anger on the part of others (manifestations that betray the qualities of reserve normally so important to Muslims); so is the cursed isolation which has resulted. And floating above it all, there is descried the hand of the West; there are all the angry beards of the mullahs and, not least, the vaguely sardonic smile of the author himself: his image floats above all this overexposed but nevertheless highly equivocal drama, swathed in shadows. Philosophers might point out here the theatrical nature of language itself, how superstition craftily moves to ensure its own efficacy. What has emerged from this is the worst kind of taboo, one that is made even worse by the intermittent way the whole thing has been treated in the midst of the other events of the day.

Everything proceeds, once more, as if the whole thing were merely a rhetorical war or a simple conflict of images in which the loquacious West goes up against an East which is characterized either by the heaviest blanket of silence or by howls and cries of the mob calling for a lynching. It is as if the whole affair did not strictly concern the modern class of petrified intellectuals who are here being put to the test; as if there were not an enormous occasion here for them to be surprised that a writer should have to live as a recluse, should be deprived of his rights, and should see the circulation and recognition of his works effectively banned. Or, again, as if oppression over here and religious zeal over there, combined with apathy and indifference just about everywhere else, had not finally prevailed in this case over the desire for freedom, over the promptings of compassion, and over what should have been intellectual rebellion against terror. What we see here is a type of inconsistency which has been chronic in our world, and which has been verified on more than one occasion.

This book aims to break into this whole unhappy state of affairs and give prominence to a school of thought that, even when it is not muzzled by state power, is both little known and largely misunderstood in the West. There have already been a number of people who are motivated as a point of honor never to let down their guard, and who are operating in their own isolated circles, whether in Beirut, Cairo, Tunis, or certain European cities. It is at this point that we have now assembled a hundred prominent names from both the Maghreb and the Arab East, as well as from Iran, Turkey, the Sudan, Bangladesh, and the Muslim countries of the former Soviet Union; included are writers, thinkers, artists, filmmakers. They are, for the most part, men and women of influence and renown, and they have all been brought together here to testify in favor of Rushdie.

The invitation issued to them was of the simplest kind: it mentioned first of all the simple desire to express support for and solidarity with the author of *The Satanic Verses*. But the invitation was also conceived both as a manifestation in favor of freedom of expression and as a political act (however minimal it might seem) bearing upon

3

the issue with which it is concerned. Space for a response to the invitation was limited to roughly two pages. The invitation was issued primarily to Muslims, but also to some Christians operating within the same cultural sphere, either those subject to the same kind of regime of censorship or otherwise possibly subject to threats arising out of religious fanaticism. The invitations were all issued from Paris, and followed one after another. Considerable cross-checking of names was done so that the choice of respondents was limited neither by hearsay contacts only nor by contacts limited to a single network; and no limitations were placed upon where the invitations were sent. Paris might as well be a Muslim capital, as is widely understood; and a Paris return address creates a very different impression than a Cairo or Algiers address, so it is not surprising that the Muslim diaspora is very widely represented in this book. Great attention was paid to the subject matter itself, both as an object of current scandal and as a private preoccupation.

Rushdie: the name echoes like a stone dropped down a well; and like a true gravitational force, the name immediately attracted many adherents, who expressed neither any qualifications, nor any uncertainty, nor even any perceptible embarrassment. It was remarkable that there were less than twenty turn-downs returned in response to the invitations sent out. Only one or two abusive responses came back. Only three of the texts in this collection, which were written earlier, have been previously published.

Thus it was that silence, indifference, and division on the issue raised by Rushdie's condemnation have been overcome and a group has been constituted—one would almost be tempted to say a possible community has been constituted—which has made its own without reservation the causes of freedom of expression and creativity and the causes of refusal of obscurantism and the death penalty—has made its own, in short, the cause of saving Salman Rushdie. In other terms, since all these causes are as interrelated as the two sides of a coin, it must be emphasized that everything said in these pages has reference to a group of intellectuals operating within the Islamic *Umma*, or religious community, and within the Muslim cultural sphere; these intellectuals unconditionally oppose the *fatwa* that was issued by imams and subsequently reiterated by them. The intellectuals who have contributed to this volume take the part and adopt the cause of a writer who, though an atheist, has been accused of blasphemy. Nor is it in any way neutral or indifferent to note that in taking such a position they are going against their own rulers and certainly against public opinion in their own countries. It is necessary to recognize that for populations for whom the values of modernity are alien, religious law explains the meaning and consistency of the world; it prevails over all purely civil norms and, in particular, over those foundational human rights we call "the rights of man." However such a traditional public opinion may be affected by an unfortunate phrase used, or even by the outrage (or what was perceived as outrage) that resulted from its use, the fact remains that such a public opinion is still normally more inclined to leave such things to a divine judgment than to resort themselves to blood.

The essential thing, though, goes beyond this, and the essential thing is that these intellectuals have broken through the magic circle of threats and isolation which were intended to strike at the condemned apostate; they are moving out in the open, thus filling the void initially created by terror. It can even be asserted that by exposing themselves to the vindictiveness of the fundamentalists (thereby putting themselves at risk of sharing the same fate as Rushdie himself), they have in a sense substituted themselves for those singled out and called to act by the *fatwa*: "the defenders of the true faith," who have in effect been summoned to commit murder by the *fatwa*. This does not mean that the texts included here in any way respond directly to the sentence affirmed by the *fatwa*; rather, they place the whole issue in a number of different perspectives, denying the authority of mere power and blind force. Often they are based on premises other than religious (even while bearing Islam strongly in mind). By enunciating principles, they signal resistance; and by the pledges they offer, they supply testimonials in favor of morality and of art; and so they constitute a new kind of authority and sovereignty. In this regard, it is not terribly important how much this book comes to be actually appreciated. Without doubt, some of the contributors themselves were offended by the work of desacralization undertaken by Rushdie. Beyond all their differences, though—religious people versus secular people, exponents of a theory of liberal universalism versus partisans of Islamic law—they form a unified group rallying around someone who has been the victim of an absolute wrong (a wrong done to the man, to the author, to the citizen, and to the literary work). They henceforth now embody the struggle that has proved to be necessary; all these protests, appeals, analyses, and cries from the heart represent so many assembled voices directed into the currently devastated city that is Islam today. In fact, Islam succumbs all the more readily to archaic practices today, where oppression remains the rule, and where destitution is allied with ignorance.

Even while they definitely point to an ideal, these intellectual voices are nevertheless very heavily constrained by the particular difficulties of our times. This collection, which was put together between October 1992 and June 1993, is thus not limited to merely reflecting the nature of the crisis. Rather, it sets forth both its causes and its effects, dwelling on them, being carried along by them, in fact, and bringing out and amalgamating events that might at first sight have been considered unrelated to the Rushdie story. These voices also betray a certain bitterness, an ancient lassitude. Four years after the event constitutes a period of time that supposedly should have indicated a critical distance. In point of fact, in these texts, the whole affair has been greatly broadened and deepened, and its salient points identified. Is it not generally a characteristic of such celebrated affairs as the "Rushdie affair" to bring out so many related difficulties beyond the immediate causes of the affair itself, meanwhile unearthing new antagonisms and implications of all that is at stake in this case?

Similarly, the question also has to be asked what there is in common among the repeated bombardments of Baghdad, the agony of Sarajevo, and the fate of Salman Rushdie. Actually, there is very little in common among them, if the truth were known—except that media projections show violent clashes taking place between two blocs, between two cultures which, formerly, lived together in peace and tolerated one another as discrete entities, agreeing to diverge from one another with neither obfuscation nor mutual rejection. Two years after the establishment of the "new world order," with its key foundation based on the West having been demonstrated by the application of incommensurable force, the very number of Iraqi war victims still remains unknown, and no analytical work has been produced taking the measure of the event itself. Elsewhere, during roughly the same time period, Muslims are being exterminated in the very heart of Europe. A wartime logic has already more or less established itself on the basis of the leonine principle of "two weights, two measures." Already the lack of symmetry is flagrant between the denial of the consequences of the Gulf War in the West, and the silent diffusion of misery and impotence in the Arab world in particular which has resulted from it.

Moreover, it is difficult even to measure the real impact of the tragedy in Bosnia, notably as regards the so-called "ethnic cleansing," except that it surely confirms within the spirit of the Arab and Muslim masses (insofar as they are aware of it) a will to destructiveness, a markedly hostile attitude that is reinforced by a multitude of other grievances, ranging from perceived consent to injustice, to plunder, and to acquiescence in simple vulgarity—indeed to all of the modern expressions of everything from ordinary racism to the enormous current prevailing ignorance of Islam as such. Then there is the support accorded to the worst of the feudal-type states under the banner of unlimited mercantilism. All these things are significant, especially when added to the phenomenon of actual armed conflict.

The malaise today in the Muslim world is immense; and it is in no way relieved—far from it—by the current internal crisis. Based on despair, it seizes on everything, whether near or remote, that tends to manifest the power of the West and prove its duplicity. Everything which evokes these realities functions like a detonator already automatically set and ready to go off. Thus, "the rights of man" in particular become fatally undermined from the start by suspicion; the very notion of universality is no sooner mentioned and treated as if it had been handed down from above than it is derided, subjected to such things as reasons of state, and then most likely pushed out of sight. Take, for instance, the basic notions of freedom of expression and the right to one's life. As they relate to Rushdie, we should recall that he is a British citizen, taken under the wing of another state; thus he is "protected." He is the author of a difficult, opaque book touching upon ultra-sensitive subjects in a time of troubles and acute religious intolerance. Rushdie could not help finding himself at the crucial meeting point of all these various runaway events. Nevertheless he found himself defended, though not without the expression of some reservations and recriminations. He was involved in an order extending far beyond himself and his situation, an order from which, as an authentic third worlder, he always kept his distance anyway.

Many of the texts collected here speak of the double constraint that exists here; it has been rendered more complicated still by internal opposition to the Islamic state. For if the West often appears as the adversary, there remains still another internal enemy more stifling yet, a common enemy; it amounts to a more or less declared form of native fascism, the true virulence of which, however, has certainly been slow to be realized. This collection includes works by certain authors who, like Rushdie, suffer from the threat of criminal penalties decreed in *fatwas* issued against them, and thus they too are subject to a veritable army of potential enforcers of justice. This book project was just about completed when the death of Tahar Djaout occurred, thus bringing to light further evidence of the fact that an overall strategy has been developed in the wake of the Rushdie affair; it became clear that his case was neither new nor isolated. Though this strategy scarcely represents a unified effort, it proceeds not only from a hatred of free thought but from a global will to eradicate minorities everywhere (women, intellectuals, homosexuals, foreigners); it can indeed change, if not actually break, the unity of the Islamic *Umma*. More than one person has paid with his life for the crime of intellectual audacity or courage in resisting fanatics: the Egyptian Farag Foda, to whom homage is several times paid in these pages; Mahmoud Mohammed Taha, the Sudanese theologian hanged by

Nemeiry; and Sadiq Melallah, the Saudi Arabian poet who was decapitated. One of the additional merits of this collection, then, is to call attention to these names. In the ruins of our deserted central cities, where idle youth with no work to do gather, these victims were among those who dared to confront the inadmissible and were thus able to declare, in effect, that Islam is not dying merely because of the dogmatism of the mullahs and other worn-out clerics; it is also dying from the terrorism carried out in its name by the official political classes.

Thus, a few intellectuals, even though divided, are still attempting to hold the line against a supposed "end of history," which alternates with an apparently irremediable decadence—or, if one prefers, against the utter caricatures of the two modern forms of nihilism. (One form, to express it briefly, refuses to withdraw from the political process, rejects any notion of anybody being able to live together, and indeed exhibits a marked loss of the sense of the reality of the world. The other form of caricatured nihilism represents a closing off of any access to the political process, a totalitarian presence in the community and over everything else, and in general, a slowdown if not a paralysis.) The media, whose role cannot be neglected, have generally identified the two polarities of the problem, though without realizing its seriousness. In fact, the stage has been set in such a way that those rare local actions in defense of human rights neither find support nor do any tangible repercussions flow from them, for it is the fundamentalists themselves who, in a remarkable way, are the masters of the media of communications in the matter. As a generalization, the Rushdie affair has focused both sides on the very worst aspects; this is true with regard to both mutual frustrations as well as all the excesses exhibited. And for the most part it has served the interests of the reactionaries and the hypocrites. However, the case can also now serve to favor new regroupings, new questionings, and new exchanges.

One thing is certain: Rushdie, a polyglot scholar and a truly multicultural man, is very much the bard of the mixed and the impure. Rushdie, who presents in his writings the divisions between human beings and the disparities between societies, is someone who both brings together and divides and separates. Or, more precisely, it is by Rushdie that are revealed the internal divisions and lacerations of the intellectuals, their general malaise, their oscillation between two extremes—a state of affairs that is ultimately untenable. Out of all this ambivalence arises the ambivalence that more than one of these intellectuals feels with regard to Rushdie. Certain of them support him; at the same time they denigrate him, dwelling on such things as his arrogance and provocative and fantastic vanity—that of a spoiled child playing with a powder keg, it is thought. Others recognize both his talent and the far-reaching literary significance of his work; at the same time they continue to regard him as a traitor, someone who has furnished arms to the enemy and sown serious disorder within an already ill-governed Islamic community. Yet others, who have had access to *The Satanic Verses*, sometimes see nothing in the book but a practically delirious jumble denoting a highly alien sensibility for which virtually everything slips away and escapes in the end: everything from the very dense arrangement and ordering of the novel to its syntax, the imaginary as represented in its Indian component, Joycean in all its postmodern jokes and witticisms—and all this is brought out without speaking of the episodes themselves. For such a stirring up and casting down of virtually everything, one might have wished for a more representative object: something classical, transparent. But for that one might as well have been thinking of other times than ours as well. On the other hand, all those who have been able to appreciate *The Satanic Verses* certainly have to be grateful to Rushdie for his ambition. With him the prophetic gesture has been opened up to the four winds of the imaginary, and the whole question of his exile has also now been freely posed in all its modalities. Those whom the book pleases know that its text was always destined for them in particular.

The Editors
Paris, July 1993

Why Is It Necessary to
Defend Salman Rushdie?

by Anouar Abdallah

I will begin with a remark of a general nature: my support for the cause of Salman Rushdie is based upon the immense admiration I have for his writings. Moreover, there exist, in our Arab and Islamic history, other great writer-thinkers who boldly undertook to mount a critique of religion on rationalist grounds. One could cite in this connection Ibn al-Rawandi, Abu 'Issa al-Warraq, and the physician al-Razi, as well as the leaders of the Qarmatians who said such things as, for example: "Let us admit that the Prophet Muhammad was the most eloquent of all the Arabs and that the Koran was his principal miracle. How is it the fault of other peoples, though, that they do not happen to know Arabic?"

One could also cite the case of Professor Abdallah al-Qasimi, who is actually a contemporary, and who has written, notably, that "it is the Universe that judges the divinity."

I must mention the fact that certain spirits even among the secularists have avoided giving their support to Rushdie on the pretext that he was probably being pushed by forces hostile to Islam all along. But this is a very fragile argument that in no way justifies their attitude. To defend this author is a question of principle, and it is of little importance whether his book is the fruit of personal conviction, or whether he somehow yielded to external solicitations. In either case

---

Sociologist, Saudia Arabia. Originally written in Arabic.

we must still condemn the *fatwa* issued by the imam, the Ayatollah Khomeini. In the first case, our support of Rushdie would rest on the principle of freedom of expression, regardless of the intrinsic value of the text being defended. Let us add too that it is up to the adversary party, the Khomeinists, to respond to Rushdie in kind, namely, with the pen, not by calling for the shedding of his blood. In the second case, the democratic and secularist forces are the ones being aimed at by the *fatwa* anyway; the goal is to intimidate them. We must in the first instance, therefore, analyze this particular *fatwa* carefully in order to show the dangers it contains and what its effects are likely to be. But let us also be careful not to allow ourselves to get bogged down in the labyrinth of what political Islam happens to be today. For the distance is very great indeed between this new Islam and the historic Islam, as I have explained elsewhere. The fact is that this *fatwa* evidences a number of very disquieting features.

The Return of the Figure of the Holy Man

It is not given to just any ulema, even a famous one, to be able to issue *fatwas* that will be carried out by enforcers everywhere. The ulemas of al-Azhar in Cairo, for example, have issued dozens of "religious opinions," including the one that authorized the shedding of the blood of Tunisian President Habib Bourguiba because he advocated back in 1965 making peace with Israel. That *fatwa* was never carried out by anyone, of course; but a fortiori nobody ever even knew about it, either. If Rached Ghannouchi or Abbas Madani had ever promulgated such a *fatwa*, nobody would have paid the slightest attention to it; or, at any rate, it would have been considered nothing but another maneuver in the psychological and media war going on. All that is required, though, is for one of those types of ulema to achieve actual political power, and then such *fatwas* as he might issue suddenly become invested with a sacred character that does call for actually carrying them out. This new sacred character resides in the fact that the *fatwa* in question is now imposed with the authority of the state and in its name. The Ayatollah Khomeini was earlier one of the religious authorities of the Shiite community;

because of this, his accession to political power in 1979 transformed him into a unique kind of authority, whose reach extended all over the world, even while he continued to be the supreme political and spiritual guide of the Islamic Republic of Iran. He thus became "the door leading to the Mahdi to come"; and he was thus distinguished both by the strength of his partisans and importance of his base. Although he has now been dead for more than two years, no Iranian dignitary—such as, for example, President Rafsanjani—has dared to cancel the *fatwa*, which meanwhile has become effectively lodged in the collective mentality of the people; and now the whole thing is henceforth inseparable from the perpetuation of the regime.

In view of all this, it is important to note the essential difference between a purely political tyranny and a politico-religious type of tyranny. Political tyranny finds a perfect model in Stalin. No sooner is a Stalin dead, however, than his comrades proceed to trample on his tomb; the same thing was true of a Franco. In the case of this new tyranny of the politico-religious type, however, the leader retains his sacred character even after his death. For a long time after his departure from the scene, in fact, the destiny of the living still remains linked to his memory. The tree of this new kind of tyranny has very deep roots; these roots are both solidly grounded and extensive, and thus they are very difficult to uproot.

The Planetary Character of the New Tyranny

Salman Rushdie published his book neither in Qum, Shiraz, nor Isfahan, but in London. He is not even an Iranian citizen. Nevertheless, the world has seen the *fatwa* issued against him move across three continents in search of its intended victim—as if, after having cut down all the standing grain in the country itself, the sickle then had to go in search of a few more stray stalks in foreign fields; or as if the solutions to the numerous and complicated problems of Iranian society were dependent upon the spilling of the blood of Salman Rushdie. Thus, the *fatwa* of Khomeini reveals to us the planetary character of this new tyranny that sets aside the laws and customs of other states.

Pride and Emulation

No sooner had this *fatwa* been issued than the Saudi-Wahhabi machinery also began to function in order to demonstrate to the world its own attachment to tradition as well as to reiterate its own character as an authentic representative of pure Islam. Indeed, jealousy, as well as the desire to emulate Iran, literally ate at the hearts of the Saudi-Wahhabi rivals of the Khomeinists; and they themselves began issuing *fatwas* too, excommunicating both the living and the dead without distinction. In 1988, a book appeared in which more than a hundred literary figures were made the object of a global anathema; implicated were, notably, such as Salama Moussa, Shibli Shmayyil, Naguib Mahfouz, Lufti al-Sayyid, Said 'Aql, and Adonis. In September 1992, the Wahhabis went further; in the great public square of the city of Qatif, they proceeded to execute Sadiq Melallah, who had been accused of being an unbeliever. They would never have gone this far if they had not been encouraged by the *fatwa* of Khomeini; this *fatwa* opened up the fatal path to this execution. The same thing is true of Egypt, where the extremist religious forces assassinated Farag Foda on the pretext of his being in favor of secularization. Earlier, it was General Nemeiry who had Sheikh Taha killed in the Sudan under pressure from the same Saudi-Wahhabi power.

Blackmail

The deadly *fatwa* is now to be found among the police records in the West, where it serves as a means of pressure and of blackmail; it provides the means to take action against this or that secular thinker or writer who, on the outs with an Islamic state, must either knuckle under with regard to the powers that be and remain silent, or else be forced out of countries where refuge has been found— and therefore with a very uncertain future ahead. By now the police in the West know how to exploit these *fatwas* for their own advantage, at the same time that the multiplication of such *fatwas* provides emigrant intellectuals with strong incentives to resign themselves to unfavorable living conditions in order to remain outside of the reach of the authorities pursuing them.

Our insistence upon affirming the freedoms of thought, of expression, and of publication for Rushdie is not aimed merely at assuring the mental and moral equilibrium of this one man. Rather, it also aims to bar the way against all who those are both bloodthirsty and apparently prepared to traffic in religion to gain their ends. Rushdie employed his pen only; those who oppose him should reply with logical arguments, not by calling on the sword of the state.

On the Subject of Rushdie

by Etel Adnan

The "affair" of *The Satanic Verses* arouses in me a flood of questions and emotions. It is evident that Salman Rushdie, who was raised in a Muslim milieu, knew very well that he was subjecting to ridicule the beliefs and sentiments of hundreds of millions of Muslim believers, and that in their eyes he was committing a sacrilege.

Nonetheless, his condemnation to death is no less acceptable for all of that. This condemnation is contrary to the spirit of Islam, in which the individual is ultimately responsible for his acts, *morally speaking*, to God alone. It is also contrary to the spirit of pardon, which is one of the divine attributes on which the Koran insists most strongly and in a constant and absolute fashion.

It would therefore be desirable if this question could be placed in a larger context—for example, by making a comparison with the genocide against the Muslims of Bosnia. People have the right to be Muslims—believing and practicing Muslims—just as they have the right not to be. Above all, people have the right to their own lives and their own possessions, whether these possessions are intellectual, ethnic, or religious. The time has come for dialogue to replace repression; the time has come for all the various inquisitions to disappear. The dignity of the human body and spirit is what most concerns me about this whole question. Such things cannot be imposed upon; they can only be lived.

Writer, Libya. Originally written in French.

Even the Sun . . .

by Adonis

1

Even the sun
Illuminates only what can receive its light.

2

Ah! The sky
That climbs the neck of the earth.

3

I know how to weave with the threads of the earth
A dress for the sky,
But I do not yet know how to weave with the threads
of the sky
A dress for the earth.

4

You will not know how to be a candle
Unless you rest on your shoulder at night.

5

Many dead around us
Where bury them except in language.

Poet, Libya. Originally written in Arabic.

6

The shadow is not the negation of the sun
But its other light.

7

O, you who rush upon the waves,
How can you hope that the shore will receive you?

8

Truth is not the sword
Nor the hand that holds it.
It is the point that ties the one to the other.

9

Everything inhabits the earth,
And the sky inhabits the sky.
Why then do you ask:
Which of the two is more beautiful, more vast?

10

May the rays and the fire of your silence
Warm you.

The Rushdie Affair in France

by Farid Aïchoun

It was Friday, the day of prayer. In a small Algerian cafe in the Golden Drop quarter, an animated discussion was going on between the customers concerning the latest news: the American air strikes on Baghdad. At the counter, a group of young men were drinking what was apparently beer. At the same time in the mosque across the way, there could be seen, through the embrasures of the windows, white-robed and hooded figures prostrating themselves in prayer. Four years earlier, the imam of the mosque in Bradford, Great Britain, approved of the burning of *The Satanic Verses* by his congregation at the same time that he declared that he could not subscribe to the "incitement to murder" that had been launched against the author of that book, the writer Salman Rushdie. Indeed, the imam in Britain had counseled his faithful to demonstrate "proof of their wisdom"; at the same time he had made clear that "Khomeini was perhaps the spiritual leader of Iran, but that did not necessarily mean that he was the spiritual leader of all Muslims."

In France, the Salman Rushdie affair never really unleashed any serious passions. The multiplicity of tendencies among the Muslims of France is such that it is sometimes difficult even to find an inter-locutor to discuss certain of these tendencies. The most important tendency is that of the Islam of the Maghreb as imported into France: there is to be found in this tendency a rather broad mixture,

Journalist, Algeria/France. Originally written in French.

including some pre-Islamic and Maraboutic (cult of holy men) traditions, and also traditions based on the teachings of the ulemas (or doctors of the faith). But even the Muslim groups that have sometimes agitated about other things here never accorded too much importance to the Rushdie affair. Sheikh Abdelhamid Zbantout, who has been installed in France since 1938, declared: "It is not for Khomeini to issue such a *fatwa* (decree). Naturally, I am indignant that anyone should write that the Prophet received his revelation from Satan and not from the Archangel Gabriel. However, when you come upon a madman, there is absolutely no point in trying to show that you are madder than he is."

Is the *Fatwa* a *Fatwa?*

by Sadik J. Al-Azm

In this brief contribution to the Arab/Muslim volume saluting Salman Rushdie the author, and expressing solidarity with his plight, I would like to put on the table the question of whether the notorious *fatwa* issued by the Ayatollah Khomeini against Rushdie is really a *fatwa* in the first place. This is neither an academic exercise nor a purely theoretical investigation, but a matter of great practical relevance to any strategy (and tactics) for helping Rushdie the prisoner, writer, and human being transcend the debilitating impasse in which he finds himself locked at present.

From the very start it seemed to me that the Ayatollah Khomeini's celebrated *fatwa* did not read like a *fatwa*; nor did it have the form, texture, and feel of what Muslims—both Sunni and Shiite—would commonly recognize as a *fatwa*. For a *fatwa* normally takes the form of a response, a dispensation, a practical solution, a way out addressed to the problems, paradoxes, anomalies, puzzles, and such that life throws up constantly in the face of the faithful, be they the high and mighty or the poor and humble. Thus, a *fatwa*'s most common function is the circumvention of the application of the letter of the law to avoid unnecessary injury to life, limb, property, family, community, and so on. This is why a good mufti is invariably a bad Muslim. This is also why the practice of issuing *fatwas* is mostly associated in common Arabic parlance with such not-quite-honorable

---

Philosopher, Syria. Originally written in English.

practices as hair splitting, verbal quibbling, vulgar casuistry, the drawing of Jesuitical distinctions, the torturing of texts, the unprincipled bending of principles and servility to the powers that be.

The above considerations are vitally important for the often-raised question of whether the so-called *fatwa* is rescindable, retractable, and/or circumventable. In fact, it would have been in Rushdie's favor had Khomeini's *fatwa* really been a proper *fatwa*, because the procedural rules and conventions for dealing with such dispensations are well known, well established, and well observed by all those concerned. Furthermore, a *fatwa* can be counteracted, diluted, moderated, or invalidated by another *fatwa* issued by an equally competent *'alim*, sheikh, mufti, *faqih*, or juri-consult. In principle any person who regards himself versed in Muslim law and doctrine and finds others willing to follow and listen to him is entitled to produce *fatwas* on this or that matter of life's affairs, large and small. His *fatwas* are not binding except to those who accept his opinions as a juri-consult. For example, the assassins of President Sadat of Egypt sought and obtained a *fatwa* from a trusted sheikh of their own, allowing them to proceed with their plan to kill the apostate president. In the end, the fact that Ayatollah Khomeini's so-called *fatwa* became so potent is an affair of the state, power politics, and revolution, and not an affair of faith, Muslim theology, and *shariah* law.

In essence, Khomeini's supposed *fatwa* is really a judgment, a call and a death sentence the imam, the grand mufti, the *faqih*, and so on authorizes himself in moments of grave danger to Islam and for the defense of the integrity of the faith and the sanctity of the *Umma*. Under such extraordinary circumstances, the jurist (*faqih*) may also call upon and permit any Muslim to carry out the sentence without further ado. Now, because such a sentence is not really a *fatwa*, it is neither revocable nor contractible. Only the disappearance of the peril to Islam that brought it about in the first place would invalidate it in the sense of rendering it obsolete and immaterial. Since it is not handed down by a properly constituted court—Islamic or otherwise—it is not appealable. In other words, it is purely political, discretionary, and in this case, of charismatic origins to boot.

What does this mean for Rushdie and for those trying to help save him? It means the following: stop trying to make the clerical hierarchy in Iran admit that they made a mistake by insisting on the withdrawal of the *fatwa*. The only practical course of action is to desist from raising the issue any further, to let the dust settle, to consign it to benign neglect; look to the future, and proceed forward after absorbing the so-called *fatwa*. In other words, the best policy is to *aufgehoben* the *fatwa* in Hegel's literal sense of the term. Thus all efforts, personal, public, private, official, political, and so on, should be directed at pressuring clerical Iran in that direction. Above all do not forget that it was only in November 1992 that the Catholic church's clerical hierarchy formally admitted having done nothing wrong to Galileo! Remember that the mills of the gods grind very slowly on both sides of the East-West divide, and try to learn a thing or two from the historical experience of the Catholic church in never admitting to a major error, but always proceeding forward to *aufgehoben* that error after assimilating it. Last but not least, do not expect the Western powers to put any of their vital interests with Iran in jeopardy for the sake of a mere writer and an individual novelist: "an author on a book tour," as President George Bush dismissed Rushdie's last visit to the U.S.

Rushdie, the Traitor

by Aziz Al-Azmeh

The Rushdie affair is many different things. Considering how it
has persisted, one of its most important aspects is how it has
revealed the development and crystallization of a new "holy family"
on a worldwide scale; it is a "family" that has arisen out of a rather
improbable combination of events whose effects have also turned
out to involve rather considerable fallout. This family has arisen out
of a misalliance between two basic partners, Western and Islamic,
each one driven and fecundated in turn by various factors, both
concordant and discordant. The whole thing is thus really an illegitimate child begotten out of an authentic Machiavellianism. On the
Islamic side there has been a temporary marriage between a radical
Islamic fundamentalism that exists on an international scale, and a
worldwide cultural type of Islamism characterized by various institutions seeking more activist roles and also characterized by the
presence of many formerly leftist intellectuals anxious to prove their
own cultural virginity (which, however, they have only recently
acquired!). For all these various elements, Rushdie appears to be a
traitor filled with self-hatred, inner-directed, transcendentalist,
subhistorical—or else as someone whose identity has been assigned
to him from the outside along the lines of Islamic finalist-type categories as a result of a rather extraordinary combination of circumstances. On the Western side of this temporary "marriage" are to be

Academic, Syria/Great Britain. Originally written in English.

found both the various enemies of Rushdie, whether they are secularist, Christian, or Jewish, and also some others in the same general
categories who, however, happen to like Rushdie and wish him well.
All of these, friends as well as enemies, like their Muslim opposite
numbers who are all participating in the same *danse macabre* around
him, see Rushdie as a reprobate, a traitor to his own kind. All of
them, indeed, if we are to believe their often expressed zeal for the
(rather exotic) integrity of what for them has to be, however, a
wholly imaginary Islam, believe that he must "face up" to what has
happened to him. At the same time, though, according to these
same "friends," it is necessary to save him; for he represents a kind
of avatar of Westernism, especially since he keeps his distance from
today's perceived barbarism, itself hearkening back to a former age,
one that was once an integral part of Rushdie's own previous
Muslim essence.

It is out of this whole welter and jumble of incongruous elements that Rushdie the pariah has been produced. He is considered
to have treated his own with condescension; he has served to expose
their crude and rough identity to the whole world as an identity that
has been fashioned out of a combination of archaism and rigid
unchangeableness; it is an identity that is seen as devoid of any hope
and bereft of the slightest trace of any modernity. Nevertheless it is
an identity that is single and homogeneous, easily recognizable, and
alien. Such are the usual terms that are employed in the characteristic discourse on the subject of this particular exotic identity; the
terms suggest a condition of congenital deprivation. All this is what
has been devoured by *The Satanic Verses*. Yet it is precisely this very
contemporary discourse on the same basic identity that is handled
so roughly in the book itself, where it is treated with a marvelously
sharp eye both as regards the past and the present; it is also handled
with a peerless intelligence and talent. There is the new and totally
"super-Islamized" Muslim; there is the new and totally "super-
Islamized" Islam—these are precisely the fantasies that are explod-
ed in the book along with a certain common type of Western narcissism. And one of the effects of this radical calling of everything into

question is to make an important contribution to a battle that is currently going on in all Muslim-majority countries, particularly the Arab countries. This ongoing battle is between religious reaction and the modern enlightened critical spirit of which Rushdie himself is such a brilliant representative. This same battle has been going on in the life of Muslims for more than a century in various guises. Certainly the Joycean and Rabelaisian features of Rushdie's work are neither novel nor marginal—except in the exotic-type discourse concerning "super-Islamized" Muslims which is to be found in some of the commentaries on this author's work, whether hostile or friendly.

The result of the emergence of the new "holy family" arising out of the temporary misalliance between East and West on the subject of Rushdie, then, is to obscure and foreclose on current reality itself; it is to preclude the possibility of carrying on with the ongoing battle; it is to conceal and mask the fact that the critical position taken by Rushdie is actually essential to the modern historical development of the Arab and Muslim worlds. This development already enjoys substantial social support in those worlds, though. So it is legitimate to ask whether the foreclosure of reality effected by the erecting of the screen of "false literature" does not, on the one hand, obscure and hide the "super-Islamization" that is involved; and on the other hand, whether it does not close off the West itself from real contact with the "barbarians" (a perception of them reenforced by the West's own racism), helping to prevent their participation in the democratic and pluralistic postmodern culture. This foreclosure of reality also serves to establish the appearance of authenticity for the "barbarism" in question. Does not all this serve to divide the world for the benefit of the North—a North that is in fact not open to the humanity of all, but that is nevertheless surrounded by a myriad of those who are different from it and who are thereby revealed to it in all their repellent and transcendentalist specificity as being barbarians easily led by the nose by dictators with thaumaturgic pretensions? Are these latter not supposed to represent the authentic identity of their own masses, their maximum historical achievement, the limits of their historicity, indeed the essence of their deprivations? The corralling of others into this same notion of a single authentic culture, and the closing out of respect for other cultures—both of these things represent new attempts to stop the course of history and to divert it for the benefit of the North. Is not a Jean-Marie Le Pen the natural complement and corollary of the FIS? Are they not really each other's doubles? And do not *The Satanic Verses*, therefore, precisely constitute a means that is both practical and attractive for exposing and unraveling the whole tangled skein?

Escaping from Both "Organized" Oppression and "Diffuse" Oppression

by Bouland Al-Haïdari

If we set aside the reasons that prompted Salman Rushdie to publish his novel in the first place—along with my own personal appreciation of its literary value. If we simply decide to remain in ignorance of the whole question of whether or not he was justified in basing his story on the ancient account of Tabari that can be found in the latter's *Annals of the Apostles and the Kings*, an account transmitted down to us by a whole series of different authorities, of whom the first is Sayf Ibn Omar al-Tamimi, who relates that the prophet Muhammad once recited before a group of Meccans the following verse: "By al-Lat, and al-Uzza, and by Manat, the third, they are high-flying birds, and their intercession is most desired." If we similarly neglect the refutations made by some who pretend that the prophet later corrected himself and replaced this verse dictated by Gabriel with another one that figures today in the sura of the Star: "Have you then seen al-Lat and al-Uzza and Manat the third? You then would have males and He daughters only? That would be an inequitable division. . . .They are nothing but names that you have created, you and your fathers, and God confers no power on them." Another verse of the sura of the nocturnal Voyage says the same thing: "If they are at the point of succeeding in turning you away by means of seduction from what We have inspired, then you

---

Poet, Kurdistan/Iraq. Originally written in Arabic.

can calumniate us." And then again in the sura of the Pilgrimage there is to be found this: "For God effaces what Satan suggests, and then He presents His own definitive verses."

And if we also go on to lay aside the definition of an apostate, which actually goes so far as to include someone who stops paying the *zakat* and to recite the prayers. And if we forget that the Prophet Muhammad himself enjoined that an apostate should be given the opportunity to repent before being condemned, and that the caliph Ibn al-Khattab once manifested his disapprobation of the execution of an apostate who had not thus been given the opportunity to repent. ("Did you ask him," he said, "whether he was prepared to repent and remember the command of God? God is my witness that I was not there when you put him to death, and that I did not give the order for it.") Besides, Muslims never did in the course of their whole past history ever carry out such a sentence— that I know of. And if Khomeini did not give Salman Rushdie an opportunity to repent, the fact remains that the latter on his own has made a declaration in that sense anyway. And if, finally, we insist on remaining ignorant of the fact that offering financial incentives to put to death an apostate is surely not a method that Islam has ever accepted. If, then, we leave aside all these considerations that I have been enumerating, so we can arrive at a formulation of the basic principle at issue here in such a way that the judgment of thinkers and intellectuals on the question will not be reached except by thinking the whole thing through; except by discussion and dialogue, which make it possible to separate the true from the false. In the situation we are in, what intellectuals should do is mutually assist one another by approving a *charter* guaranteeing their right to freedom of opinion. Freedom of opinion has practically disappeared today; or, rather, it has wrongly been snatched away by methods that sometimes include outright murder.

In our world the role of the intellectual tends to be exercised in accordance with three basic models. According to the first, the intellectual simply chooses to collaborate with the regime, receiving in exchange the various gifts and honors it can give him. The second model can perhaps best be expressed by recalling the well-known image of the three Indian monkeys: the first covers his eyes in order not to see anything; the second covers his ears in order not to hear anything; and the third covers his mouth in order not to say anything. Today's literary man operating in accordance with this second model at least assures his own security.

Finally, there remains the third model, which can lead the same intellectual to choose to flee his own country in order to seek freedom and thereby be able to express what he both sees and hears and what he has the duty to say, even if he only does so it in a whisper.

To speak truly, our intellectuals do not merely suffer from that form of oppression we may style "organized"—the kind imposed by dictatorial regimes. Our intellectuals also undergo the effects of another, even more terrible form of subjection, which we may style "diffuse" oppression. It extends over almost all our territories today, and its power arises out of and is nourished by our own retrograde social heritage. This kind of "diffuse" oppression demands total submission to a kind of tyranny that knows how to hide behind the intimidating facades of old traditions as well as behind those of confessional, partisan, and national affiliations; and it is this kind of oppression that withdraws from us the right to sample even the least of the dishes served up at the banquet of power. Our intellectuals might more profitably begin to try to understand the message transmitted by the whistling of the bullets that have already pierced the hides of several dozen of their own.

The moment has arrived for drafting and adopting a *charter* for intellectuals, a charter that they should sign and thereby undertake to defend. This is a necessity today, in fact, one brought about on the one hand by the imperative to revolt against the barriers that everywhere hedge intellectuals in, and on the other hand—and more profoundly—by the conviction that taking positions of conscience among peoples can be realized only when intellectuals are able to act effectively in their own societies.

It is a *charter* that we need, then, not a party, an organization, or a league. More than that, we want to be able to cultivate a spirit that will lead us to better positions that can then help assure the victory of greater human and cultural values. And it is only in the name of such a spirit that, finally, Salman Rushdie can be judged, whatever the outcome of his trial, whether condemnation or acquittal.

Concerning Repression, Liberty, and the Affirmation of the Right to Be Different

by Eduard Al-Kharrat

I see in the freedom of culture and the freedom to write a necessary condition, indeed an essential possession of the poet's and the novelist's art or of any kind of artistic creation. Without freedom no creative work is even conceivable. It is not sufficient that the artist should merely consider himself essentially free; the work of art itself must become a freedom—of choice and of construction. It must also appeal in its turn to the freedom of the reader; it is in this respect that the kind of freedom I am talking about differs from mere anarchy or absence of law. In addition, the creation of poetry and fiction is by its nature dissociated from either actual historical context or sacred meaning. When these very different kinds of things become confused, we inevitably enter into a vicious circle from which there is no exit. Without doubt respect is owed to sacred texts long consecrated, just as respect is also owed to the believing community itself, as far as religion is concerned. And, understood within its proper domain, the freedom of the novelist should in no way suffer from any of this. A work of art should not be perceived as a religious text that must be either refuted or subscribed to. The only criteria by which we are allowed to appreciate a work of art should be purely artistic criteria; and they arise neither from religion nor science nor ideology nor even from the moral and

Writer, Egypt. Originally written in Arabic.

social conventions of the community. Freedom is either absolute or else it is not freedom. Freedom is a starting point; it is both means and goal. It is absolute in that it arises out of a law that is implicit, hidden, and related to responsibility rather than to constraint, to choice rather than to any charge imposed from the outside or by some other authority alien to the laws of art. If a work is born in liberty, it will be received in an atmosphere of equal social and cultural liberty, which has to be a total liberty, without reservations. None of this is possible except on the basis of respect for the rights of others, for dialogue, and for reason; there cannot be any surrender to obscurantism, fanaticism, or a narcissism that is blind to the existence of others and the light of tolerance.

Even though fear, self-censorship, and the absence of interior liberty can proceed out of the subjectivity of each person, they are not any less the products of external and collective powers. The power exerted by sacred texts and the effects of social injustice and the dominant ideology often show themselves to be more determining and even more ferocious than the official measures of repression. I do not doubt that, in order to achieve freedom of culture and of artistic creation, it is necessary that all these internal and external factors, all these individual and collective centers, be interrelated and function in some kind of competitive fashion.

To achieve all this, the creative artist must be prepared to pay the price without hesitation. There must be a true pluralism of works and opinions that are not required to fit into any definite framework, but must instead arise out of the interaction of all the relevant factors, such as rationality, an ideal of justice, and the dignity of human beings. This pluralism will come about only if other people and other values are accepted. Nor can these values be limited to those held to be revealed and fixed forever in the tables of the law; rather, they must be continually enunciated for the benefit of all and constantly renewed in their basic formulation. Others—even if they are obscurantists themselves—can be treated only in accordance with the same principles of freedom and reason. Only then can we prevent a perhaps irremediable breaking of spirits. The unity of a culture does not require that everything be poured into the same mold of a closed and monolithic system. The unity of creativity is, on the contrary, pluralistic, diverse, dialectical. Simply put, this unity must be based upon a right to be different, and not on the power of any ancient texts, dogmas, or for that matter, on the established order. We must therefore continue to summon everyone to take part in the dialogue.

Those who wish to interrupt the dialogue, on the other hand, can only be considered to belong to the camp of terror and repression, whatever the reasons for their choice might be. To call for murder in the name of the law can only give rise to blind violence and other effects that can never be anything but deadly as far as creativity is concerned—even though, as I understand it, creativity *cannot* be destroyed. Nevertheless, the right to be different must be held sacred.

Night

by Omar Amirallay and Mohammed Mallas

If there are those who believe that these closing years of the twentieth century have been marked by the triumph of democracy, the rights of man, and freedom of thought, they will rather quickly be refuted by the facts. It is enough merely to cast a superficial glance at what is going on in the world today in order to perceive the breadth and seriousness of marked regression that concerns practically everything related to enlightened thought. In spite of the hopes raised by the great lessons of contemporary history, it is becoming more and more evident that we are about to take leave of a century where henceforth the only things likely to reign and prosper appear to be the most primary kinds of proselytisms, especially those that arouse the most intolerant kinds of religious and nationalistic passions, imbuing the masses with fanaticism rather than awakening individual consciences and encouraging the free exercise of the human faculties of reflection and creativity. In other words, there is no longer any place today where the individual voice can be properly raised and heard; there are only vast stadiums where the multitudes shout out a single cry in response to a single spectacle.

Our societies in the Arab and Islamic world have not witnessed a sufficient change of structures in the course of the past few centuries to enable us to bring forward anything new today. If, from a distance, the message of a few rare voices that are truly free do suc-

Filmakers, Syria. Originally written in Arabic.

ceed in penetrating the shadows and making themselves manifest, this occurs only when occasionally the usual "hyenas" are absent, or only when they are weakened for some reason.

Perhaps it is our duty today, more than ever, to try to rediscover the means by which, over the course of centuries, the breath of resistance and freedom has even been able to be drawn—that this breath of freedom has been able to be drawn even when it has also often been interrupted. The same person who can distinguish a shadow in darkness may also be the one who can discover the torch that will illuminate things to the point where others can also see that the shadow does not represent total darkness, and that the sinister phantoms perceived in that same shadow are nothing but other human beings whom the light has not yet reached. Meanwhile, the torch fails to illuminate because the wind is still too strong and continues to blow dust in the eyes. This same situation, it seems, is one that the enlightened Muslim philosophers who came along after the appearance of the final revealed Books understood perfectly.

For our part, we must attempt to learn the proper lesson from the fierce tempest that blew so strongly after the publication of the novel by the great writer Salman Rushdie. What happened then surely had to happen; and thus we have to understand that nothing essential has really been changed in our world. However, the anger that has taken over in some spirits risks carrying us along with it, if we cannot learn how to master it; in the abyss of today's collective illusions, we risk the extinction of the flame itself, and this would bring us to a situation of utter defeat. That is why we have no other choice but to take up again the work of being stubborn ants, fashioning our own underground passages and channels of communication, meanwhile undermining the very ground on which the imams of darkness operating in today's land of delirium are standing.

Concerning the Rushdie Affair

by Mahshid Amir-Shahy

It has already been four years since a writer born in India of Sunni Muslim extraction, though English in language, was condemned to death by a Shiite Iranian religious leader who recognized neither any frontier to his realm nor any limit to his authority.

This event surely rates being considered one of the more bizarre episodes that our century has witnessed. How did we all react to it? Naturally, with confusion and disorder. Declarations flowed from the pens of intellectuals of great prestige and sincere good faith. Unfortunately, however, this prestige did not influence anybody much; and all the good faith exhibited was pretty much obliged to yield to "faith," period. Since then, little, if anything has changed.

Many have been able to accommodate themselves to this situation, considering the whole thing as a kind of game which has ended in a tie; some have even made the comment that Rushdie is still alive, after all. In my view, however, the whole thing represents a kind of delayed-action defeat, for I am obliged to point out the unhappy fact that the sentence has not been lifted from the interested party, Rushdie. And the question still remains whether we can really be satisfied with this.

Up to this point those who have been giving the orders for this murder to be committed have enjoyed certain advantages, the most

---

Writer, Iran. Originally written in French. Speech delivered before the meeting of the League of the Rights of Man, Paris, February 11, 1993.

obvious of which, of course, is the element of surprise. By acting so methodically, they have succeeded in getting the attention of the entire world, especially on account of the utterly spontaneous and unpredictable ways in which they have acted. Nevertheless, in one sense, their methods have certainly been well thought out; they have first been tried out inside Iran, and then they have been exported. They have first terrorized their enemies by invoking divine retribution upon their heads. Then, if fear of this divine punishment did not suffice to disarm all resistance, they have promptly set in motion their own means of vengeance. We may imagine that we live in a desacralized world, yet we are now at the mercy of such "divine threats," transformed into a simple method of operation.

The Rushdie case is only the most flagrant and best known current example of this method of operation. Nevertheless, in the launching of this particular affair, at least one great blunder was committed. In attempting to impose their own law on the whole world, the mullahs aimed too high, and in so doing, they prepared the ground for their own defeat. Their attack on the whole modern world over the past four years has already reached its culminating point; from this point on it is bound to fail, and we are now in a position to help precipitate that defeat.

To this end, I think, there must be developed a sort of division of labor between the intellectuals of the Muslim world—particularly the Iranians—on the one hand, and Western intellectuals on the other hand. Such a division of labor is dictated by the particular configuration formed by the weaknesses of the regime with which we are dealing, and which the mullahs themselves describe as a theocratic regime. It is an anti-modern regime, deficient in its real cultural ideology, though it attempts to ground its "otherness" in Islam and to become "sacralized" thereby. This ideology has long been taken quite seriously; it has even attracted the approval of some, and it has certainly known how to gain the respect of others. To discredit this ideology, and to violate the taboo of its "sacrality" (imposed with whips, stonings, and bombs)—this is something only the Iranians themselves could have done, and now they have done it. The appeal for support for Salman Rushdie, which they first launched last year, and which continues to attract signatures, aims to put an end to all the cultural blackmail that has been operative and to let the whole world finally know that certain universal values are not absent from the land of the "sacred terror."

No matter how universal these particular values might be, however, they still cannot dispense with concrete representation in persons of flesh and blood. To defend the most celebrated victim of the intolerance of the mullahs is at the same time to mark the path that leads out of our present difficulties—to put the mullahs on notice that, as the heirs and successors of an old man who, up to the end of his life at the age of ninety, was still unable to master the proper use of auxiliary verbs in his own native language, and who surely got into the field of literary criticism way too late in the game, they are hardly the ones to be invoking Iranian culture and attempting to justify their crimes by doing so! The reaction the Iranian appeal aroused within the Islamic world was immediate and very consequential. What the Iranians who signed it were able to do was point to the contradiction at the heart of the whole fundamentalist enterprise and thus offer an additional source of moral support for the defenders of Rushdie.

But what about Western intellectuals? They are the ones who have been most active from the very beginning of the Rushdie affair. They have not failed to denounce with appropriate vigor the abject character of the *fatwa* condemning Rushdie (without, however, really being heard by those who have made it a point of honor to offer up the head of the insolent author). It is to the Western intellectuals that I now address myself. The mullahs, of course, will denounce all their various appeals for clemency, as well as their denunciations of intolerance, on the grounds that all these initiatives are part of a Western plot. Shielded behind the buckler of their ideology, they will not consider these denunciations as having really scored any hits on them. However, if Western intellectuals will now focus their efforts on Western governments, either by direct intervention or by means of influencing public opinion, and get them to call for a complete and unconditional withdrawal of the *fatwa*, they can by this means succeed in making the Iranian government bend. For the fact is that, in spite of its arrogant and bragging ways, the Iranian government is beset with numerous internal difficulties; it is not in any position at all to stand up against serious international pressures. Ideology can protect for a time against contamination even by true ideas, but it cannot indefinitely escape from the constraints of reality.

I would like to conclude with a final comment. No country has ever been large enough to have at one and the same time both tyranny and freedom of expression. By being too ambitious, Khomeini committed the imprudence of linking the fate of his regime with freedom of expression, not only in Iran itself but in the world at large; this link will prove to be deadly for the regime. We must actively continue both our efforts to defend the rights of Salman Rushdie and to promote the idea of a secular democracy among the Iranians because, believe me, the Iranians have no illusions about the supposed virtues of political Islam.

I do not believe we can separate these two causes, and I dare to think, therefore, that we will stand together in this double battle.

Appeal of Iranian Artists and Intellectuals in Favor of Salman Rushdie

The signatories of this appeal, who have already manifested their support for Salman Rushdie in various ways, believe that freedom of expression constitutes one of the most precious goods of humanity; and, as Voltaire said, it cannot exist in the true sense unless there is also freedom to blaspheme. No individual and no group has any right to limit this freedom of expression in the name of any sacrality whatsoever.

We underline the intolerable character of the decree of death that the *fatwa* is, and we insist on the fact that aesthetic criteria are the only proper ones for judging works of art.

We unanimously raise our voices in order to support Salman Rushdie, and we remind everyone that writers, artists, journalists, and thinkers in Iran are daily undergoing censorship and that the number of Iranians who have already been imprisoned, or even executed, on the charge of "blasphemy" is far from negligible.

To the extent that the systematic denial of the rights of man in Iran is tolerated, this can only further encourage the export outside the Islamic Republic of its terroristic methods which destroy freedom.

Chahnaz Aalami (poet), Mahasti Afchar (researcher), Kouroche Afchar-Panah (actor), Reza Allameh-Zadeh (filmmaker), Nasrine Almasi (comedian), Mahshid Amir-Shahy (writer), Michanch Amir-Shahy (researcher), Mansour Anvari (journalist), Mary Apick (actress, producer), Ali-Mohammad Arbabi (journalist), Aref

---

On June 2, 1993 there were 127 signatures.

Arefkia (singer), Kouroche Aria-Maneche/Reza Mazloumane (university professor), Bijan Assadi-Pour (caricaturist), Touraj Atabaki (university professor), Assurbanipal Babela (playwright), Houchang Baharlou (filmmaker), Habib Behdad (journalist), Chahine Behraveche (psychologist), Ali-Asghar Behrouzian (writer), Shahram Broukhim (actor), Kamran Chahgaldi (university professor), Mohi Chaïchi (actor), Hayadeh Daragahi (university professor), Ali Dasta (actor), Mahmoud Davoudi (director), Mohammad-Reza Djalili (university professor), Mehranguiz Dowlatchahi (sociologist), Khanak Echghi-Sanati (jurist), Homa Ehsan (radio producer), Sadredine Elahi (journalist), Nasser Enghetae (journalist), Azar Fakhr (actress), Masser Fakhteh (writer), Farhang Farahi (journalist), Cyrus Farmanfarmaïan (architect), Faramarz Farshad (journalist), Chahla Fatemi (political analyst), Hamid Fatemi (journalist), Maryam Ghafari (archeologist), Ali-Akbar Ghanbari (journalist), Parviz Ghazi-Saeed (journalist), Djamchid Golmakani (filmmaker), Mahmoud Goudarzi (journalist), Avideh Hachemi (architect), Safa Haeri (journalist), Ali-Asghar Haj Seyed Javadi (essayist), Hormoz Hekmat (university professor), Dariush Homayoun (journalist), Homayoun Houshyar-Nejad (journalist), Fereydoun Hoveyda (writer), Mohammad Jafari (actor), Iraj Janati-Atayi (playwright), Ramine Kamrane (sociologist), Parviz Kardane (actor), Behzad Karimi (journalist), Ahmad Karimi-Hakak (university professor), Rafi Khachatourian (actor), Nasim Khaksar (writer), Jean-Yahya Khakzad (journalist), Behrouz Khaligh (journalist), Bijan Khalili (editor), Mouloud Khanlary (essayist), Fereydoune Khavand (university professor), Khosrow Khazaï (university professor), Ahou Kheradmand (comedienne), Manouk Khodabakhshian (TV producer), Esmaïl Khoï (poet), Morteza Latifi (journalist), Ali Limounadi (TV director), Amir Maenavi (journalist), Sousan Mafi (TV journalist), Hossein Malek (researcher), Ali Massoudi (journalist), Mehdi Mehramouz (poet), Dariouche Mehregan (journalist), Morteza Miraftabi (writer), Ali Mirfetross (researcher), Mansour Moadel (sociologist), Ardavan Mofid (actor), Hossein Mohri (journalist), Taghi Mokhtar (writer),

Taher Momtaz (journalist), Esfandir Monfared-Zadeh (composer), Assadollah Morovati (radio producer), Marva Nabili (filmmaker), Mohsen Naderi-Nejad (filmmaker), Nader Nader-Pour (poet), Firouz Nadji (poet), Hassan Nazieh (jurist), Djamileh Nedaï (drama critic), Farrokh Negahdar (journalist), Javad Nouri (journalist), Parto Nouri-Ala (poet), Kamran Nozad (actor), Mahmoud Ostad-Mohammad (playwright), Abbas Pahlevan (journalist), Younes Parsabenab (researcher), Kouchiar Parsi (writer), Darioush Pirnia (university professor), Mansoureh Pirnia (journalist), Ali Pourtash (actor), Iradj Rahmani (poet), Hassan Rajabpour (journalist), Zohreh Ramsey (actress), Manouchehr Razmara (physician), Noushin Sabeti (school director), Morteza Saghafian (poet), Ali Sajjadi (journalist), Satar Salimi (archeologist), Homa Sarchar (journalist), Hassan Sattarian (university professor), Parviz Sayyad (playwright and filmmaker), Massoud Sefatian (urbanist), Alireza Sepasi (editor), Chojaodine Shafa (writer), Cyrus Sharafshahi (journalist), Ali Sharifian (writer), Behrouz Souresrafil (journalist), Soussan-Abadi (miniaturist), Barbad Taheri (filmmaker), Djamchide Taheri-Pour (journalist), Nasser Tahmasebi (physician), Hassan Tehranchian (university professor), Houchang Vaziri (journalist), Ileen Veegen (actress), Mahdi Younesi (university professor), Hassan Zerehi (journalist).

Back to the Rushdie Affair Once More

by Mohammed Arkoun

In his didactic broadcast entitled "The March of the Century," Jean-Marie Cavada awakened in many memories, at least in the memories of many in France, the realization that the Rushdie affair is still very much with us. This writer is still living under the threat of the famous *fatwa* condemning him to death which was reaffirmed by the Iranian authorities after the death of the imam, the Ayatollah Khomeini. During the program, a very serene Salman Rushdie was shown on French television screens bearing up with a great deal of dignity under the burden of a personal drama which, at this point, has taken on the dimensions of a historical destiny: the destiny of an immigrant Muslim now living in Europe who is being pursued in his refuge there both by the ancient heritage of Muslim societies and by their more recent heritage as well.

It is even less possible to escape from this double heritage of both ancient and modern than it would otherwise be when we consider that both the current political situation and the economic and social disorders in the world impose the whole thing more and more on all concerned. And if, like Rushdie, one has undertaken to stir things up further—if only by producing a work of art, by electing to touch upon a system of basic religious symbolism that gives support to the hopes of millions of human beings marginalized by a history that is blind—if one attempts this, then, one is only too likely to

Islamologist, Algeria. Originally written in French.

unite against oneself forces of vengeance directed against a destiny that will necessarily be less and less subject to any kind of mastery.

It cannot be said that the participants on Jean-Marie Cavada's program raised the level of the debate to a point where it was possible to understand what is truly at stake in the Rushdie affair. For historians, I believe it is an affair that will mark an important milestone for the end of this twentieth century. I myself attempted, in an interview published in *Le Monde* on March 15, 1989, to indicate what was at stake in the whole affair. However, the storm that blew up at that point was so violent, passions were running so high, and the threat of actual physical force was so agonizing, that what I had to say then was rather arbitrarily classified as just one more opinion belonging on "the fundamentalist side." It was classified thus even though, for the last thirty years, I have not ceased to work for a true rational critique of Islam—and this precisely in order to make possible not only a favorable reception by the Muslim public of such works as *The Satanic Verses*, but also to multiply the kinds of intellectual and artistic activities that help to liberate certain kinds of mentalities from "knowledge" that just happens to be false, from mythological-type representations to which they are also prone, from fideist prejudices, and from various other primitive and often undisciplined beliefs.

My whole experience with the Rushdie affair provides rather convincing proof, though, of a current intellectual weakness in the West which is only too evident, and also of an ideological drift on the part of the intelligentsia, which is way too heavily influenced by the media, and which also refuses to consider what the real problems are at the same time that it feels quite able to give lessons in freedom of conscience to the Muslim world. It feels quite able to give such lessons even though, at least from the nineteenth century on, practically everything possible has been done in that Muslim world to downgrade and render inoperative and even ridiculous any such thing as an appeal to respect "the rights of man."

I do not wish to repeat my earlier offense, that of stirring up again the same old "defenders of the West"; nor do I wish to provide another occasion for people to decide to believe that I actually accept the condemnation of Rushdie in order to protect "the sacred values of Islam." What I do say is that the condemnation of this author was a political act, which sought to amplify its effect both by resorting to a certain method of operating and also by insisting that there was a serious religious issue at stake in the whole thing. I also want to say that, given the present state of religious psychology in the Islamic context, making a distinction between an essentially political strategy and act and a religious commitment aimed at protecting spiritual values is not one that was ever going to be accessible to a very large number. The imaginary collectivity was bound to react blindly, immediately, and with fury when it was made to believe that the prophet has been made to look ridiculous, and that God himself had been blasphemed.

Now in politics, I contend—even in the West—nobody has the right either to ignore or scorn the psychological dimensions that are necessarily involved in the public perception of events. So it is perfectly vain to proclaim in the abstract the universal rights of man in societies that for centuries have been subject to all forms of arbitrary power and denial of the dignity of the human being—including during the long period of colonial domination by the West itself, which only very recently has suddenly become the defender of freedom all over the world (and this still remains perfectly true, whatever necessary correctives or reservations the most lucid observers in the West might raise in this regard).

It is necessary that Salman Rushdie should be able to recover his full liberty—his freedom to live his life, to move about, to express his thoughts, to publish his books, and, in general, to enrich by means of his talent as a writer the great debates of the present day, and precisely on questions of politics and religion. I would like to see *The Satanic Verses* made available to all Muslims in order that they might be able to reflect in a more modern fashion on the cognitive status of revelation, not only as regards Islam, but also as regards the other monotheistic religions which profess belief in the same phenomenon that Islam does, namely, that the very Word of God has actually intervened in human history.

At the same time, however, it would seem to be equally necessary that a serious debate take place in the West concerning the legitimacy of brutally dismissing an entire culture, a historic world religion, in fact, entirely on the basis of supposed philosophical *postulates* that, even in the West, have not been subjected to any real tests of intellectual validation or cultural efficaciousness. But now suddenly they have been transferred into entirely new religious, historical, and psychosocial contexts. I refer in particular to certain ideological forms and modalities understood in certain European countries as the separation of the *temporal* from the *spiritual*—to be distinguished clearly from the separation of church and state, of one power apparatus from another. This question of the separation of the temporal from the spiritual is today in need of a radical philosophical reconsideration. Yet it is precisely here that a truly violent form of Western arrogance takes root which, under the cover of a defense of "freedom of expression," in fact seeks to debase Islam and prove that all the old talk about the civilizing mission of the European colonial powers is and has always been fundamentally valid.

It is time to cease treating the Rushdie affair by moving in one direction only, by taking one side only. The demonstrations, manifestations, and rejections that have been characteristic of certain Muslim milieus have been directed much less against the person of Rushdie than they have against a book that very quickly became a symbol of all of the aggressions of recent history, especially from the time of the eighteenth century on, directed against Muslim societies. The forms of domination that still weigh upon the national states that have issued from the Muslim wars for independence are currently experienced and interpreted as nothing else but a prolongation and aggravation of the domination that had earlier been imposed by the colonial empires. Thus, merely to protest against the intolerance of Muslims alone means covering over with a veil of silence some things that represent a decisive aspect of the whole battle that has involved Rushdie.

Take, for example, what happened during the Gulf War. What was said, what protests were launched, what promises or justifications made, what petitions were circulated in the West against the Gulf War? Is there no connection here between the flood of passions that was unleashed—the violence, the rages, the destructiveness, the desire for vengeance—and the desire to do away with an enemy? Is there no connection between all of this and the similar phenomena that have been manifested in the Rushdie affair? Or the affair of the scarf that followed so closely upon it in France?

The fact of the matter is that all of our discourses, our commitments, our analyses, our denunciations, our warnings, our predictions—none of these things even begins to suffice to deal with the challenges of history opened up by what has been called—so absurdly!—decolonization. The social sciences, which are supposed to throw light on the complexity of our present history, instead take refuge in mere expertise, in descriptive studies, in summing up developments after the fact, or simply in peddling a kind of "futurology." Philosophy, meanwhile, has simply retired from the field, leaving it to the various social science specialties to focus on such narrow and severely limited issues as those related to studying ancient clans or tribes, for example. As far as speaking seriously about ethics or spiritual values, even the religious authorities no longer really dare to do it—so great is their desire to speak in no language but the language of the media, because that is the only language anybody listens to anymore; hence it is the only language that finally comes to be imposed.

How then, under these conditions, is it even possible to speak of an affair such as the Rushdie affair, which brings out, precisely, all the failures, incapacities, humiliations, and rejections from which the intelligence of our day suffers?

Freedom

by Aïcha Arnaout

To write or, in general, to create, means to lay bare one's soul, indeed, to lay bare pretty much everything. Thousands of different flights are possible in order to embark upon the great adventure of the imaginary. And it is precisely at the point where this laying-bare process takes a particular flight that the created work emerges. The process of creation is incompatible with absolute values. Each step forward in the process of undertaking artistic creation calls for the abandonment of certitude, and from that fact alone, all limits are abolished. Freedom of expression therefore constitutes the very essence of creation, just as it constitutes the primordial genesis of any created work. It is because this principle was violated in the Rushdie affair—hardly a unique occurrence in history—that we are now summoned not to give up in this case, but to maintain a position that is firm and unyielding.

It seems to me useful to note, however, that the implications of the Rushdie affair are not limited to the question of freedom of expression. I consider it a manifestation of a very complex situation, in fact, one that has resulted from a number of different factors: (1) the abyss that separates two ways of thinking and two modes of existence (an easily manipulable mob on the one hand, and a creative writer and his work on the other); (2) the steadily increasing rupture or fissure between the Muslim world, itself an integral part

Poet, Syria. Originally written in French.

of a Third World that is largely disarmed and powerless, and the powerful Western world with its superiority either already over-whelmingly manifested or obviously in place not far below the sur-face; and (3) the current state of virtual incommunicability between these two cultures (which, however, is not necessarily ineluctable).

A supposed Islamic authority pronounced a sentence of death against Salman Rushdie; motivated by fanaticism, it then manipu-lated the mob in order both to signal its own presence and demon-strate the chaotic extent of that presence. The Western world promptly interpreted this gesture as a provocation. Basing its posi-tion on the principle of the freedom of expression, the West then greatly amplified the whole affair, especially through its media; it thus delivered a largely justified response to the fundamentalist uprising. At the same time, though, the West seized upon the occa-sion to portray Islam one-sidedly and in largely reprehensible terms, and this further aroused the anger of Muslims. The whole issue hinges on the relationship between the two camps, and is per-meated by a cause-and-effect duality; because there are so many variable and even reversible factors, the whole affair is much more complex than one might imagine at first sight.

In the midst of such a ferment, Rushdie quickly became a scapegoat and served as an ideal target in a long-suppressed con-flict. Every death sentence, on principle, is unjustified and open to question. So what, then, can be said about a death sentence that is both arbitrary and without any persuasive juridical foundation? The Rushdie affair reminds us once again that the struggle is permanent and never-ending, not only for freedom of expression, but for the freedom of man in general.

Rushdie on the Edge of the Abyss between East and West

by Liana Badr

I was born in the city of Jerusalem where the heart exults to hear both the church bells and the praise of Allah which rises up each time the voice of the muezzin is heard. It was in this city, whose name is associated with the Canaanite god of healing, Salem, who is said to have lived under its olive trees, that I learned that the remedy for the ills of life is man himself, whatever his religion might be. It never crossed my mind that I had to boycott our neighbors during their Christmas celebration; like their children, I too awaited with impatience the gifts of Father Christmas. Nor did it cross my mind that my Christian girl friends would decline to put on their necks the gilt-edged Korans that we were accustomed to wearing then. When, much later, I was in Lebanon, and I first heard the word "confessionalism," a word so jarring to the ear, I was ashamed—by then I was a student—to discover what it meant. Still more years passed before I was absolutely astounded to discover that religion, which for us had always represented a celebration and a glorification of life, was something that could become the source of political conflict and even the pretext for the settling of ethnic scores.

It is in this context of a highly political abuse of religion that I understand the sentence of death meted out to Salman Rushdie. The basic situation is that the East has felt itself the victim of injus-

---

Writer, Palestine. Originally written in Arabic.

tice inflicted by a powerful West. Rushdie simply got into the middle of all this; he was on the frontier between the two camps—on the edge of the abyss between East and West. But is this justice? Is it in any way just to inflict upon him a punishment merely for having produced a literary work of fiction? This author, in making such a great effort to express himself without taking any a priori positions of any kind, has surely proved that his work does not originate in any kind of bad faith. Or is it justice never to make any judgments against the Muslim nabobs who squander fortunes on the green felt gambling tables of the West at the same time that they are mortgaging the future of their peoples by their subservience to colonialism and multinational corporations? Is it justice to remain silent, in the name of political pragmatism, in the face of all the crimes against humanity, in the face of the brutality, torture, and assassinations perpetrated by so many governments against their own peoples—and then to turn around and judge the man and the writer, Rushdie?

As a Muslim I can attest to the fact that Islam differs from other religions in not investing the earthly representatives of God with absolute power. Did my teachers deceive me in teaching me that there is no shadow of God on earth, and that it would be simply impossible for Islam to have an office such as the papacy, for example, or a center such as the Vatican? Who can pretend to be able to apply divine justice with absolute certitude? I am well aware that Islam is associated with the system of Shura, or "consultation with wise men." On what kind of consultation is the condemnation of Rushdie based? Do the many violent incidents unleashed by the publication of his book truly represent our commitment to our traditions, or even our feelings of having been wronged? Was it not possible to respond to Rushdie's writing with other writing, to subject what he advanced to discussion and debate? Was it not important to spare the lives of those who fell in the course of all the incidents of protest that have broken out? Should we not always have resorted to rational argument rather than declaring sentences of death? I do not accept that it is possible to remain silent concerning the many repressions and humiliations of all kinds that the Islamic regimes regularly impose on their citizens. But then, meanwhile, they proceed to condemn a writer who merely embarked upon an adventure in the realm of the imagination—carrying it even to the point of confusion, in fact. Merely to limit sanctions to writers is in itself an ineffaceable injustice.

Rushdie's novel is an example of a literary genre that actually took its raw material from the world of dreams; it attempted to describe the contours of a strictly unreal world. Is it not strange that we should be indicting dreams and putting literary productions on trial? As a Muslim born in the Holy Land—holy to all the monotheistic religions—I find it entirely unjust to attempt to settle scores between East and West in this fashion. Even supposing Rushdie may have been insulting in a certain way, we must still take the part of right reason. In my country, Palestine, I was educated in traditions that called for the rejection of religious violence. I therefore consider it absolutely necessary to revoke the sentence against Rushdie. This affair must be normalized by listening to the voice of justice and good sense. The countries of the East will achieve greater credibility in facing the modern challenges that confront them by aligning themselves with the spirit of the age and putting aside for good fanaticism, repression, and clenched fists.

The Sanctification of the Patriarchate: Outline of a Theory of Intolerance in Religion and the Family

Halim Barakat

My interest in explaining tendencies toward intolerance in human behavior and violation of freedom of expression rights has led me to explore some aspects of the interrelationships between family and religion. Notwithstanding areas of conflict between these two institutions, I reached the conclusion that they tend to be mutually supportive and complimentary. Inasmuch as each one has served as an instrument of the other, I would argue that originally it was the family that shaped religion in its own image, rather than the other way around. Yet, religion in turn has constantly reinforced and strengthened the family in its original forms.

In order to explain tendencies toward intolerance and limitation on freedom of expression, I concluded that one of the most significant aspects of the process of mutual reinforcement between religion and family is the great similarity between the images of the father and the image of God in the mind of believers. This came about, I say, as a result of a historical process of sanctification of patriarchy. Such a process of abstraction, as I indicated in my book *The Arab World: Society, Culture and State* (University of California Press, 1993), may have passed through four basic stages. In the first stage, the father and ancestors were objects of veneration and worship, and

Writer/Sociologist, Libya. Originally written in English.

religious practices were conducted at home and led by the father, who played the role of priest (*kahin* or imam). In the second stage, the god of the family (*rabb al-usra*) became the god of the tribe or city as a result of the extension of the tribe's influence and control over others. In the third stage, the god of the tribe or city became the god of the society due to the same process of influence and domination. In fact, the unification of the society required such a transition from tribal gods to a more inclusive god of the society as a whole (Mecca, for instance, represented this sort of tension between oneness and plurality in the pre-Islamic period). In the fourth stage, the one God (Allah) became the ultimate divinity, totally eclipsing earlier localized gods originating in family or ancestor worship.

This four-stage process leading to the establishment of God as an extension of the patriarchal father is demonstrated most clearly in the great similarity between the image of the father and the image of God in the minds of believers. Both the father and God are endowed by the believers with two contradictory sets of traits. On the one hand, both are categorized as *rahum* or *ra'uf* (merciful, compassionate), *ghafur* (forgiving), *hanun* and *muhibb* (sympathetic and loving), *jalil* (dignified), *karim* (generous), and *'adel* (just). On the other hand, the father and God are also both described by the believers as *jabbar* or *qawi* (forceful, strong), *sarim* or *qasi* (strict, severe), *mukhif* (fearful), *muhaymin* (hegemonic), *ghahhar* (subduer, coercive), *muntaqim* (revengeful), *mutassalit* (domineering, authoritarian), *ghadub* (quick to anger), and *muta'ali* (condescending). These seemingly contradictory characteristics were originally those of the father or family patriarch. The fact that they were extended to God suggests that He is an extension, abstraction, or symbol of the father. "Our father who art in heaven" must be a magnified portrait of our patriarch on earth.

This process of sanctification of the earthly patriarch must be at the roots of religious intolerance and persecution throughout history. Rushdie's *The Satanic Verses* and Mahfouz's *Children of Gebelawi* represent instances of such victimization (to a much lesser degree in the latter) by divine right and the divinity of rulers.

The Metaphors for God

by Salim Barakat

From the time of the earliest miseries of our childhood, we never really escaped from unhappiness, even though, at that time, we scarcely had any real experience of it. It was for this reason that we were really constrained to find in music, that is, in song—which represents a kind of eclipse of the physical body—a means of escape from the harshness of the world. All by itself the singing voice can harmonize and reconcile us to life; it represents a kind of divine call; indeed, it represents the celestial trumpet which, at the moment of the Resurrection, will reveal to us the full text of Misery and will finally permit the Spirit and Eternal Life to attain their true perfection.

These earliest miseries of ours taught us, those of us who were assailed by other and more mediocre visions—and usually having only a narrow and tenuous hold on reality—how to lose ourselves in music that was sung, hiding ourselves in its capacious folds, so much sweeter than the true appearance of things. Meanwhile, actually understanding the words did not even greatly concern us. But we knew Naris and Dilip Kumar, Mahighal, Sayra Banu and Sunal Dutt, the Aboor family and the Raj Kumar family, Div Anand, and yet others. The were all actors, playing out for us a life of pain that would otherwise have been inexpressible; they were simple, unaffected figures for a simple, unaffected age. They all sang either in

Writer, Kurdistan/Syria. Originally written in Arabic.

their own voices or through the voices of others. And we were fiercely attached to the images that went along with those voices; they made us weep, in fact.

The darkness into which the movie houses featuring these singers and actors inevitably had to be plunged helped us enter progressively but ineluctably into the world of the images themselves, every other reality becoming less important. The suffering that enveloped our own lives took on the mask of the actors (even if it meant sometimes degenerating into an irresistible kind of buffoonery); and the sobs that filled the movie house often covered the sound of the applause. Every gesture of the actor could fill us with tears, every dance reduce us to sobbing. The victories and defeats, indeed, each instant of beauty—all these things constituted a delicious torment for those of us who were seated there in the movie house (fleeing from our own history in order to follow these stories coming to us out of India!).

There were all those Indian actors and songs then, and in a language we could not understand. But all of that merely increased the enchantment of the hidden effects we felt. And even if Salman Rushdie is hardly Sharmy Kapoor, he is nevertheless connected in our minds with the same kind of enchantment that once touched our lives, less by its own power than because of the accumulated misery in us which was like a dike battered by the waves of oppression beating up against it— oppression suffered in the family, the school, even in God himself—all these things having been snatched away from us by those who dominated everything.

I am not good at the art of interpreting, but I do make reference to the spirit behind the works of speech of which each age must have its own verbal manifestations, all founded on a worldly basis. May each person, in the end, accept God as his judge. And since God cannot be subject to any qualifications, since He is duration without determination, every effort to try to enroll Him in any worldly cause can only be an effort that does injury to a Fullness that is really beyond our reach, a Fullness whose power of enchantment resides, precisely, in its secret, its mystery. Everything related to the hidden magic of the divine being also perforce enters into a whole that is perfectly just and equitable.

No one can make the claim of being able to prevail by acting as the supreme authority in matters of life and death. Islam teaches that all the divine messages to be delivered have already been delivered. It is in the gradual unfolding of our lives that this mystery will be progressively revealed—that same mystery which, by the way, has not revealed to anyone any denunciation of any person by the name of Salman Rushdie.

The Combat between the Demon and the Fire

by Abbas Baydoun

The great majority of Arab and Muslim liberals and men of the left have not been greatly concerned with the Rushdie affair. The author writes in a foreign language and is therefore suspect anyway where the treatment of the Arab and Islamic heritage is concerned. Rushdie is a writer on whom weighs the same suspicion that attaches to orientalists generally, namely, that he is already working out of a tradition that includes the colonialist mentality and all the arrogance that goes along with it. But it should not be forgotten that Rushdie is the author of texts treating the backwardness and collapse of postcolonialist societies; his two great novels, *Shame* and *The Children of Midnight*, have been translated into both Arabic and Persian, and readers have found in both of them a severe critique of the colonialist legacy.

This common lack of interest in Rushdie on the part of liberal Arabs and Muslims is surely a regressive thing, and it rather clearly expresses the low estate into which a certain failed type of liberalism has now fallen. It is a liberalism that is ignorant, however, and represents a type of secularism that is mere snobbery. To the abdication of basic principles it joins the absence of any solid foundations; in many respects, then, it is just about reduced to zero. Nevertheless it does sometimes seem that the intellectuals have

Poet, Libya. Originally written in Arabic.

59

almost wholly abandoned to the religious leaders any concern for anything having to do with religion and with the history of Islam.

And if the religious leaders conclude from this that the intellectuals have indeed adopted such a total hands-off policy toward religious questions, then there will no longer be any possibility of dealing with Arab and Islamic history, laws and questions of the state, language and literature, morality and sexuality, or even without doubt the origins of man and of the world without running into a religious ideal that will henceforth be untouchable. It will become equally impossible to deal with questions either of current events or of the past without running up against religious limits beyond which it will then be impossible to go. At that point we will be in a situation of having to leave to the religious authorities alone— whose openness of spirit has always varied according to the personality and the age, but today it has become narrower than ever—any concern for interpreting and defending our own history, image, and relationships with the rest of the world.

And when all these current religious views are combined with a populist ideology and a cult, either open or implicit, based on "tradition" and formulas from the past, then what we will be faced with will be a culture of mullahs, imams, propagandists, and storytellers in the village or quarter. In a situation such as this it will scarcely matter whether the storyteller in question is a fundamentalist, a nationalist, or even a communist. To such, then, is to be left the struggle for the renaissance of the Arabs!

Secularists, liberals, leftists, and nationalists have all thus regressed to the narrowest possible positions, and henceforth they must share their domains with religious leaders holding views that can neither admit any limits themselves nor otherwise allow any limits to be imposed on them. As a result of the Rushdie affair, and of the way in which it has most commonly been understood, the power of the mullahs has now reached into the narrow domain that used to be reserved for the modernizers. Henceforth no intellectual can really pretend to represent an independent culture, writing, or art. It should not be surprising that the "teachings" of the mullahs are now everywhere, in fact, and that they are now even pronouncing judgments on such things as literary metaphors, metonymy, and the meaning of books and other works of art.

We no longer possess the courage of our ancestors when we write on such subjects as religion, history, literature, sexuality, and morality; it is no longer possible for us even to take up again a work as ancient as that of Al-Jahiz. In this situation, perhaps the theologian is not the unhappiest person of all. Nevertheless when a popular ideology takes over in his domain as well, not even research on spiritual subjects can rise much above the level of slogans and shibboleths. The culture as a whole is then at the mercy of the streets and the propagandists of the streets; transgressing the limits set by them, even if it is advocated by religious people themselves, then becomes heresy and apostasy.

Perhaps the very worst thing about all this is the built-in tendency to confuse words with acts; writing becomes deprived thereby of its normal immunity. When no distinction is made any longer between a line or an article that is written down on paper and assassination, destruction, and other acts expressing undying hostility, it becomes lawful to respond to writing with knives and bullets. And when, furthermore, an idea is actually attributed to a demon, then exorcism by fire does finally appear to be the easiest possible solution: ideas themselves appear as a combat between the demon and the fire.

Hello, Salman Rushdie

by Riad H. Beïdas

"Hello, Bernard Shaw."

"Welcome to our brilliant journalist."

"We are well acquainted with the mordant irony of your language. But tell me: what do you have against our Lord Jesus Christ?"

"There no longer are any 'lords' in this twentieth century. But you will still note that I am always there to talk to people, in spite of what I may have written against them."

"But don't you fear God?"

"Which god are you referring to?"

"The One Who is on high."

"Should he not rather be down here among us?"

After looking up toward the sky, he added: "The sun is bright. It is better to look toward men. Everything that I have written, I have written out of conviction, and if you want to know what I think of Jesus Christ, well, I believe that he was certainly not any Christian!"

"Professor Renan, don't you see where you have gone wrong?"

"How wrong?"

"You have written things that have shaken the faith of many, and yet you go right on acting as if you have done nothing at all."

Writer, Palestine/Israel. Originally written in Arabic.

Renan burst out laughing and then pondered for a few moments. "The door always remains open for discussion. It is always possible to debate with me in the press. My ideas can be opposed, argued against; there are plenty of theologians around who can do it. As far as I am concerned, all my travels have simply reinforced me in my convictions."

"Don't you fear God?"

"'God' is my own spirit."

"Can we see you again?"

"Certainly. Pick out the place that suits you."

"Are you Kazantzakis, the writer?"

"Yes."

"How can it be that you are still at liberty in your movements, considering what you have written about Jesus Christ?"

"Please! Leave me alone. I want to be alone, away from everybody."

"But you have denied, abolished, the faith of our childhood!"

"I did it first of all for myself."

"Don't you fear that someone will attack you, do you harm?"

"You can see for yourself that I come and go as I please."

"What are you afraid of, Mr. Kazantzakis?"

"Of myself, of my own spirit."

"Lord have mercy!"

"Yes: mercy as regards this odious conversation. Give me some fresh air!"

"Good-by, sir."

Note: In view of the importance of all the atheists on our list, and in order to prevent any freedom of expression or artistic creation on the part of writers and poets, we call for the suspension of the examination of the case of Salman Rushdie for a period of one hundred years, beginning from the time of our own detestable era, characterized as it is by impiety, free thought, and atheism. This delay will enable us to finish beforehand with all the other atheists who have preceded him.

Meanwhile—hello, Salman Rushdie!

Theft of Fire

by Tahar Bekri

At Seville the works of the theologian Ibn Hazam were burned. The mystical poet Al-Hallaj was crucified. The writer Ibn Muqaffa was killed; the licentious poet Bashshar Ibn Burd was condemned for heresy. The philosopher Ibn Rushd (Averroes), the historian Ibn Khaldun, and the poets Ibn Sharaf and Al-Husri all had to go into exile. The list of instances in Arab and Islamic intellectual history where tyranny won out is a long one. How many intellectuals were pushed into hermetism, for example, in order to escape from the sword of the prince or from other forms of political, religious, and moral censure? The pen against the sword! Rather, the pen broken in two in the name of truth, when it came too close to the latter! Truth, ideas, personal opinions: on these subjects, unfortunately, despotism has been our common legacy. If we thought the present era was going to be more clement in this regard, we should have remembered the works of Gibran burned by the church and the words of dozens of Arab writers condemned by the mosques. It is as if repression were an integral part of our landscape or scenery, as if the kind of humiliation we suffer represented absolutely nothing out of the ordinary. Truth weighs down upon us like a lid. Even partial doubt, such as that of Al-Ghazzali and the Mu'tazilites, became a narrow box in which the beautiful and generous human adventure we call writing became confined; it has become demo-

Writer, Tunisia. Originally written in French.

nized. It should be recalled that the Arab poets who came before Islam all communicated with their genies, and poetry itself was seen as the parchment of the devil, pursued only by those who themselves were somehow offtrack.

The intolerance which has now come down on Salman Rushdie's head is more than a violation of his personal freedom of thought; it is an ill omen for any of us attempting to establish tolerance as a fundamental human value. Milan Kundera has attracted attention to the danger that can threaten the novel when morality wins out over humor. There is an even greater danger in store if the *fatwa* of the Ayatollah Khomeini becomes the rule; it will lead to the construction of new scaffolds for today's writers.

The only thing that can cancel out this unfortunate *fatwa* would be another *fatwa* rescinding it—thereby effacing the violation of international law represented by the original and also helping the Muslim world get beyond this latest of its ordeals. In the meantime, any authentic writing surely amounts to something like the theft of fire from the gods: anyone who tries it badly risks getting burned.

The End of an Illusion

by Rabah Belamri

Long before the Rushdie affair ever broke out, we were all well aware that censorship both of many types of thinking and also of many types of artistic creation was a fairly regular thing in the Muslim world. The current powers that be, whether monarchies, oligarchies, one-party states, or pseudo-republics, are not only sure of possessing the truth themselves; often they are also the only dispensers of the means of artistic production, culturally speaking. However, they have always tended to keep a rather tight rein on any productions of the spirit anyway; and generally, they have succeeded in maintaining a rather rigorous ban—employing methods up to and including assassination—on any serious criticism, on the posing of certain questions, or indeed, on boldness or nonconformity of any kind that might in any way undermine their monolithic system. Those intellectuals who would neither keep silent nor moderate their voices to the extent necessary generally had to emigrate to the West in order to make themselves heard at all. In the West one might still continue to believe in the possibility of free speech. And even if works of the spirit produced thusly outside, as it were, were themselves of limited influence, nevertheless it was important to Muslim intellectuals to be able to continue to conduct their own processes of reflection, to create works of their own, to mount a resistance, in other words, and finally, to be able to hope. It is this last illusion that

Writer, Algeria. Originally written in French.

the condemnation launched from Teheran has now reduced to nothing. Henceforth we now know that any artist or thinker who is born a Muslim, whether living in his country of origin or abroad, is pretty much, once and for all, condemned to silence.

It is as much the monstrous character of the sentence issued as it is the fact that it does mark the end of an illusion that has brought me on this occasion to descend into the street to express my indignation and sense of utter rebellion against this state of affairs. I have not taken part in any public protest since the end of the Algerian War. Nevertheless I owe it to the truth to state that intellectuals of Muslim origin—those who ought to have been the first to be concerned about this affair—have not been very numerous in joining the protests. Indifference to, or even tacit acquiescence in, this death sentence emitted by Iranian power has been all too common. Is this itself a reaction to the reaction in the West?

The Rushdie affair has very clearly revealed to the entire world that Islam—its values, mythology, and powers—has now demonstrated its incapacity to undergo with impunity any serious kind of examination, whether one based on reason or the imagination. In effect, the Iranian religious leaders have, by means of the Rushdie case, now issued a warning to anybody who might possibly be thinking of ever trying to lead Muslim societies out of the age of theology, to introduce any pluralism into them, or to replace the idea of dogma with that of free debate.

Muslim societies, handicapped for centuries in their intellectual and political torpor, are encountering an extreme difficulty in attempting to effect any kind of cultural change (change in their ways of being and thinking); such change is experienced by them, rather, as a loss of identity, a loss of one's own essence or substance. We must not forget that Muslim opinion, whether intra- or extramural, has very largely been prepared to confirm the sentence pronounced against Salman Rushdie. A society that refuses to question its own premises and denies its own artists and writers the opportunity to raise any doubts whatsoever; a society that does not dare to laugh at itself, and seeks to banish all impertinent questions—such a society has no chance at all of ever flowering again. It will no doubt continue to slumber amid all its tiresome idols, which it habitually goes on praising, and its sclerotic ancestral values, which it continues to exemplify; but that is about it.

The Target of the *Fatwa*

by Murat Belge

I want to draw attention to a certain aspect of the complex situation produced by the *fatwa* on Salman Rushdie. I do not mean to say that this aspect is more important than the individual horror to which Salman Rushdie has been condemned, but a lot has been said about that horror.

It took a long time for people, even democratic and progressive people, in the West, to come to terms with a multicultural mode of existence in their own societies after the Second World War, when so many emigrants from the old colonies came to settle down in European countries. The actual progress is not so easy as it looks in the abstract, and individuals have to fight their own cultural egocentricism on a day-to-day basis to understand, to tolerate, and then to respect a culture alien to them.

Khomeini represented the opposite pole: he wanted Islam in its most orthodox form and hated any kind of reconciliation between Islam and whatever was non-Islam. He issued the *fatwa*, shortly before he died, precisely to blow up any grounds for cultural interaction, which could lead Moslems astray.

Those Westerners who had stood for the necessity of understanding modes of thinking and value systems other than their own were thus confronted with a very grave challenge. It is relatively easy to defend, persuasively, the right of a Moslem girl going to

Writer, Turkey. Originally written in English.

school in a veil because this is her religious belief. But the liberal, democratic leftist—whatever—who speaks for this kind of toleration believes in the inviolable right of freedom of expression, and usually the latter is the basis upon which the former is cultivated. And this is the target the *fatwa* is aimed at. How can you tolerate a "different" faith that declares it a religious duty to kill someone for betraying?

There is no easy way out of this question. By advocating liberalism in this case, you are undermining the basis of your values.

This is what Khomeini wanted to achieve, and this after all is what he did achieve.

The private destiny of the writer (a brilliant one, too) is now inextricably tied up with this general problem. I do not know of a remotely similar case in history.

We cannot accept this destiny ordained for Salman Rushdie, nor can we accept the general cultural/political impasse. On this second aspect of the extraordinary problem, the intellectual and moral leaders of the Islamic world bear the greater portion of responsibility.

In some ways the crisis resembles the debate between Gazzali and Averroès. The way that debate was settled, or allowed to settle itself in history, did not lead Islam to intellectual or spiritual "victories." Maybe now is the time and this is the opportunity to settle that question as well.

The Liberty of the Word

by Emna Belhadj Yehyia

Thought is a key that opens out upon the unknown, out upon risk and the confrontation of possibilities. One of the reasons for the frequent defections of thinkers and artists in the Arab and Muslim world is fear: fear of the very adventure of thought, as well as a continual fear in the face of threats from the politico-religious world. These defections and quiet attempts to dodge responsibility are really traps; they lead us to absurd conclusions and are actually contrary to the order of the world. Our personalities bear the stigmata of a too-long-reigning law of silence. We are of course conscious of this, though, and so we seek to efface these stigmata by brave words intended to put an end to the tragedy of silence which truly does weigh down upon our lives.

You will say: let him express himself anyway, this Arab and Muslim writer, even if liberty is lacking. Let him show great signs of docility and adhesion, let him give full voice to the grandeur of obedience and value of acquiescence! Nobody will attempt to impede him in this; indeed, everybody will support and applaud him. However, such voices as these would have no power to touch us, much less persuade us. And the only way we could ever relate to them would be to remain deaf to their pleadings. So what is the upshot of it all? Can nothing at all be said on our subject? Is there nothing but silence and indifference, faint echoes in an endless desert?

Writer, Tunisia. Originally written in French.

Such a judgment as the one rendered against Rushdie is difficult to accept. It is absolutely revolting, in fact, that it should have been issued in the name of Islam, a religion in which my forbears found the meaning of life, built their world, created their visions, developed their morality and human relations, chanted both their harmonies and disharmonies, and built their palaces as well as their hovels. It is also the religion of my mother, a woman coming from a family of Hanifite theologians who, having practiced down through the centuries, developed a solid substance composed of piety, readiness to listen, moderation, tolerance, a certain ingeniousness, as well as strength of soul combined with intellectual modesty. My mother reads the Koran every evening, and the immensity of her faith can only be guessed by this essential tie that unites her to others. How can it be that this oxygen I have breathed from birth, which formed my first impressions of the order of the world—something still associated with the smell of amber, sweets, and milk—has been so thoroughly betrayed by censors breathing fire, who apparently want to unite in a tyranny under the banner of Islam everything that is dry, cruel, and confining? How can the very air have been so poisoned by men who want to associate Islam with their own bitter resentments and harsh, pitiless judgments? How can they pretend to transform it into a prison from which no one can henceforth escape?

Such muddle and confusion are not acceptable. For us the loss of liberty corresponds to a loss of memory—and to the progressive extinction of the voice that once defined both our wisdom and follies, our certitudes and fantasies, our heights and depths. It is through the word "liberty," and through the liberty of the word, that man makes himself, and that there is born into this universe the promise of escape, no matter how bogged down in reality we might otherwise customarily be.

Islam and Literature

by Jamel Eddine Bencheikh

A call for the murder of a British writer issued by an Iranian imam, handed on by an organization of Indian and Pakistani gangsters, then complacently given credibility by the media—all these things have naturally provoked some reactions that need to be analyzed with care. Let us note, for the moment, that this call for the assassination of an individual was legitimized in advance by a rabbi of Israel, who thus manifested for Salman Rushdie the same sort of compassion that is regularly manifested for Palestinian children in the occupied territories. The archbishop of Lyons, for his part, carved out for himself a role of unprecedented solidarity with those who have been "injured," leaving it to other priests to treat Muhammad as a lubricous satan who had preached a criminal religion.

In the university, words can change their meaning and concepts their allegiance with the same brisk ease. Expressing a thought that is tortuous in its length, contradictory in its argument, and ridiculous in its conclusions, Professor Arkoun of the Sorbonne (see *Le Monde* of March 15, 1989) believes that to invoke the rights of man in this case would be to "lock oneself into a western model of historical development." For him, an Enlightenment philosophy and dogmatic secularism would simply constitute a replay of the kind of discourse historically typical of European colonialism. Another

Professor, Algeria/France. Originally written in French. This text was published in *Le Monde* in April 1989.

view is that in order to resolve the crisis, there is only one way to go: create a theological institute so that, according to B. Étienne, also a university professor, Muslim preachers could be recruited and formed in order to counter the accelerated current Iranization of the Muslims of France. Thus, even the French university would be arrogating to itself the right to form Islamic preachers!

But what does literature have to do with all this? This is a rather easy question to answer. Let's face it: no Muslim is ever going to agree to read a burlesque exercise about a Muhammad who has been placed at the heart of an existing Islamic reality. This fiction, which substitutes for the true Islamic reality its own representations, necessarily constitutes for a Muslim a major attack on his religion. This literary composition makes use of the prophet in order to project dreams about him in a way that harms not an individual but rather a whole order of the world; it is an order that gives a significance to prophecy and fixes limits to the writing about it. Naguib Mahfouz, a Nobel Prize winner, is well aware of all this. In December 1988, he interrupted on his own initiative the serial publication of his *Son of Medina*. Back in 1959, this book only appeared at all as a result of the personal invitation of Nasser (there was also a pirated Lebanese edition). Why? Because God appears in the book (Djabulawi) in the midst of three prophets represented by the local political boss of the quarter. Sharkawi ran into similar difficulties in 1962, when he tried to depict in a rather Marxist fashion a Muhammad in the guise of a leader of the poor.

Let us recognize something else here: in Arab countries fiction is not fictive. Literature can only speak of realities that leave no room for any criticism or that end up with what is not said. At this point, of course, the muzzlers of the literary word have changed; they are no longer so many learned old men in the mosques as they are some of the much younger new wolves representing the new totalitarianism. It is a lesson that the new political regimes have learned from history; for these new regimes have, in about equal measure, enslaved consciences, obliterated liberties, reduced the intellectual classes to nothing, and emptied the university. In this situation, what free thought is there any longer that is not nourished in silence, exile, and "going it alone"? The "new Islam," in rejecting the power structure currently in place, confronts a stupefying cultural void out there. Arising out of a mixture of pride and frustration, and apparently more anxious to wield steel than promote faith, it fits rather crazily into the void created by the new authoritarian governments. In essence, the battle opposes against each other tyrants who are of the same general type. The recent experience of the Mahgreb, and the free and lively debates that have taken place there, have perhaps constituted the last chance anywhere for Islam to emerge as a religion of free men. But it is not in any institute of theology that these free men are going to be formed.

All this naturally constitutes a very real problem. But it is one that is effectively obscured when, suddenly, the scarcely hoped-for example of a book that happens to be too iconoclastic appears and is then seized upon in order to make one's points. If, as was affirmed at a recent Islamic conference held in Riyadh, there truly is "a cultural and ideological invasion aimed at the destruction of Islamic culture," then we need to be told what indigenous conception of freedom is guiding the current dispositions of the politicians in power as well as the ferocious current holders of positions of religious leadership. For these latter are certainly not being guided by the faith. Rather, they are dragging the faith into the labyrinths of their own Machiavellianism—and into the convulsions that have arisen out of their own ambitious fury. What is this murderous kind of virtue that we are presumably supposed to take from the works of an Ibn Taymiyah (who, so far as I know, was scarcely sent by God)? In the year 1293, this extremist Hanbalite, who was also a very severe judge of Ibn Arabi, was imprisoned for the intransigence that he exhibited at the time of the affair of 'Assaf Al-Nasrani, a Christian Arab from Suwaydah, who had been accused of insulting the Prophet. It was on this occasion that the same Ibn Taymiyah composed the *Book of the Sword Unsheathed in Defense of the Insulted Prophet*.

Once in place, such a system as the one we have now never lets go of its prey. The interdict issued by Khomeini extends its sway like an inoperable cancer not only over the whole realm of the sacred but also over the realms of morality, politics, society, sex, the family, the fatherland—it extends its sway everywhere. Literature, reduced to silence, becomes nothing but something dictated by the false devout, who believe that they alone know the truth. In this situation, virtually everything ends up falling into the category of being an insult: an insult to figures of history and mythology as well as to people still living. Even the paths of reverie are forbidden, even those of pleasure—just four years ago a tribunal in Cairo ordered the destruction of three thousand copies of *The Thousand and One Nights* which had been seized. Everything is henceforth subject to be plunged into the abyss of disaster, and at a moment's notice: sculpture, painting, cinema, what have you.

Moral principles and social rules are henceforth wielded like clubs; they stifle creativity and render sterile the very power of invention—that is to say they stifle and render sterile precisely those things that might have been capable of ensuring the survival of an independent culture, or at least capable of resisting aggression. If there is indeed "an imperialist and Zionist plot," it is by the action of free beings that it is most likely to be effectively opposed, not by corrupt leaders who show more courage when confronted by a single, solitary writer than they ever do when faced with the multinational corporations, the armament industries, or the traffickers in the resources of the Third World. Meanwhile, in the Middle East and elsewhere, it is today apparently possible to gas people, torture them, violate women, and drive children crazy without—God be thanked!—ever being accused of blasphemy!

However, the art of writing cannot really be reduced to a condition of slavery. Writing arises out of the shadows as well as out of well-lighted places; it is born out of the pleasure of life as well as out of its sufferings; it shares the torments undergone by all as it shares the wounds suffered by each individual; it can be disarmed but it cannot be reduced; and it cannot but lay bare what it does treat, even though it can, of course, fall into a pitiful parody of it. Literature lives on grandeur as it does on failure; it creates both beauty and honor; it treats dreams as well as reality. Nobody can make its choices for it externally.

Of course literature can also be criticized, even violently. Indeed, to practice criticism actually develops the spirit of liberty. But can we threaten authors with death? Never. If we were ever finally to accept such a thing in the world of today, we would logically have to start passing a very different type of judgment on many glorious pages of Arab literature. Thus, we would have to judge Bashshar Ibn Burd differently, along with Abu Nuwwas, Muti', Abu l-'Ala Al-Maari, Al-Hallaj, Ibn Quzman, and dozens of others. We would have to ban Ibn Rushd all over again, along with Ibn Bajja and many others too. We do not go to literature merely in order to venerate it, obey, and then be silent; rather, we go to literature to help us open our eyes to the world. There is no such thing as a poetry that is not always in open rebellion against lies, as a matter of fact.

Meanwhile, during exactly the same period of repression we are currently undergoing, think what true and great challenges of the twentieth century are being neglected! Mathematics, biology, medicine, astrophysics, the information sciences—all these things are opening up prodigious new perspectives for our times. The scientific power of the future is already in the process of setting everything in place and distributing all the various roles of what is soon to be. The great economic and military complexes are currently dividing up the world. For our part, are we merely going to specialize in the production of whirling dervishes?

In any case, we are certainly not going to commit our irrepressible desire for spirituality either to any church or any inquisition; we are in need of no rabbinate of fanaticism, nor of any lugubrious type of messianism which, as a matter of fact, celebrates nothing but death. As far as the Islam of France is concerned—and it no longer seems to be a temporary phenomenon here—it should *never* allow itself to transgress the laws of the republic. These laws cost the people who put them in place a very great deal. They permit the Muslim community to live here in peace. Although it should make its voice heard, the Islamic community of France should *not* be specifically connected with any political power, much less a tool for foreign governments to manipulate. Under the conditions we currently have, the Islam of France can still nourish a faith as exemplary in its practice as it will be enriching in its thought. There were great Christian Berbers such as St. Augustine, after all. Why should there not be Muslims as great in France?

There certainly does exist an open, fraternal, compassionate, and generous Islamic tradition that not even the furious howling of today's hyenas can succeed in silencing. This tradition lacks neither refinement nor elegance nor concern for human joy. It is an Islam with feasts that do not resemble mourning; rather, they are replete with songs, laughter, and pardons exchanged between men and women who, as evening falls, still love to listen to Andalusian love poetry before they finish the day by reciting the suras of the Koran that speak of mercy.

Those who believe in God need his own tenderness. They do not need the hatred of some of his zealots. We must be vigilant against these zealots. We must not let them cut off our own souls.

Verse of the Mirrors

by Mohammed Bennis

1. Say: this writing is blood that points
   trembling into a distance that is out of joint
   This blood and the name that gathers us together.

2. It is a cloud on a wall
   It hastens the meeting with the wind.

3. We begin to exist by dreams
   Then the lances lacerate two necks.

4. Steps cross one another
   Silence is an archipelago of shadows and knives.

5. Two blind factions assassinate the moon
   on the edge of words
   Never will we be silent.

6. Your breath, your breath
   The sea liberates a bird
   and we divide up the horizon.

Poet, Morocco. Originally written in Arabic.

7. Blood alone seizes upon the instant
   By your hand protect your own hand
   and renew the vow not to betray.

8. The fatherland is no longer possible
   nor is exile
   And you, are you the madman of the frontiers?

9. Henna, rose water, incense
   Alchemy of dead writing.

10. What difference between a tree oozing
    the blood of Hallaj
    a river whose sources are the blood of Lorca
    a land that cries I am the blood of Husayn Muruwa
    the blood of the young Algerian
    the blood of Tahar Djaout.

11. A cigarette, leaves, pure embers
    such is the ceremonial of blood.

12. And they kill in the name of all the Books
    Yes my friend Ghassan Kanafani.

13. Strange voices for a time
    caught between blood and blood.

14. Greetings to cruel windows
    closed upon a hand that does not kill.

15. I hear the scratching of the pen
    recalling passages that they do nothing but pass down.

16. Distances are abolished
    the dark age lasts
    and the lock of hair of Abu Nuwwas
    mirthful and stubborn in his desire.

17. They knock on the door
    The poem unfolds in successive waves
    The fact is that your clash is mine.

18. We no longer belong to the line
    of blessed stars
    And you, tongues, you will not die
    It is for that that we write.

19. In an equivocal calm
    Omar Khayyam dictated to me a cloudy language
    which was lost without reaching me.

20. Who threw me in this place?
    Orphans are consecrating their fraternity
    neither East nor West
    has anything but blood and place.

Rushdie, or the Textual Question

by Fethi Benslama

The Salman Rushdie affair raises what we may call "the textual question" in its most acute form; it is an eminently instructive case for the world of today. First of all, it is instructive for Muslims, who are summoned in this end-of-an-era period in which we live today to make some fundamental revisions in their ancient way of seeing things. More than that, though, Rushdie has come to constitute a crucial symbol of what is at stake in the game between Muslims and those who primarily affirm European values. And what is at stake in this case has even taken on the character of a significant world crisis, of which the underlying factors are well worth analyzing, especially since it is quite foreseeable that this kind of case can only too easily be repeated, perhaps with even worse consequences. We are confronted here, in fact, with two different manifestations of the "unacceptable," and both are related to a textual question. A literary text is accused of defaming the figure of the Prophet and of committing blasphemy by evoking a certain episode in a way that casts doubt upon a text considered sacred. On one side, the view evidently is that literature cannot ever be subjected to any kind of prohibition, certainly not by any prescriptions of a moral character; according to this view, literature enjoys the contingent strength of an unlimited freedom, and from this very fact *it* therefore is "sacred." On the other side of the controversy, an author has been accused of unjustified attacks on something that is

---

Psychoanalyst, Turkey. Originally written in French.

supposed to be absolutely prohibited, he is accused of violating an absolute law that extends beyond mere human reason. Thus, in the Rushdie case, the rights of the imagination are flatly opposed to a religious necessity that is perceived to be absolutely imperious and wholly necessary to preserve both a highly symbolic institution as well as the great written account on which it is based (the Koran). One side of the controversy sees in the scandal experienced by the other side precisely the matter of the scandal *it* experiences! Both sides have put forward something as absolutely "untouchable." Thus there is a core substance here that goes far beyond a case of mere manipulation of the masses and public opinion. Even granting that such manipulation is going on, the whole affair would never have achieved the prominence it has if there were not serious reasons behind it which move and motivate those manipulating or being manipulated.

The very title, *The Satanic Verses,* immediately strikes at the heart of the Islamic textual question. It refers to a well-known episode much commented upon by numerous traditional sources. In the middle of a revelation expressed in a sura affirming the absolute oneness of God, it seems that Satan was momentarily supposed to have taken on the traits of the Archangel Gabriel, the angel by whom the revelation was conveyed, in order to extol certain goddesses found in the pre-Islamic Arab pantheon. The Prophet corrected this text in due course, but the memory of the apparent aberration was not forgotten.

On the evidence, the whole incident touches on a nerve point at the junction of the human and the transcendent where a sacred text was once produced, a point therefore marked as one standing between the purely human and the absolute to which men are also dedicated. In such a case, a definite "construction" or "installation" set up or put together in the same way, that is, as something given or handed down, would always seem to be an absolutely necessary thing; in fact, every symbolic foundation claiming to be the basis of any law always has to be put together in this way. Whether we are talking about a religious system or merely an ethical or political system, its successful installation depends upon its having been made "in the name of"—in the name of the higher cause or higher law or principle, even the highest, on which the foundation has been made. It is only by a "text," in other words, that one is ever considered authorized to name, to found, to legislate, to judge, to give life, to decree death, and so on, and it is for this reason that "the textual question" must always come to the fore. When such a foundation is made, it is necessarily sacred, idealized, venerated; love of a basic "text" therefore lies at the very origin or foundation of every community. This is, of course, true of such diverse texts as the Bible, the Koran, the myth of corporal ancestry found among certain Australian tribes, the Declaration of the Rights of Man and of the Citizen of 1789, and so on. Naturally, in view of all this, the means by which a foundational text was originally created or came about is always, therefore, of the greatest importance; for it is here that transcendence "immanentizes," and immanence is transcended. It is the place or area of "mediation," and therefore the location of its great secret.

Now, while modern systems are content merely to be assured of the *legality* of such an origin of foundation, traditional cultures still insist upon expunging any impurity thought to have affected the process in any way or at any point. The "construction" or "installation" has to be as perfect as the cause or law or principle from which it is supposed to have proceeded. For example, the incarnation of the Word in Christianity must be seen in terms of the operation of the Holy Spirit (and, much later, also of the dogma of the Immaculate Conception).

Thus, the episode of *the Satanic verses* designates a situation where the purity of the Koranic revelation has been fundamentally called into question. That such an episode could actually have been mentioned and treated by ancient Muslim authors whose authority is not doubted merely proves that at the heart of the foundation of Islam, what we have called here the textual question, the question of mediation, that of divine-human "construction" or "installation," had already been satisfactorily settled for that time. In fact, great debates took place on the subject; and even some rather radical positions were taken on the question, since the Mu'tazilites went so far as to deny the uncreated origin of the Koran. I cannot go into all the ins and outs involved in the emergence of the definitive text of the Koran here. What can be said is that this text was at one and the same time human, all-too-human, as well as divine—at times excessively divine. We see this in the case of the *Nabi*, the Prophet, passing through the great ordeal of melancholy with the help of his wife; we see it in how he fell prey to anguish and hallucinations even to the point where he feared for his own reason, before finally receiving the dictation from the archangel. In fact, the history of Islam passed through several phases where the "all-too-human" thus predominated. The episode of *The Satanic Verses* illustrates this; what this episode tells us is that even the law cannot escape from the discontinuity of otherness, from usurpations of one's basic identity, and even from interference in the most privileged relationship among man, the angel, and God.

There were also other periods, of course, when the "excessively divine" predominated and a primitive faith was propagated, a faith ignorantly based on the presumption of the proximity of God—a faith all the more ignorant in that God was made to seem so vulgarly close. It was forgotten that in Islam there is a very important distinction between the Book (*al-kitab*), as a concept bringing together in the writing of the Koran the absolute Book; and the book itself as a concrete work (*al-mushif*) that refers to the Koran, which is actually available to us in the official edition brought out by the Caliph Uthman, having thus definitely passed through human hands in its transmission. As a matter of fact—and remarkably so—the Koran itself affirms that the absolute Book, "the mother of all books" (*um al-kitab*), resides with God himself and is inaccessible to both men and angels; the Koran as a concrete work is nothing but a readable copy of the timeless original. Thus, nobody at all has access either to the original or to the totality of the Book! The text, in fact, adopts a plurality of laws, languages, peoples, and readings.

Most of this has as a practical matter been largely forgotten, however. Muslims stopped studying and reflecting on their origins centuries ago; they stopped making use of the open features of their own system which once enabled them, by means of the text of the Koran itself, to continue to maintain an actual relationship between the human and the transcendent. Thus, the actual "construction" or "installation" of all this which we have spoken about has become the source of many anachronisms which have sometimes even been tragic—but also sometimes comic too! Sometimes, when Muslims make use of European techniques, the gap between their ancient "construction" and the modern viewpoint becomes so yawning that they can easily become dizzy. Many Muslims then either become immobilized by it all, or else they have to resolve to move forward, whatever the risk. To be a Muslim today is to dance along the edge of an abyss.

Europeans who have extended to the textual question one of the modalities of modern techniques, namely, the disclosure or uncovering of all origins, sources, foundations, and so on, are now no less deprived of their former ancient and firm relationship with the absolute than are today's Muslims; but the Europeans have the advantage of already having identified and analyzed the whole process of what we have called the divine-human "construction" or "installation." For the Europeans, the question becomes reduced to one of what we may call the human "writing machine." Everything becomes the product of a human "author." Nevertheless, for them, all literature, along with everything else connected with the textual question, has to be subjected to a painstaking process of disclosure or uncovering, in the course of which nothing at all is ever to be spared. In Europe, there no longer are any absolutes maintained; or, at any rate, such absolutes are maintained only through the legality of their forms and images. Works of fiction since *Don Quixote* have been recognized to be basically extravagant in their essence, and hence capable of being mocked or derided; and a new "ethic" of insolence has even been introduced, which destroys all the former conventions. Texts, like subjects, are now based on a principle of auto-foundation. Such a viewpoint cannot but clash fiercely with the traditional "constructions" and "installations" which give support to the great hidden work of God and to the status of man who is subject to God.

All the great traditional systems are characterized by dissimulation of their own origins; the obscurity or opaqueness of their historical condition is always vigilantly to be kept under wraps. So when modernity attempts to remove these wraps, to show the "human" artifice at the origin of every "construction," a clash becomes inevitable. In fact, one can say that the modern spirit consists of the—usually rather terrifying—enjoyment involved in the deliberate unmasking of such origins. This is one of the sources of the self-sufficiency that secular literature enjoys today and that it also spreads, perhaps more effectively than any other medium (though with an exigency made up of a kind of omnipotence and an extreme fragility, both mixed inextricably together). The individual *author*, after all, is really a rather singular modern invention. He affirms himself only by placing his own signature on his work; but he actually spends himself in writing a text that really expropriates his own true identity from him at the same time as it transforms him into a kind of "power" of dissemination existing within an imagined multiplicity. The author can only become the hand of someone by becoming the hand of no one.

Salman Rushdie is a victim of the basic clash described here. What is involved in his case goes far beyond any individual insult and outrage, and even beyond any individual innocence or guilt. What is involved here is a fatal encounter brought about by a piece of writing. Rushdie was not the first to fashion such a piece of writing, but perhaps he was the first to carry to the extreme the whole European textual modality applied to the ancient "construction" of the Koranic text. The nature of this encounter is something we must understand; it constitutes one of the principal manifestations of what today is so often called "modernity," in fact. This modernity is now worldwide, and it consists in the near universal diffusion of the irrepressible European practice of exposing and uncovering all sources—disclosing all origins, exploding all myths—including, first of all, of course, those on which its own civilization was based. It consists, in other words, of something I like to call "European extremism." We can certainly verify that the power that resides in this practice of questioning everything has now passed, by means of the operation of a kind of "parabolic machine," which consists of the diffusion of a modern literature based on modern attitudes, into the hands of just about everybody in the world; it has already crossed all the frontiers. There is, however, a dwindling of the power inherent in the working out of the textual question, as it goes along, just as there is a weakening of its effects. It is in this latter sense that modern literature can even provide some resistance to the corrosive power of the textual question itself, even as it sometimes participates in its liquidation. For what we see is that writers more and more write for the express purpose of feeding the "parabolic machine" itself, along with its cultural adjuncts, and thus producing on a grand scale what Georges Bataille has styled "the slide of thought into impotence, which is then turned into literature."

In this situation we need to pay particular attention to all the immigrants and refugees—an entire humanity belonging to the ancient traditions of "the text," and hence fundamentally affected by the textual question—who now find themselves resident in Europe. It is through these refugees, and especially, considering their condition, their anguish and the various manifestations they exhibit, that we see revealed all the ingredients that went into the creation of the Salman Rushdie affair—the confrontation between the modern Western approach to the textual question and the ancient unencumbered view of the phenomenon of a sacred text. In fact, it may be only now—now that its own past is coming back up against it in the person of living human beings—that the West too can ever become capable of grasping the extent of what it has done. The mob in the suburbs of London that began to burn Salman Rushdie's book at the very beginning of the whole scandal was composed of a few hundred persons, each of whom in almost every way was very similar to the main character in the book: "they had all fallen out of the airplane," so to speak. Salman Rushdie, of course, created a character who fell out of an airplane and put him in a modern book that described how this same character had fallen away from the Book (the Koran) as well. However, the people of the Book did not accept this particular fall, and so they burned the modern book describing all the tribulations of falling away from the Book. They condemned it as another "crime," committed before our very eyes, by the "modernity" to which they too now henceforth belong. The following phrase, which appears in a letter by Kafka to Max Brod, resounds eerily here: "The writer is the scapegoat of humanity;

thanks to him, people can sin innocently, or almost innocently."

Modern literature began with the falling away from the Book, and its continuation now perhaps depends upon its being exiled from the sacred Text. This is a situation that, on the evidence, the Rushdie affair brings out very well. However, this evidence should not lead us to be satisfied with the explanation provided as to what the real transgression consists of. The transgression does not merely consist of acts that are the negation of or that are contrary to the law. Rather, the transgression involves the affirmation of something beyond, something that the Salman Rushdie case should now lead us to examine further. It should now lead us, as a matter of fact, to re-open the whole dossier on literature itself, and consider again its action, necessity, and stormy promise. There are no doubt many of us who have had more than a presentiment that in this shaking up of the whole Muslim world by a work of literature, in this pronouncement of a death sentence on a man for producing that work, and in the sacrifice now being demanded of *one man* in order to appease millions of others, there is to be found something considerably more significant than a mere case of blasphemy involving the aberrant judgment of a tyrant. Let us not attempt to place outside the range of reason something that rather reveals to us some of the actual workings of reason in human history.

To assert that by means of literature we move from being a humanity made by a text to being one that makes its own text— indeed, a society that even pretends to mass-produce its own basic texts as a kind of industry—is really to assert something quite banal. Yet this is precisely the principle upon which the novel of Salman Rushdie is based; it is the story both of a particular turning in human affairs and of the writer's own personal torment. In appropriating materials from the original Islamic text, in reworking and refashioning these materials as he pleased—or rather, in working them up into an entirely different story than is found in the original, a story of falling away from the Book—Rushdie, in one stroke and within the compass of a single novel, has exemplified one of the great modern suppositions of literature: *the fiction of the common origin which has now been demolished.* Rushdie effected his act of destruction of this common origin in order to substitute an artifice or invention of his own imagination, one he asks us to believe in merely for the short period of time it takes to read his text. Moving away from his own origins and his own community of origin, Rushdie is a writer who thus projects a blank space in order to be able to provide free rein for his own imagination.

All the great experiences of modern literature testify to this same supposition concerning the destruction of origins, by the way; it might even be possible to assert that the modern West *affirms* the right of all of us to fall away from our own origins as we please. Everyone can adopt the same supposition for anybody else at all, by the simple gesture of opening up the book and accepting the fiction that the common origin has now been demolished. Thus, moving from novel to novel, we can then go on to other stories of the same kind, continually piling up more debris from the now destroyed origins. It was this basic supposition of modern literature that made the clash inevitable in the Rushdie case—and also made it so menacing.

In his book Salman Rushdie went the whole way, once and for all, as if he really wanted to be, all by himself, all the different authors who had never been able to exist in the history of his tradition. Without flinching, he chose the Satanic suras where the affirmation of the Oneness of God is clouded over by a reference to multiplicity. And again without flinching, he undertook to caricature holy figures in the history of Islam by turning them into perverse figures and showing them wandering around in foreign parts as if he wished to see realized the entire project of hate concerning the exile of the gods; for according to this view, the demons were nothing but ancient gods who had been exiled. Without flinching once again—and again at one stroke going straight to the extreme limit—Rushdie produced modern literature's typical shattering affirmation concerning the infinite distance from human origins that modern literature habitually assumes, indeed demands—and requires that others demand as well!

To speak truly, unless we want to remain at the level of puerile declarations of innocence, we have to recognize that there is something really frightful in all of this—as there is something really frightful in some of the corollaries of it: for instance, considering the protests of

Muslims as something merely absurd, or equating the totally unacceptable death sentence with the maintenance of an ambivalent facade of interests and insulted dignity which is contrasted with the image of an Islam composed of madmen. There is something frightful in all this, then, but it is the same kind of frightfulness that is actually a condition of, even the possibility of, modern literature, as it also is a condition of its characteristic ecstasy. It is frightful because the original clash confronts the frightfulness of stripping the cover off of everything, of calling everything into question, of featuring the unbelievable and promoting the unnameable, of encounters with creatures of terror who have no other reason to exist except to move away, to go outside themselves—but of course without ever having any identifiable destination.

The current political exploitation of the Salman Rushdie affair has consisted mostly of spreading fear among the masses—a fear all the more intense in that the text of modernity proposes no reconstruction or restoration of the common origin or foundations. The book speaks of no origin except its own—it has no end in view except its own; it enters into the dubious wager that any real speech is possible without beginnings and without ends except those it asserts itself. This is the scandal of the individual word which has now become the declared enemy of the collective. The author too, therefore, necessarily appears as the exact negative counterpart of the idealized leader—the same leader who pronounced the sentence of death. If we recall what Freud wrote in his *Psychology of the Masses*, we can see how the negative version of the leader is one of the sources of the present disaster. People were surprised that Salman Rushdie provoked protestations by great masses of Muslims when all he did was merely produce a work of literature. People should rather have been surprised that, absent any possibility of a common origin or foundation, simple words should still have existed and proliferated to the extent that they have. The West endeavors to go on on its own, but it has become so accustomed to the way that it is that it forgets to be surprised by some of its own bewildering inventions—until they double back upon it from a world it once attempted to conquer. And they double back on it, of course, in forms it no longer recognizes as its own.

A New Human Illness: Fictionalizing Salman Rushdie and His Critics

by Reda Bensmaïa

In an article he published in *The Observer* (October 1, 1989) on "The Rushdie Affair," Umberto Eco observed: "One of the effects of the mass media is that they have brought fiction to people who have never before even read a novel, and who have never accepted 'the contract of fiction,' that is, the willing suspension of disbelief." Then he added this rather frightening remark: "There are probably no more than about 50,000 people in any given country who belong in the category of novel readers."[1] And in truth, all the din that has been stirred up around the novel of Salman Rushdie, *The Satanic Verses*, has come from the fact that what his detractors—and among them, those who eventually became his persecutors—have chiefly reproached him with is not so much that he wrote abominable things about the Prophet, his wives, and his morals, but rather that he lied about them, or rather, that he did not tell the truth about them—or even worse, that he distorted historical reality about

---

Writer, Algeria. Originally written in French.

1   Umberto Eco, *The Observer*, October 1, 1989, quoted by Malise Ruthven in *A Satanic Affair, Salmon Rushdie, and the Rage of Islam* (London: Chatto & Windus, 1990), 60. In the context of his article, it is clear that in speaking of "novel readers," Eco is referring to readers who are capable of seeing the difference between what a writer might think, desire, etc., and what he might wish to try, experiment with, or bring about the release of pent-up emotion through in a work of fiction.

them. This is how this author has been seen by people who essentially have no idea of the types of relations an author might have with his created characters. For such readers, everything has been taken as if the extremely elaborate and complex form Salman Rushdie imposed on his novel had to be considered entirely secondary to one, and only one important fact, namely, sacrosanct historical reality.

The other aspect of the problem raised by the novel is how clearly it reveals the reactions to its appearance as resting upon the belief of many readers that Rushdie, a man of flesh and blood, is one and the same as his work and belongs to it "in the first degree."[2] For such readers, Rushdie can endorse only what his characters do and say. In vain can Rushdie cry from the rooftops that his book has been grossly "judged and indeed misjudged because a standard of historical method has been applied to it when in fact it is nothing else but a work of the imagination." In vain can he repeat to whomever might be willing to listen that "the true aim of fiction is in no way to distort facts but rather both to explore human nature itself and also to explore the ideas with which the human race supports itself." A movie actor might well present us with acts or words that are "blasphemous," for example, but the question of the exact status of those words or acts, whether they are true, referential, or perhaps merely fictitious, still remains to be settled separately. It is possible to maintain *mordicus*—that is, stoutly or vigorously—that the man in question is a congenital renegade and blasphemer, and that it is always necessary to defend the well-known principles of Islam against all comers from every quarter. In vain can Rushdie then plead that he was outside any Muslim country; in vain can he say that he did not even write in the language of the Koran; in vain, finally, can he protest that his novel has not even been read by many of the very ones who are crying out the loudest against him. In spite of all these things, however, the most virulent kind of hatred has

---

2   My analogy here is with the Anglo-Saxon juridical expression "murder in the first degree."

nevertheless descended upon his head—and an actual price has been put upon his head as well!

Perhaps, "all this" does explain "all that." We are not, after all, simply talking about "good reading" in this case, nor even about "good writing"; rather, we are above all dealing with a new "human illness"—although it is a kind of illness that is in reality probably as old as the world. It has no doubt been there all along, incubating, until the Rushdie affair came along and allowed it to burst out in all its virulence. Such an illness is only too human: in no way does it consist in not being able to read—literally being illiterate. It consists in not being able to identify the fictional in what one is living, and inversely, in not being able to understand what is real and what is not in what one is reading. In this connection, it is perhaps useful to recall that it was not after having actually *read* the novel that the Ayatollah Khomeini was moved to summon his secretary and dictate the fateful and deadly *fatwa* that would soon transform one of the most inventive of today's "minority" novelists into an international renegade. No: the Ayatollah Khomeini acted only after seeing on television the persecution and death of Muslims protesting in Pakistan against *The Satanic Verses* (which, by the way, they could never have read in that particular country, as in many other countries).[3]

Thus, Salman Rushdie appears to have been less a victim of an ideological conflict than moved by a kind of a "blind spot"; like

---

3 The following is what Daniel Pipes has reported on this subject in his book, *The Rushdie Affair* (New York: Birch Lane Press, 1990), 27:
   Accounts differ as to how exactly Khomeini learned about the novel. According to one version, he was in his house on February 13, watching the evening news on Iranian television, as he did every night, when he saw pictures of the rioting in Pakistan. The scenes he witnessed moved him deeply. Indeed, it is hard to imagine news more affecting for someone with Khomeini's sense of Islamic solidarity than the Muslims outside and American Cultural Center crying out, "God is great," then proceeding to die at the hands of the police. A second account has him hearing about the rioting in Pakistan from a small transistor radio he took with him on his three daily half-hour constitutionals. The final version has him alerted to the existence of the book by a petition, accompanied by translated excerpts, sent to him in January by a group of British Muslims via the

those he pitied—who, in effect, fashioned the *fatwa* for him at a distance—the Ayatollah evidently believed it to be perfectly legitimate to do as he wished based upon what he had seen and not upon what he had read. In acting thus, however, he effectively made it impossible for anybody henceforth to *read* any longer what could no longer so easily be *seen*, namely, the very complicated plot of the novel. This is a novel in which, perhaps for the first time in such a radical and systematic manner, a writer of Muslim origin attempted—not to call into question the historicity of the Prophet or his legitimacy; not to blaspheme, nor even to denigrate, the Islamic faith—but rather to ask questions concerning the outer limits that separate fiction from reality and to cause to be explored regions of the imaginary by a spirit taken out of the one and unique Book. When all this is realized, it is easy to understand why Rushdie so often complains in his interviews, in phrases recalling the poet Mallarmé, that his contemporaries simply "do not know how to read."

If it is true, as Umberto Eco contends, that there are no more than 50,000 true novel readers in any given country, it is equally true that there are perhaps millions of people around today who have no access at all to what is contained in many, many books, except what they happen to have heard about them on radio and television programs. It is in this sense that the Rushdie affair thus constitutes a truly significant phenomenon—an event?—which is all the more disturbing in the degree that it represents a symptom

---

Iranian embassy in London. Ahmed Khomeini then brought the matter to his father's attention, and the latter was said to be "shaken utterly" on reading portions of the novel. The testimony of Khomeini's daughter, Zahra Mutafavi, confirms the likelihood of the first or second scenario. According to her, Khomeini tuned in to the radio through the day for news broadcasts, both Iranian and foreign. "He listens to news all hours except when sleeping or praying . He has a portable radio which he carried even during the fast, believe me, and even during meals. He's careful that he himself hears the news rather than hearing it from others."
What clearly emerges here is that all this bears no relation to any *reading* of the incriminating book at all. What motivated the dictation of the *fatwa* were reports in the media.

of one of our more harmful contemporary evils—what I call "fictionalizing." Fictionalizing is an evil and a malady that does not merely consist of no longer realizing the fact that life still is a "novel" in the sense of being a "romance" (or an "adventure"!); it consists of failing to realize that, without "novels," we are in danger of losing sight of what it means to dream. And when we lose sight of what it means to dream, we also lose sight of an important part of the meaning of life itself. So long as Rushdie is obliged to go on living his current clandestine life, we will have to realize that we are victims of this same current malady: it is a malady of fatigue that, as Artaud would say, makes us believe we have been successful.

Being Open to the Imaginary

by Zhor Ben Chamsi

From whichever side it is approached, the Rushdie case would seem to present some uniquely new elements. It is the first time, I believe, that a writer has ever been sentenced to death without any kind of trial (even a hasty or simulated one). The trial of Al-Hallaj went on for nearly ten years before he was finally condemned to death. In the Rushdie case, though, a judge—a mortal man—has declared it to be a sacred duty of every Muslim to proceed to a murder and thus to substitute himself for God. So it is the *fatwa* itself that is the blasphemy. This is all the more the case in that Islam considers faith to be a fundamentally personal thing. For his part, Rushdie, for the first time, made use of certain elements from a Koranic text and from Muslim tradition; he did this for purposes related to the writing of fiction. He treated the sacred word as it happened to affect both the real and imaginary worlds of a modern Muslim living in London. Given the reigning orthodoxy, however, it would appear that the word of God could never germinate in this way; or ever be fecundated by the imaginary; or ever be made to appear as a myth from which to continue indefinitely building on. Yet this is exactly what is said in the Koran apropos Mary. Mary was fecundated by the word or breath of God after her cousin Joseph had been presented to her by the angel. In the metaphorical interpretation of this particular figure, the imaginary too enters in with all its components.

Psychoanalyst, Morocco. Originally written in French.

Today, however, the symbolic tends to be afflicted with sterility, indeed, with a kind of death. And the law is then confiscated and taken over by fundamentalists on all sides and yoked with the iron collar of official commentary and exegesis. Rushdie understands this: he understands the great effort that has been exerted in the course of history in order to construct walls and dikes intended to contain the word and impede the spirit of the law. The logic works itself out here in the same way as it did in the case of women: what was originally progress in recognizing an enhanced status for women, who for the first time were even accorded a status, became transformed by the interpreters of dogma, working with an intense, almost desperate energy, into a status that henceforth imposed almost pure conditions of subjection upon them. Why have no plays ever been written on the tragedy of Muhammad after he married his own daughter-in-law?

There are those who have reproached Rushdie with having acted like a spoiled child with no common sense. But it is precisely as such that he permitted himself what others could not; others have been unwilling to call things by their real names, or to take effective aim at our contemporary sclerosis. We should really be grateful to Rushdie for having opened up the imaginary for Muslims once again.

For Rushdie

by Tahar Ben Jelloun

Fiction is more frightening than reality. Literature seems to be more dangerous than the facts of real life that inspire it and on which it sometimes likes to dwell in order to explain a particular era and bring out its incoherences. A novel can never be simply "realistic," no matter what the intentions of its author may have been— that is to say, a novel can never be at one and the same time as precise, as unpredictable, and quite simply as crazy as the real lives we live, believing we understand them. Fiction presents real life in rather smudged lines. Its attempts to render reality are sometimes even laughable, because reality is so much more complex and unfathomable; and fiction is usually only nothing but a very pale imitation of it.

In real life we accept without protest that things such as prostitution, misery, and violence all exist. But to treat prostitution, misery, or violence in a story is often considered intolerable. It is a notable fact that censorship exists in certain countries concerning things that nevertheless do visibly occur in those very same countries; they occur and yet this arouses no apparent shock. What arouses shock is to describe those same things in words.

There is no doubt, then, that words are very dangerous. Even so, few would ever have imagined that words alone could have provoked a reaction as cruel and relentless as a *fatwa* of an Islamic

Writer, Morocco. Originally written in French.

republic pronouncing a death sentence on a writer. Islam has never as a rule advocated the death penalty. Men have no right to pursue justice in the guise of imagining they are God. However, the problem is not really a problem of religion at all, but rather one of politics. The death sentence visited upon Salman Rushdie was a political decision. It was linked to Iran's relations with Pakistan, which at that particular time was headed by a woman; it was also related to the Iranian commitment to Lebanon.

The fine details of the whole affair no longer matter today. Certainly they hardly matter for someone who can no longer even go out to a café to get a cup of coffee! What has really been called into question here, though, is literature itself. What is being aimed at is the very faculty of being able to create characters and place them within a particular space and time chosen by the author. To attempt to act upon the hidden face of reality, to spin out unbelievable tales (and those included in Salman Rushdie's novel are surely that), to invent strange and improbable situations, to try to rise above the hard facts of reality, to confer importance upon dreams and upon the extravagances occuring in dreams—all these things are possible only when one is free. Without freedom there is no artistic creation; there is no life; there is no beauty.

That Salman Rushdie may well have gone too far and produced something actually shocking to people's faith and convictions—all that is understandable. A book certainly can irritate and annoy, stir people up, even do harm; it can cause both laughter and tears. But a book should never be the pretext for an incitement to murder. No book should ever be the cause of a death sentence being pronounced upon its author. The very idea is intolerable, inadmissible. It bears no relationship to the tolerant Islam I was taught.

Respect for Freedom

by Khédija Ben Mahmoud Cherif

The death sentence meted out to Salman Rushdie and the murder of Farag Foda have represented a double setback along the difficult road toward democracy, tolerance, and freedom of opinion in the countries of today's Arab and Muslim world—where the works of Rushdie have been banned, and those of Foda burned. Such actions simply evidence failure on the part of regimes that pretend to legitimize themselves by imposing censorship as well as by carrying out political repression and other arbitrary acts. These measures have even been considered a privileged means of governing; but they really indicate the bankruptcy of the societies that employ them. These societies have taken a drastically wrong turn on the road to modernity and democracy. Repression proceeds from state power while censorship arises out of the prejudices of a particular society, but both repression and censorship go together. And they point to the existence of a society and political culture that continue to be based on the ideas of a fixed divine and natural order, ideas representing a fundamental impediment for contemporary man attempting to take his own destiny into his own hands.

In this dawn of the twenty-first century, there is an urgent need for a kind of democracy that guarantees man the ability to be an actor in his own history as well as a true initiator of ideas that can lead to freedom and justice. It is not the individual alone who gains

---

Sociologist, Tunisia. Originally written in French.

by the satisfaction of the desire for freedom; it is society as a whole. For it is by this means that society becomes the master of its own destiny, and also that society is able to develop harmoniously in accordance with its own dynamic, not just remain fixed and static within a particular traditional meta-historical framework.

According to Touraine, democracy is "associated with a society's capacity to develop, that is to say, to liberate those acting in society in accordance with the values of modernity." To be able to come to be, democracy supposes "a secularization of thought"; it supposes a secularization in the life of society, a separation between religion and politics; and it supposes autonomy for individuals with respect to the public authorities. And all these things, in turn, require respect for freedom of opinion, respect for the individual conscience, and an end to "crimes of opinion."

The new political culture born at the end of the Middle Ages, which became fully developed in the Age of the Enlightenment, allowed the emergence of the rights of man; it also guaranteed various freedoms in a way that implied tolerance and respect for the opinions of others. These developments were not entirely alien to the Arab-Muslim patrimony; Arabs and Muslims had also participated with their own particular genius in these same developments. Many who worked within this patrimony always vigorously emphasized "the role of reason," whether in the domain of philosophy, religion, or science. The spirit of innovation was present in literature and poetry, as it was in the sciences. As examples, Ibn Rushd, Al-Farabi, the Mu'tazilites, Ikhwan Al-Safa, and Abu Nuwwas can all be cited.

Arab and Muslim societies and public authorities today, however, clearly suffer a form of amnesia with regard to this aspect of their own traditions; they have turned their backs on this part of our patrimony, just as they have turned their backs on the now universal legacy of the rights of man. Instead, they demand unanimity, absolute certitude, received truths, and monolithic discourse, all of which represent the legacy of dictatorships. They nourish aggression; they encourage religious extremism; they favor sectarianism.

In doing all these things they oppress the individual, emasculate the critical spirit, inhibit creativity, literally terrorize the free individual, and reject everything in any way related to progress. Such an attitude cannot but foster obscurantist forces, meanwhile reducing the domain of those freedoms that nevertheless continue to constitute the most effective weapons against absolutism.

It would be very dangerous to allow apathy and indifference to set in in such a climate where human dignity is not respected and the irreducible freedom of man is denied. For it is not merely democracy and development that we risk losing thereby; the very future of our societies is at stake.

Mourning, Sorrow!

by Latifa Ben Mansour

Before being led to the scaffold where he was put to death in the most merciless fashion, the great mystic Hussein Ibn Mansur, known as Al-Hallaj,[1] the Wool-Carder ("the Carder of Consciences"), recited these terrible verses:

> I cry out: Mourning, Sorrow! For souls whose witness goes away to the beyond to join the Witness of the Eternal!
> I cry out: Mourning, Sorrow! For hearts so long watered with the rains of revelation from clouds holding oceans of wisdom!
> I cry out: Mourning, Sorrow! For the Word of God, since the time it died, its remembrance is a nothingness in our imagination!
> I cry out: Mourning, Sorrow! For the Demonstrators before whom all the discourses of orators must yield with regard to the dialectic.
> I cry out: Mourning, Sorrow! For all the converging Allusions insinuated by various minds; nothing any longer remains of them in books that has not been reduced to ruins.
> I cry out: Mourning, Sorrow! In the name of Your love, for

Writer, Algeria. Originally written in French
1   Al-Hallaj was born around 244 Hegirah (A.D. 857) and was executed in 309 Hegirah (A.D. 922) under the reign of the Abbasid Caliph Al-Muqtadir.

the Virtues of the group, those for which mounts were readied to obey.

They have all gone already; they have crossed the desert, without leaving any tracks or wells; they have gone like the tribe of 'Ad and the much regretted city of Iram! And behind them the crowd, abandoned, gropes without direction, more blind than the animals, more blind even than a troop of camels.[2]

Al-Hallaj was given Hussein as his first name by his mother, who named him after the martyr Hussein, the grandson of the Prophet Muhammad. Today I feel like saying—I who am a descendent of the Prophet Muhammad—I feel like crying out against our own grandiose and magnificent civilization: "Mourning, Sorrow!" It is a civilization that apparently feels so threatened and closed in upon itself that it is prepared to remain silent before the unacceptable.

I cry out, "Mourning, Sorrow!" in the name of Al-Jahiz, the one with his pen dipped in vitriol; he would surely have known how to reply in a civilized way to Salman Rushdie. I cry out, "Mourning, Sorrow!" in the name of Ibn Hazm, Ibn Al-Arabi, and Sidi Abu-Madyane, all of whom would have known how to reply to the author of *The Satanic Verses* in a calm and serene manner.

I cry out, "Mourning, Sorrow!" in the name of Abu-Abdallah Ach-Chuzi, the grand *qadi* of Muslim Seville in the thirteenth century. One day while he was dispensing justice, he suddenly began to tremble before the gravity of all his responsibilities, namely, "to apply and cause to be respected the law of God[3] upon this earth . . . [he was engaged] in judging individuals each of whom is a *banu Adam*, 'a son of Adam,' that is to say, a 'human being.'" Following that realization, he preferred to resign his office and go off to wander by himself in the desert of the Maghreb. He finally settled for

---

2   Ibn Mansur Hallaj, *Diwan*, trans. Louis Massignon (Paris: Editions du Seuil, 1981).
3   The *Sharia*.

good in Tlemcen in western Algeria. Although he had been a grand *qadi*, he now became a seller of sweets, and he even began to call himself Sidi Al-Halwi, "Master of Sweets." He composed these verses, which many today should meditate upon:

> When existence itself begins to speak,
> There are people who will listen.
>
> There is nothing unintelligible about its language;
> It is merely too fine for imbeciles to understand.
>
> Be intelligent and attentive,
> And this same voice will speak to you from some place very near.
> Don't be one of those who has to be called from a distance.[4]

There are very few people living around Oran today who can remember the name of the ruler who was on the throne in the time of this Master of Sweets; but the mosque where he is buried today is the one most frequently visited on Fridays by those whom life has crushed.

I also cry out, "Mourning, Sorrow!" in the name of Ibn Msayab, who bore the premonitory name "the son of catastrophes." An Algerian poet who lived in Tlemcen around the end of the seventeenth century, he also had a price placed on his head by the Turkish authorities of the day, after he wrote some verse like this:

> God has willed
> After these prosperous days
> That the death-knell of Tlemcen
> Should be sounded!
> That misfortune should be unleashed on her!
> She needs to be annihilated;

---

4   See Ibn Khaldun, *History of the Berbers.*

She alternates between thieves and tyrants.
They possess no benevolence.
They are without pity for those they govern.
The markets are empty;
Injustice is rife everywhere.
In Tlemcen:
Once a city of repose and pleasure.

As a result of this kind of writing, a *fatwa* was issued against this Algerian poet by the authorities in Constantinople, but the men and women of that epoch were not listening to *that* particular voice ("Swords and gunpowder speak plainly"). Ibn Msayab found refuge in the sanctuary of my own ancestor, Sidi Abdallah, at Ain al-Hout, a sacred parcel of land belonging to the descendants of the Prophet Muhammad, located a few miles away from Tlemcen. It was in this sanctuary that he wrote the poem that became a classic, beginning, "O, Friends of Allah, Succor the Fugitive!" It was from this same sanctuary that he also wrote his poems denouncing the tyranny of Turkish rule, "monsters living off the blood of a people in chains." Naturally these same Turkish authorities, along with some local bigots, accused him of *zandaqa* (apostasy).

Ibn Msayab, heartsick, finally had to go into exile in Morocco, but there still remained time for him to compose more poetry, always going back to his own roots. No one today remembers who the Turkish ruler of the day was, but the poet Ibn Msayab remains immortal.

And so I cry out, "Mourning, Sorrow!" in the name of another Algerian poet, Ibn Triki, who was a contemporary of Ibn Msayab. He also came from Tlemcen and suffered the very same fate, for he lived "a careless, easygoing life," in every way different from the lives of "good Muslims." "His nights he filled with the sound of the lute on which he was rather proficient; he also drowned himself in wine, perfumes, and beautiful women." Thus it was that various bigots and hypocrites reported on his life-style to the Turkish authorities in order to have him exiled. Nevertheless, even in our own day, the Darqawa, the largest mystical confraternity in the Mahgreb, begins its meetings by reciting a poem composed by this same Ibn Triki, also known in his own time as the poet who was "perverted," who had "gone astray," and who was also "the loafer and the libertine of Tlemcen." This is the poem:

Ya kirama al khalqi
Min aurbin wa min 'agamin
Wa ya khayra adamin
Bi ayatin wa qu'anin
'Afaka 'afaka, ya khayra
Al khalq Allahi...

You noble creature!
Whether you are Arab or foreigner,
You, the best of the sons of Adam.
By the verses of the Koran,
I beseech you,
I beseech you,
You, the best of the creatures of Allah,
To pardon me
On the day of the resurrection,
For I have sinned much . . .

Thus, following Hussein Ibn Mansur, "the Carder of Consciences"; following Ibn Msayab; following Ibn Triki; following so many other men and women—I cry out, "Mourning, Sorrow!" And I offer the poem below to Mr. Salman Rushdie, to whom I would also like to say that, even though I felt offended by his book, my faith was never shaken, even for a single moment. I therefore dedicate to him this poem written by the "no-good," the "profligate," the "libertine" of my city, namely, Ibn Msayab. It is chanted

5   Al-Ghawth and Al-Qutb are considered "the Grand Succor" and "the Pole," respectively, of Sufi mystics.

by our women today before his tomb, and echoed by our men when they participate in long procession, going out to prostrate themselves before the tomb of Al-Ghawth and Al-Qutb,[5] and of Sidi Abu-Madyane, the master of the great Ibn Al-Arabi. I also offer this poem to all of those who have made themselves into judges and pretend to be able to exercise the right of life or death over other men:

> Mortals succeed one another,
> But God alone remains.
> What has happened to them,
> Our moments of happiness?
> I no longer have a body,
> For my heart is enraptured
> By the one whose Mourning
> Will fill my whole life . . .

Literary Form

by Mohammed Berrada

I have understood since the 1960s that it is no longer acceptable to appeal to the concrete nature of Moroccan and Arab society in order to justify the "social and ideological commitments" inherent in the profession of writing. It sometimes seems as if literature is merely a means destined to bring about direct, concrete, and measurable change in society. But how can literature commit itself in advance to any particular ideology, or to any point of view whatsoever, and then go on pretending to be working for the discovery of true freedom, freedom both for individuals and for language, at the same time that everything is in flux and, indeed, is engaged in a battle where no quarter is given?

The commitment involved in writing (not the commitment of the writer) resides in the freedom proper to writing: this is the liberty through which virgin territories can be explored, which specifies and spells out that of which common discourse is ignorant, which brings out the contradictions inherent in both words and behavior, and which ceaselessly lays bare the ego itself. I had to modify considerably the Sartrean conception of commitment with which we had become imbued during a period of great national and ideological effervescence. The experience of Arab societies, confused as it is by modern ideologies with their typical slogans, permitted me to distinguish between a literature of mere indoctrination

---

Writer, Morocco. Originally written in Arabic.

and the preaching of received ideas, and a literature of freedom and true artistic creation; between rote, subservient texts, and those texts that, grounded in liberty, contained unique, irreplaceable form and content.

I believe—although I do not have space to go into any detail here—that the question of literary form is, in an essential way, the touchstone of both the freedom and the commitment that must characterize any authentic writing. When we consider the infinite multiplication of mere texts, the a priori positions taken, the various kinds of wooden language incessantly repeated, and the many preconceived opinions and certitudes of all kinds that continue to flourish, authentic forms of literary expression come to be seen as the things allowing new space to be opened up; they also allow a means of escape from whatever forms of censorship society and social institutions are habitually imposing upon individuals. Literary art that refuses to be domesticated remains the only anarchy really possible, and can resist every attempt to direct and channel it. Thus, to speak of the death of literature and of art, or of their incapacity to survive modern technology and the new computer age, or the new rationalizations of life and death—to speak of such things is to state an absurdity. All I have to do in order to regain confidence both in literature and its necessity is to read one good novel. To read one good novel is to remind myself of its necessary freedom as well as its great importance in a society otherwise burdened with so many highly visible constraints and limitations, which are so often disguised by systems attempting to impose uniformity, not to mention being impeded by the simple spirit of gregariousness. For the freedom of the reader begins and is necessarily grounded in the freedom of the writer: without the boldness of the latter continually striving to present things and relationships in their true dynamics and multiple possibilities, a literary text loses its vital sap; it loses the power of suggestiveness it should retain concerning all that is still possible.

A true writer cannot serve as a substitute for a preacher, a jurist, or even an independent thinker proposing various alternative theories. Rather, the true writer finds both his reason for being and his strength in functioning as an observer who never sheds his neutrality except to be a partisan in favor of a plurality of the possible, whether we are talking about the real world or some world of the imagination. It is in this sense that we must understand what Milan Kundera meant when he said that "the novel is an area where moral judgments must be suspended." Such a suspension of moral judgments does not imply the immorality of the novel, of course. Rather, this kind of suspension *is* its morality: a morality opposed to the habit so deeply rooted in humanity that too often pushes human beings into making instant judgments—of trying to judge before one has come to understand or, worse, trying to judge without ever understanding at all.

This whole concept of the necessary freedom of literature leads us to ask yet another question: how can we manage things so that all the problems, experiences, sentiments, scenes, landscapes, fantasies, and so on that constitute the raw material of the novel, and all of which are equally important in its makeup, derive their status and value not from external factors but only from their own artistic form and the way in which they are used in the novel itself? The necessity of finding an answer to this question is what motivated me to become interested in what I call "the life of the text," and various aspects of the composition of the text, such as the successive drafts, the different versions, and the various stages assumed before it takes on its definitive form; the reception of the text, the "life" that it experiences through being read (for example, in the cases of Mallarmé, Flaubert, and Gide); and the various forms and sponsorships that even move some writers to write parallel texts (letters and memoirs) revealing yet other ways they could have opted for in order to produce the definitive text. The novelist Julien Green, for example, has spoken about "the novel that could have been written"; he described it as an obsession that continues to pursue the writer even after the actual novel has been written—and that sometimes stimulates him to write yet another text in the hope of succeeding a second time.

Do not such considerations manifest the strongest kind of proof of the need for freedom in the act of creation and, indeed, in creative writing of any kind? Often I have envied painters; their medium of expression allows them to make use of various ideas and expressions in their various preliminary sketches, thus allowing these ideas and expressions to be part of the total creation; this permits multiple actualizations of the same work. In writing my second novel, I found it necessary to have a second parallel notebook at hand in which I dealt with my various relationships to the text and with the problems I was encountering as I went along.

At the conclusion of this testimonial I must touch upon the whole question of the relationship of the writer to what he writes on a deeper level, especially as regards the freedom with which he writes. I make reference here to what Jean Genet in *Giacometti's Studio* called "the secret place within ourselves"—that place from which another and different human adventure could always rise, an adventure that would be an essentially moral one. If I am not able to probe this "secret place" even in myself—and it can assume a number of forms—then I can surely affirm that it would be simply impossible to separate it from an aspiration toward freedom that helps us transform our secret wounds into many different possible worlds, worlds woven out of the desire of "what could have been."

Concerning a Memory:
Of a Photo of Salman Rushdie, with Eyes as If Painted in a Miniature, and with His Right Hand Raised to His Lips

by Kamal Boullata

During the eleventh century, when Ibn Faris described calligraphy as "the tongue of the hand," the practice of chopping off hands and tongues was not an uncommon punishment. An illustrious victim who underwent such mutilations was himself a calligrapher who, a century earlier, had already entered into legend. Known as Ibn-Muqlah, he is remembered for being the technical inventor of the six major styles of Arabic calligraphy. More importantly, Ibn-Muqlah was the veritable pioneer who established the system of proportions governing the aesthetics of Arabic script.

Legend tell us that during a period fraught with political troubles and instabilities, Ibn-Muqlah was serving as *wazir* and scribe in the Baghdad court of the caliph al-Radi Billah. One day, he was accused by a rival *wazir* of being involved in a political plot against the court. Confidential letters Ibn-Muqlah had written were used against him by the rival *wazir* as evidence supporting the accusations. Instantaneously, the caliph commanded that the calligrapher's right hand be cut off.

Undaunted by the loss of his hand, Ibn-Muqlah continued to

Painter/Writer, Palestine. Originally written in English.

produce exquisite masterpieces of calligraphy. Some sources claimed that while serving his sentence in jail, he taught himself to write with his left hand. In time, Ibn-Muqlah's challenge met with his sovereign's order for re-incarceration; this time, the calligrapher's left hand was ordered chopped off.

To the surprise of all, Ibn-Muqlah went on to produce unsurpassed examples of his matchless script. Legend claims that he continued to create what were to become the prototypical models of excellence in calligraphy by strapping a pen tightly to the stump of his right forearm. Other sources determined that this resolute man learned to hold the pen with his toes. Such an acquired skill, it was presumed, was the pretext for the caliph's order finally decreeing that, before imprisoning him a third time, Ibn-Muqlah's feet be chopped off right at the ankles. The ultimate mutilation involved the severing of Ibn-Muqlah's tongue.

During his last days in jail, one can only imagine the slow death endured by whatever was left of our legendary calligrapher.

And yet, Ibn-Muqlah's tragedy did not cease with his death in jail. The site of his grave, we are told, was changed three times, and remains of his disfigured body were reburied in accordance with the wishes of the rivaling men at court.

Not a single page of Ibn-Muqlah's calligraphy survives. What do survive instead are a legend and the unfading memory of his written forms. Nine centuries later, anybody tracing the body of that memory begins to *see* parts of the legend (in Arabic *muqlah* means "eye"). Thus, before all beautiful writing today, each one of us bears witness to how a fellow human being once lost his tongue in the process of building a permanent dwelling fit for the majesty of God's own voice.

The Transformation of the Past

by Abdesselame Cheddadi

The Rushdie affair raises two essential questions. The first bears upon the possible limits of freedom of thought and expression. The second concerns the relationship of the Arab and Muslim worlds to their own past and, in general, to their own culture. Regarding the first point, it is not possible to insist too strongly that the freedom of thought and expression is an essential historic "given" of the movement that began with the bourgeois capitalist revolution; at this point in time, it is irreversible. It forms a necessary, integral part of human society as such. It is constitutive of most modern social, political, economic, and intellectual activities, and can no longer be called into question without undermining the very bases of modern society. In this perspective, the situation into which Rushdie has been placed must be considered very grave. In the case of Rushdie, we are dealing with a man who lives abroad, and who has actually adopted a second nationality; and although he is a "Muslim" in a cultural sense, he actually professes to be an atheist. By what right and according to what logic can a so-called Islamic *fatwa* therefore be issued against him? Even if some might question the universality of the principle of freedom of thought and expression, they must still surely justify their position on the basis of principles universally accepted today, and they must surely attempt to persuade the world that their position is indeed reasonable and well founded.

Historian, Morocco. Originally written in French.

In this case, however, not only do they refuse to do this; they take refuge in their own brand of logic, which turns out to be both limited and narrowly confined to a specific region. Nor do they in any way fear to contradict themselves; they accept certain of the assumptions of the modern world merely in order to be able to reject some of its other assumptions, as they decide. They have not understood that it is impossible to disassociate modern technology (and the exact sciences on which it is based) from the general principles upon which all modern culture is based. All these things proceed from a common type of rationality, and to attempt to distinguish between them and separate them from one another is really to place oneself henceforth in a position of marked inferiority from every point of view. This is all the more the case when it is realized that the modern world is more and more dominated by the problems of communication.

As for the second point concerning the relationship of the Arab and Muslim worlds to their own history and culture, it is time for these countries to begin to recognize that their past is, quite simply, dead. It is only when this is recognized that a dialogue with that past might become possible again. The past, after all, is not something we can just go on belonging to, naturally and spontaneously, because we want to; nor can the past be simply repeated. Rather, it must be continually re-created. As a matter of fact, the same thing applies to the present: we believe ourselves to be in possession of the present by the simple fact of living in it, but in reality the present will irretrievably escape from us too unless we prove ourselves capable of transforming it.

The present consists essentially of modern culture. It consists of a perpetual re-creation of the past and a continual transformation of the present. On the one hand, there are those states that demand a national authenticity or superficial kind of Islam—an "Islamic" front, in effect—that does not encourage any serious, in-depth study or research concerning the past. Such states are an obstacle to any real thought or reflection on the present, in fact; and, as far as the past is concerned, these states are content to repeat the extremely slight kind of research into the *Salaf*, or generations of early Muslims, which has been all too typical, and, whether they realize it or not, the studies no less superficial and tendentious of some of those who are nevertheless considered to be first-class orientalists.

On the other hand, those Islamists who present themselves as the defenders of a true and essential Islam live, in effect, off the capital from these same works, which they manipulate as they please, meanwhile occasionally citing such classics as Al-Ghazzali or Ibn Taymiyah. In reality, though, the knowledge of historical Islam in the Arab and Muslim countries is in a really sad and deplorable state today. We must admit that we are living in a rather paradoxical situation at the present time: there is infinitely more serious research on the subject of Islamic culture and the Islamic past going on in the United States or France, for example, than there is in Arabia or Morocco.

For the most part, then, the most rudimentary means that would allow us to know ourselves are lacking in our own countries. In this situation, how can we dare to speak of authenticity? How can we confront others and assert ourselves on the world scene without simply looking ridiculous?

For Salman Rushdie

by Andrée Chedid

No work can be fecundated
under the yoke
No questioning
arises from subservient lips
No soul grows and prospers
under a sentence
No look penetrates
out of an eye that is oppressed
No spring of water surges
under the paving stones
No cause is honored by making threats
No future is molded
under an interdict

No God of the living agrees
to a sentence of death
No cry for death binds
a man of the living

Writer, Libya/Egypt/France. Originally written in French.

They Want Me Dead

by Mahmoud Darwish

They want me dead in order to be able to say: he was one of ours and belongs to us.

I have heard these same steps for twenty years striking on the wall of the night. They approach but they do not open the door. But now they do come, and three men come out: the poet, the assassin, and the reader.

I asked: Will you have some wine? They said: Let us drink. I asked: When are you going to shoot me? They replied: Patience! They lined up the cups and began to sing for the people. I said: When are you going to kill me? So then they said: It has already begun . . . Why did you send footwear for the soul? I said: So that the soul could walk on the earth. Then they said: Why did you write that the poem is white when the earth is so black? I replied: Because thirty seas empty into us; and they said: Why do you love French wine? I said: Because I deserve the most beautiful of women. What kind of death do you want? Blue like the stars that come down from above. Would you like to have some more wine? They said: Let us drink. I said: I want you to go slow, to kill me a little bit at a time, so that I may write a final poem to the one who has wedded my heart. But they laugh, and only the words I will say to the one who has wedded my heart circulate within the house.

Poet, Palestine. Originally written in Arabic.

It's Time to Reverse the Condemnation of Salman Rushdie

by Hichem Djaït

I have already written an article in *Al-Yom al-Sabi'* on the subject of the condemnation of Salman Rushdie by the Ayatollah Khomeini and of the outcries that it provoked in the Western world. My sense is that we are dealing here with a conflict between two worlds that do not understand each other. What is new in this particular case, in my view, resides in the pugnacity exhibited by Islam as affirmed by Khomeini; it is also to be noted how "ecumenical" the whole affair has turned out to be. Islam has been attacked and maltreated many times before in the past, but the reaction has usually not been quite so vigorous as this time. This degree of reaction has introduced a new note of fear, with both positive and negative effects, into the whole contemporary historical situation and into our recognition of the proper place of Islam within it. For at least a century, the Muslim world has tended toward two principal goals in the course of its development: to participate in the modern world, but at the same time to demand recognition for its own special historical, cultural, and religious heritage. These two goals frequently converge; but they can also diverge. In fact, the search for recognition, through both nationalism and Islam, has always taken priority over everything else.

In Rushdie's case, his work never attracted any thunderbolts from the likes of Khomeini until after public agitation had surfaced

Historian, Tunisia. Originally written in French.

in certain Islamic regions or in lands where Muslims lived. The book itself, which is a work of fiction and fantasy, and in no way an anti-Muslim pamphlet, does contain for the attentive reader certain elements that are certainly irreverent but not, in my view, really harmful. The book's title cannot by itself be considered anti-Islam, since the Islamic tradition itself recognizes the existence of the Satanic verses in question—verses excised later on. Should the whole thing then be considered merely a political-type condemnation, since the book also contains two or three rather vehement pages directed against the government of the imam, Khomeini himself? This is quite possible, yet is equally clear that the author is writing against governmental autocracies in general.

Why, then, must this condemnation be reversed? It is certainly not a question of simply attempting to please the West; all the protestations there have had no effect. In a sense, the continuing stubborn maintaining of the condemnation has really been a way of demonstrating that the West is being taken into consideration. For Rushdie's situation recalls nothing so much as an American "Wanted" poster.

Moreover, from the Islamic point of view, the notion of *riddah*, or apostasy, cannot really be applied to Rushdie. It is true that the apostasy of individuals, that is to say, the return of an individual to paganism following conversion, is rigorously condemned by the Koran; but this condemnation was delivered in the context of a new religion that was still both fragile and threatened. And even then, repentance was considered sufficient to efface the offense, according to the text of the Koran itself. As for the apostasy of a number of Arab tribes after the death of the Prophet, this was frankly understood to be a political and collective thing of a totally different nature than the act of any individual. The case of Rushdie belongs in the latter category; at the same time, nowhere in his book is it explicitly stated that he rejects the Islamic faith.

Beyond the sphere of religion as such, the entire Arab and Muslim tradition of humanism preaches pardon for offenses and respect for the human being. The Prophet himself set the example in this sphere in the case of Ka'b Ibn Zuhayr, to speak of only one. How many times has pursuit of satiric poets by political power had to be abandoned? The Arab tradition has always granted a certain latitude where the nonconformity of poets and artists is concerned; it is part of their essence.

Today, though, going beyond what is already past, we can also speak of the requirements of universal reason. The West has no monopoly on this. What is needed is a proper historical synthesis, combined with a strong ethical affirmation in favor of what is good for both the heart and human reason; for life in general; and certainly for the destinies of culture and civilization. What is at stake in the Rushdie affair is not just freedom of expression, which is concerned principally with politics and action, but rather freedom of conscience, thought, and artistic creation; the fight is really against hypocrisy. For a generation now the elite in the Arab world have in practice rejected Islam both as a belief and as a particular type of sensibility; but they have largely done so in a spirit of indifference, of *taqiyah* (religious dissimulation) and lastly, of hypocrisy. I have always strongly deplored this whole approach. It even seems to me, paradoxically, that Salman Rushdie continues to be haunted by Islam; if he has revolted against it, it is because he has revolted against himself.

In the end, every complication that enters into our act and into our thought can always serve as a good antidote against a too monolithic approach that would surely to dry up everything it ever touched. In the case of Rushdie, we are confronted both with the revolt of an individual and a definite case of nonconformity, all of it molded in the crucible of creative power. Elsewhere this might have led to hesitation, misunderstanding, even devastation. Even if the contemporary era remains one of conflict, searching out, and seeking recognition, though, the trails actually being blazed through it by our writers and thinkers will still be there when, once cultural recognition has been achieved, the time comes to create the high culture without which we will simply find ourselves empty-handed.

The Solitude of King Salomon

by Assia Djebar

Solitude and sun. Black sun.

I do not speak of the persecution of this writer who was born a Muslim; I do not speak of this four years after his condemnation. Rather, I speak of the four years of his enforced confinement. From the time of his condemnation by Khomeini, I have been especially attentive to everything Salman Rushdie has said. His novel *Shame* actually caused me to burst out laughing once in the Paris Métro. Then there was the piece "In All Good Faith," which he published in *Liberation* a year after his condemnation; this brought me great joy. I thought: "It is evident that he is resisting, because he is writing something. Writing itself, after all, is always the essential where literature is concerned." Before, I was simply one of his faithful readers; but now, from that time on, my respect for this writer has not ceased to grow enormously.

What a misfortune his celebrity has turned out to be. Before this affair, it came only as a result of his literary gifts. But now! What a desolate prospect for the life of a mature man at the very height of his creativity. And how long is it fated to go on? What a snare his whole fight has turned out to be, carried out, as it necessarily has been, before our own impotent eyes, at least in one sense (but also hidden from our eyes as if in a fog, in another sense).

Salman Rushdie resists as a writer should; he writes in order to

Writer, Algeria. Originally written in French.

live; his writing, first produced under the banner of an affirmation of total freedom, and in a blaze of intelligence all his own, has assumed a much greater and more serious kind of significance now. I sense in it much heavy labor—denoting suffering, denoting the proud and poignant despair of someone who is carrying on, who is not giving up, even though he cannot see how it is all going to end.

Solitude and sun. Black sun.
More than anything else, though, there remains his forced confinement; he continually has to contemplate in darkness his own state; he is continually under constraint. Or perhaps, if I might dare say so (and I actually feel this more and more), this prince of a writer, with the highly symbolic first name of one of the companions of the Prophet, is nothing else but perpetually naked and alone. He is not only the most vulnerable among us—that is, modern writers born Muslims—he is the first *man* to have to live in the condition of a Muslim *woman* (and since, for him, his life has now become essentially writing, he is also the first man to be able to write from the standpoint of a Muslim woman):

> *Under the sign of extreme separation,*
> *in the most dangerous clandestine state,*
> *under the pillowcase of a silence*
> *of the most compact type*

Solitude and sun. Black sun. A gnawing within.
So while Salman Rushdie still goes on talking, before our eyes, with his lively words and his tireless pen, I find it hard to imagine that internal respiration stemming from a profound isolation which must nevertheless be there.

Always excepting Rushdie, perhaps the women of the Muslim world still do not yet truly write; perhaps they only believe they write. *Solitude and sun: a sun with blackness deeper than that of Salman Rushdie.*

FOR RUSHDIE

P.S. In order to express my woman's compassion, I regret not being able to write in the language of my mother, Arabic, and in that of my faith, Koranic poetry. Nevertheless I address myself in French, the language of my immigration, to the whole chorus of today's migration (hegira).

Tatou

by Hanan El Cheikh

Animal covered with a thick carapace, you who bear the name "Tatou," *armadillo*, there is someone today who needs you, someone who has actually been banned from participating in real life, someone who must necessarily have become caught up and enveloped in frustration, who is undergoing a mental siege as well as much suffering, who is not only suffering from fear but also from the drying up of the soil of his thought: the soil that was formerly so fertile—soil now too many times and too violently plowed up and plowed up again. Thus, there is someone who has become an object of opprobrium, who has had to take refuge in silence, and who has had to abandon himself to impotent anger. There is someone who lives in such isolation that the walls around him reflect his anguish and echo his sadness, the windows his fears and suspicions, and the door conveys the continual threats lodged against him. So he remains where he is, immobile, even though this is hardly natural to him. He still tries to grope his way ahead, but he still runs into fanaticism here, injustice there, and their contraries somewhere else. He oscillates continually between knowledge and ignorance, between certitude and doubt.

Naturally, this perplexed inquietude exerts its influence on the secretion of adrenaline; heartbeats speed up; pearls of sweat break out upon the back; pupils dilate; facial expressions become troubled; blood both races and is stagnant in the veins; foam appears at

---

Writer, Libya. Originally written in Arabic.

the lips as with a carnivorous plant. Blood chokes off the breath, which attempts to escape, but the throat is deep and dry; even the vocal cords are gone.

You, Tatou, *armadillo*, equipped with your carapace, there is someone who has great need of you; he has suffered much. No doubt you cannot heal him; his exhaustion, extending throughout his whole body, is only too visible.

Do not be deceived by the proud and dignified manner he has been able to maintain; do not be deceived by his smile, by the elegance of his suit and tie. Incessant threats have succeeded in planting fear in him; it is like a veritable wound, and it affects both his body and his spirit. And the absence of dialogue with his peers has also discouraged him and made him somber.

Approach nearer to him, then, a little bit at a time, and give him the benefit of your counsels, not so that he will double himself up with his head touching his feet in order to hide, as you are able to do when confronted with enemies. Rather, teach him, and teach us too, how it is that you are able to suspend inside your body the growth and development of your unborn young, how it is that you are able to hold back the moment of giving birth until the most favorable time arrives for both you and your offspring. And then you suddenly open up the barrier again; you liberate the circulation of your blood; you unleash the movement of your strength; and giving blessing to your own entrails, you pursue the process of gestation to the end and you give birth.

Teach him, and teach us too, how to watch out for undue shocks, and how to deflect them in ways that reduce their force; teach him how, in short, you safeguard yourself—and are not corrupted. Teach him, and teach us too, how to go beyond anguish, beyond evils suffered, and beyond the overwhelming feelings of loss and wrong suffered.

Teach us, O, you animal equipped with a carapace, teach us how to hold ourselves back, how to preserve our strength—because the freedom of thought and expression for which we live, which is life itself for us, is besieged and surrounded today, and awaits more favorable circumstances in which we will finally be able to act.

Concerning Salman Rushdie: Notes for a Project of Secularization

by Driss El Yazami

1. The Salman Rushdie affair raises some very formidable questions for intellectuals, as it does for political elements in the Arab and Muslim worlds; and there are only a very few isolated voices who have treated these questions up to now: what should be the relationship between political and religious power in Islamic lands, and on what historical and juridical basis should the state itself be established in those lands? To these questions, the Iranian state has given an answer that is now known to all; the *fatwa* issued against a writer who is British is only too illustrative of the answer the Iranian state has given. In some other countries certain politico-religious elements claiming to adhere to the same Islamic faith have defended a social project that is more or less the same as that of the Iranian state. These religiously inspired political movements combine massive street demonstrations and equally overwhelming electoral performances, and they have now become a regular and recurrent feature of our political life. Moreover, such movements are encountering at least a responsive echo in surprisingly wide sectors of our society. Their success is even apt to disorient us and leave us prey to an especially strong temptation: simply to remain silent ourselves, and hope that our various illegitimate and authoritarian governments currently in place will somehow succeed in putting down all these "obscurantist movements" by force.

Journalist, Morocco. Originally written in French.

Salman Rushdie makes us uncomfortable because he drags us back, whether he wishes to or not, to the same urgent issue: what kind of project of secularization can we conceive, and how can we then in practice move beyond the mere theoretical proclamation of "our firm adherence to the principles of secularization"? Salman Rushdie annoys us because he forces us to face the question of the real alternatives to the theocratic state, just as he forces us to face that other question that we have been evading for so long: what do we do about Islam?

Even viewing these things from this perspective, it would be a serious mistake to believe that in our societies there are two well-defined "camps" opposing each other from within impervious borders: the "fundamentalist" and the "secularist" camp. For even though the fundamentalist camp is stating rather plainly exactly what it is aiming at, the secularist camp can only really oppose this to the extent that it offers its own counterproject and to the extent that it decides to speak in precise terms about what its own aims are. To reject the vision of the world being put forward by the Islamizers really means, sooner or later, to affirm the kinds of values we do favor; and, especially, it is to affirm the type of positive historical construction and rhythm required to achieve the kind of secular state we wish to have. This means, in a word, that we must abandon the purely defensive posture that has been ours for a very long time.

2. If the debate over secularization thus really does not in fact pit two well-defined camps against one another, this is also because there is a "third thief" involved—one that can in no way be ignored. I mean the State as it exists in Islamic lands. The state intervenes in at least two important fashions.

The state has actually served to help Islamize the political debate because it has almost always favored the religious movements, at least in their beginnings; it has done this in the hope of countering the left, which the state has seen as too influential in certain key areas, especially among the young. But the state has also been involved in another way; it has itself disputed with the

Islamizers, who have become influential and threatening only with its help, their monopoly on the interpretation of religious dogmas. Fortified with ministries of religious affairs, and itself employing cohorts of theologians and preachers, the state now regularly appeals to a certain religious legitimacy (even if it is only homeopathic in its effects). No leader has entirely escaped playing this role, including even Bourguiba and the Baathists. Since these leaders make an appeal to a certain Islamic legitimacy in order to buttress their authoritarian power, they also end up necessarily injecting religion into the political process, thus preparing the terrain on which the fundamentalists can then outbid them and beat them at their own game—thus contributing in a very real sense to the success of Islamization.

And it is this very same state that legitimizes these Islamizing movements in yet another way, namely, when it finally gets around to suppressing them, and goes about doing this by violating the most elementary human rights in the process. This action by the state itself against the militant Islamizers catches opposing militants for the rights of man off guard and entraps them in another sort of way. For in numerous countries the Islamizers have been victims of regular waves of repression, and meanwhile, the militants of the rights of man either do not protest these human rights violations at all, or else they protest them very weakly, perhaps hoping that the violence of the state will indeed settle by force what in fact should be considered a fundamental issue of civilization—an issue human rights militants should be the first to defend.

Following such a road as this may be efficacious for the state in the short run; but nothing prevents this same state from one day allying itself with the Islamizers. Acceptance of such repressive action by the state also precludes any democratic project whatsoever. To accept the practice of the politics of "two weights and two measures," and not to demand freedom of expression for everybody, Islamizers included, means to retard the necessary political modernization of Islamic societies; it means to fail to impregnate them with democratic values even in embryonic form. And thus it is the

Islamizing movements themselves, which emerge from their "ordeals" even stronger than before, that reap the advantage. After all, they were the only ones really to oppose the state power, which then became totally discredited in the eyes of public opinion.

3. The debate about secularization cannot in our case avoid going back to a history that weighs heavily upon us because we continue to live the fiction that "in Islam there is no separation between the spiritual and the temporal"; hence, secular values supposedly have no future in our countries. This "evidence" is repeated ad nauseam by the Islamizers—to the point where almost all researchers, not to mention the media, also tend to parrot in the most solemn tones the same line, namely, that Muslim law, so often invoked using the scholarly term *Sharia*, is indeed of some kind of divine inspiration. Muslim law is not accepted as a human construction that can be situated and explained historically; it is taken as a sort of divine code, immutable, that can never support any kind of human intervention, modification, or reform. This fiction obviously serves the Islamizers well, since it allows them to succeed in further mystifying a public opinion that is both credulous and only too apt to rely on mere hopes and desires in the absence of facts. But when militant secularists too are found repeating the same "evidence," we must truly and seriously ask ourselves how this strange "consensus" ever came about.

Various thinkers of Muslim origin, along with certain orientalists, have already dealt with some of these same particular "truths," each in his own way; they have demonstrated to us how, in Muslim history, it was actually politics that managed to annex religion and place it at its own service; it was not the other way around. By decreeing a quarter of a century after the death of the Prophet a definitive text of the Koran "the integral authentic collection, in its integrity, of the divine word" (Arkoun), the political power itself succeeded both in creating yet another dogma and in arrogating to itself at the same time the power to suppress heresy and ban any reading matter that might possibly compromise its power.

We also know, whatever the Islamizers might say about it, that there is nothing like an explicit juridical code in the Koran. The existing Muslim code is a purely human creation. Similarly, there is not in the Koran any theological model of the ideal state either, even though every state in these Muslim regions has been in the habit of invoking religion, on any and all occasions, in order to legitimize its own power. But there is no a priori reason why the Islamic heritage in these regards could not be critically reexamined and very different conclusions reached. The only thing that prevents such a reexamination are the prohibitions already in place decreed by the states in power, usually with the approval of the Islamizers in their countries, against any critical examination or any innovative interpretation whatsoever.

4. If we adopt, following Jean Baubérot and others, the necessary distinction between the meaning of secularization "understood as denying any religious influence on the life of society," and its meaning of simply secularizing or laicizing certain institutions and separating them from direct religious control, then a number of possible roads open up that might well be followed. For the fact is that certain Muslim institutions have already been undergoing a considerable degree of secularization; this has been true for some time now. It is true in a number of areas and in spite of the whole modern "religious renewal." Both individuals and groups no longer make reference exclusively to their faith, for example when deciding certain attitudes and matters of conduct. Similarly, there are many references to secularization and to the laicization of certain activities to be found in the discourses of numerous associations today and also in the productions of many intellectuals. There is a wide rejection in such quarters of what the Islamizers have put forward. Such references testify to the fact that many, many people today are prepared—and legitimately so—to decide certain questions of their lives outside the framework of religion. In meetings between associations and individuals, in projects of micro-development, in various other links and activities, in university exchanges, in translations— in all such things we see manifested, even if only in subterranean fashion in a good many cases, the slow but necessary opening up of the Muslim world to the rest of the world and its concerns.

To contribute to this process means, among other things, a greater opening up to Europe. Nothing permits us to say that we are going in that direction (while at the same time the fortresses of the rich north appear to be tempted to draw back). Every temptation for us to close either the frontiers or the minds in the Muslim world, like every other upheaval that occurs along these same lines, simply increases the advantages the Islamizers have.

5. Moreover, when we consider the battle for secularization, we realize that it cannot be reduced merely to a battle against "fundamentalism," meanwhile avoiding any serious reflection on the continuing role of the state in all these areas. Seen in this perspective, it is clear that militant secularists cannot acquiesce in the idea that the question of Islamization can be resolved only by being suppressed by state power. It is a very safe bet, in fact, that Muslim societies are going to be confronted with this problem for a very long time to come; and it is not a problem that is going to be solved either by repression and violence or by simply issuing decrees. The real solution, even if it seems to be impossible of realization today, is to begin to allow the open public expression of all the real concerns these Islamizing societies have, and then to begin to organize some peaceful means of debating and resolving some of these same concerns rather than simply driving them underground. This, in turn, presupposes the emergence of some neutral and impartial power points, just as it presupposes the establishment of rules governing the political process that must be clearly spelled out and applied impartially to all political forces, including the Islamizers themselves.

The proper functioning of a political process that is truly democratic does not mean that the state must be denuded of all means of coercion, or that it must never react against the enemies of democracy itself. The question is not one of simply remaining inert or passive in the face of antidemocratic initiatives. It is rather one of clearly defining and spelling out the legal conditions—which will be applicable impartially to all—in which a repression *will* be carried out if the democratic rules are broken.

In opposition to today's authoritarian governments, which in one way or another all attempt to challenge the Islamizers on their own religious ground, what we are pleading for here is a disengagement or drawing back of the state from religion to the extent possible—the adopting of a strict neutrality by the state where religion is concerned. What the state must ensure is liberty of conscience for all—for nonbelievers or adherents of minority religions, of course, but also, certainly, for believing Muslims as well.

6. What is mainly at issue here is the need to think through the necessary terms of a real secularization of institutions. This will require a depth and kind of reflection that cannot be limited merely to proclaiming principles, including those principles we have been enunciating and discussing here. If we survey the various institutional arrangements to be found in Europe to accomplish the same ends we are speaking about here, for example, we will find that there is great diversity; they range from radical separation of church and state, as in France, to other arrangements in other regimes, including relatively close association and sometimes even "cohabitation" of the spiritual and temporal. In most cases in the European countries secularization came about only after a long and almost always painful evolution. In almost all European countries, a historical compromise with the religion that happened to be dominant had to be forged; this was true even in the cases where the most acute conflicts raged.

But in all these European countries it was on the initiative of, or under pressure from, those who favored secularization that the various political arrangements were arrived at. It is easy to foresee, for example, that in Muslim countries it is not likely to suffice merely to write into constitutions and laws the principles of the separation of the spiritual and the temporal, and the principle of the necessary religious neutrality of the state. Rather, the consequences of such measures must be carefully thought through and many things provided for at various levels: in the organization of education, in the preparation of school curricula, in the financing and administration of religion itself, in the training given to imams and theologians, and so on.

The workplace in which all this is to be accomplished is practically virgin territory at the moment. However, many elements do exist that would enable the work to start. If there is not any actual broad organized movement for secularization as such in existence, there are certainly tendencies in that direction: there are women's associations, associations for the defense of the rights of man, associations of writers and creative artists, and more, all of which from one angle or another could participate in the hatching and making use of new ideas that could contribute to the development of truly pluralistic societies in the Muslim world. The battle for Salman Rushdie and his inalienable right to write with his security assured is itself a contribution; it contributes to the laying out of the road that needs to be traveled.

Asselman

by Ahmed Essyad

[This text consists of a musical composition. Following this musical text, there is the following inscription by the author]:
For Salman Rushdie, in order that an artist might write that with which I disagree.

Composer, Morocco. In the Berber language, "asselman" means "fish".

ASSELMAN

flute basse amplifiée

Ahmed ESSYAD

For Salman Rushdie, in order that an artist might write that with which I disagree.

Against

by Nabile Farès

Whether it was a stratagem or truly intended as a rejection of an indigestible element, the *fatwa* issued against Salman Rushdie, especially as it has now been reiterated, is a misfortune for Islam, civilization, culture, and the human mind. There should not be a single Muslim who is not shocked by a decision such as this, which appeals to their religion in order to preach intolerance and murder in its name.

But there are other contemporary events requiring even greater boldness of imagination if they are really to be understood and condemned: for example, the violation of women that has taken place in Bosnia. By what detour of thought or humiliation have we arrived at the acceptance of such barbarism? The question especially touches those victims who have now come to seem almost unreal, so thoroughly does the mere image of what is visited upon them preserve us from any real comprehension of what is really involved in death—death that people are all too easily tempted to allow to be inflicted on others for whatever good reasons of politics or civilization. Should it not be recalled that the primordial folly lies in this: to believe oneself to be the master of life and death? What is this perverse enjoyment, which denies to the living the right to singularity and self-expression? And what stage of abject regression have we reached when we are even asked what we think of a supposed sacred

---

Writer, Algeria. Originally written in French.

formula to which Muslims alone are thought to be committed (and hence are also thought to be unlike all other people)? Are Muslims alone guilty of crime, when all their writings and the thoughts they have expressed indicate how definitely they still belong to the human community in spite of all the colonialist or other efforts, cultural or ethnic, of *de*civilization that have been inflicted on them? Should we be satisfied to accept this abject status, this too opportune indication of regression that fashions the failed triumph of the living out of death itself? Do we thus have this power over life, over ourselves, over others? Taking one's own life, while speaking of sacrifice.

To kill others, calling it justice or a benefit: this is an unexampled turning around of the real truth and the sacred object itself, as if one were specifically legislating, either on one's own or hiding behind a collectivity, for the accursed portion of humanity. There are so many hatreds today that have developed out of ethnic, religious, and community conflicts that one can no longer be scandalized by a process of condemnation that denies the involvement of any humor, mind, and spirit in the development of living peoples. What attachment to the power of death is it that is revealed in so many books, current beliefs, and states insisting on the reality of death instead of the reality of creativity and becoming? No: there should be no Muslims out there at all who can be sent out to assassinate anybody whatsoever, certainly not Salman Rushdie.

Why should Persia, source of so many great works, have now given herself over, as so many others have also, to such murders and exclusions?

Exile

by Safa Fathi

The language of the emigrant belongs to an era that is now completed. He comes from one of those countries currently undergoing a "national renaissance"; it is nonaligned, has a national liberation movement, is committed to the fight against imperialism, is ruled by a one-party state, and is only too familiar with chants for independence and calls for the nationalization of industry and the provision of free universal education. Millions of people have left these former colonies and moved to the former imperialist countries in the First World. For them exile has actually served as a kind of armor, protecting them from the various afflictions and confrontations of daily life in the Third World; they live in a no-man's-land between an early upbringing and education that has become, so to speak, innate, and a new "culture of adoption."

This kind of exile is also supposed to entail the sort of freedom where language itself is liberated from some of its ancient significations, where there is more room to move about, to identify oneself, to imitate and analyze the past freely; it is also supposed to comport only a partial belonging to one's society, indeed, even a nonbelonging; and, finally, it can mean a veritable rupture of old filial ties.

But this kind of exile also means always having to walk on a tightrope; always having to seek the proper measure or balance in order not to fall into betrayal or treason; always having to avoid

---

Filmmaker, Egypt. Originally written in French.

falling either into a facile prestidigitation on the one hand, or, on the other hand, into a noncommunicating autism or things strongly resembling it (such as religion and language).

For Rushdie, the question of the hour is the question of betrayal: betrayal of both his forebearers and his fellow emigrants in the course of conducting his own inquiries into modern migratory movements, their cultural and religious roots, and the political and social reasons behind these simply massive contemporary displacements of the South to the North, and of the East to the West. To find the kind of mask persona, or identity one's country of adoption will accept often implies, as has been said more than once, a form of renunciation of, or treason toward, that which one has left behind. But it is a kind of treason where shame no longer haunts one; it even becomes itself a kind of craze or infatuation—a temptation one yields to because it may even seem required by one's new land of adoption: it can show up like an indelible mark, yet the person himself may meanwhile have actually lost his former points of anchorage or orientation, and may no longer even perceive the new way he is now being judged.

To betray means to put down permanent roots in a land belonging to others and give up on one's own land. In one's own land of origin, the exile that finally does lead to this is perceived as shame, a blemish that requires a justification, and that only such a justification can render legitimate. From the standpoint of exile, the past consists of deep wounds, the present is a continual irritation, and the future a very large question mark; one no longer even enjoys the luxury of being able to fall or fail. As Rushdie himself has said, exile transforms us—or, rather, we transform ourselves in order to become "transformed."

Are all those who have left their own countries traitors then? For the millions of Muslims who have never read *The Satanic Verses*, is Salman Rushdie a traitor? Many other exiles—notably, those who live in Bradford or Brick Lane—definitely see Rushdie as a traitor. His "treason" eclipses the voice that speaks their language and enunciates their own ambiguous situation. In an interview with an English journalist, Rushdie once remarked that he had greater sympathy for some of those who had burned his book than he did for certain of his defenders. Would this be an answer to the whole question?

A Point of View on the Ordeal of Salman Rushdie

by Soleiman Fayyad

I have not read *The Satanic Verses*. Many readers of Western languages, though, have had that opportunity, whatever the artistic level of the book might be and whatever the attitude of those readers might be toward it. I do not believe the book has even been translated into any of the languages of the Arab or Muslim world; if it has, it must have been done in secret and the text of the book must be circulating clandestinely, in the manner of traffic in drugs. By the mere fact of its publication alone, though, this book has brought upon the head of its author, a born Muslim, an accusation of something considerably more than ill will toward a sacred belief as well as an accusation of what has been taken to be mockery toward holy persons. However, the book has not been published in any Muslim country, only in Western countries which, historically—and over many centuries—have regularly warred against Islamic countries, mounting more than a few crusades and colonial wars; this latter fact, in particular, constitutes an important supplementary grief this author did not need to be saddled with.

With regard to the whole question of the liberty of thought, opinion, and artistic creation, it is important to point out that in the Islamic world, limitations are still customarily imposed on the public expression of ideas; this is done in the name of both law and cus-

Writer, Egypt. Originally written in Arabic.

tom. These limitations apply in particular to Islamic religious questions, and also to persons belonging to that tradition. If such a book had appeared in one of the languages of the Islamic world, especially at the present moment when that world is itself confronted with a rash of extremism and terrorism, there is no doubt at all that both the author and his publisher would have been subject to the gravest consequences.

The ordeal the author must be going through—in spite of the fact that he lives in the Western world and has acquired another nationality than his original one—may be even worse and crueler, especially since an imam, the Ayatollah Khomeini, himself an extremist and a terrorist, promulgated the *fatwa* against both the novel and its author, a *fatwa* the followers and disciples of Khomeini apparently have no choice but to carry out, sooner of later—even years later.

Even though it is possible to produce films on Jesus Christ, it is apparently not considered acceptable to produce representations either of the Prophet Muhammad or of any member of his family; this ban appears to hold outside the frontiers of the Arab and Muslim worlds as well as inside them. We only learned of the existence of this novel through the Arab press, of course; and the Arab press was certainly in no way neutral on the subject. It must be conceded, however, that the information media in the Arab and Muslim worlds as a whole have largely reflected real public opinion in those same worlds. This public opinion has been quite decisively directed against the author and his novel from the beginning of the affair. Nor has the taking of a position in his favor on the part of a number of Arab and Muslim writers been able to change very much the ordeal this writer continues to suffer. It also remains true, though, that to take a stand at his side is currently another way to defend the freedom of thought, opinion, and artistic creation within the Arab and Muslim countries in general.

We Arab and Muslim writers are surely overwhelmingly with Salman Rushdie in spirit, then, even if we are not necessarily in favor of his novel, which the majority of us have probably not read. Furthermore we have surely read little about it that was not rather strongly misleading and tendentious. Nevertheless, there does exist among us an almost unanimous attitude of solidarity with Salman Rushdie as well as one of support for freedom of thought, whether religious or profane, and of artistic creation.

Nevertheless I would address one reproach to the author on at least one count—nothing more nor less than a reproach—and it is this: that he published the novel in a Western language. This is a question that concerns Islamic culture as a whole. Heroism, for an author truly exercising his creative freedom, would have consisted of writing his work in the language of his land of origin and publishing it there; this is all the more true in that, both by blood and faith, he is truly a child of this region. If he had done this, he might have received more support from all the writers in this part of the world, and the pressures exerted by them in his favor might also have been much stronger. They might have literally flown to his side against his judges, and they might also have helped him win his case. Of course they might not have too. All causes have had their martyrs, always and everywhere: in literature, science, religion, philosophy.

But a writer such as Salman Rushdie should not have given the Islamic media the opportunity to accuse him of exploiting, and in the West no less, causes and beliefs detrimental to his own country, or to accuse him of seeming to seek thereby literary success through a work written in the language of those whose unfavorable attitudes toward Arabs and Muslims have been around for a long time and show no signs of changing.

However, we writers of this region also believe that there was no call to launch a media campaign against a lone writer such as Rushdie; nor, certainly, was there any call at all to issue a *fatwa* against him, condemning him without a trial. Both the *Sharia* and the civil laws of Muslim countries require a trial in such a case; the principle of freedom of thought and expression also applies here and should in no way be limited by the kind of criticisms to which Rushdie's work has been subjected.

I believe that Khomeini—who was a partisan political figure before becoming an ayatollah, after all, and apparently he became the latter only in order to escape the surveillance of the shah—never read the novel. Nevertheless, he condemned it. This was how he repaid the institution he himself had created, and also the little group of ayatollahs who had done him the honor of integrating him into their ranks.

I myself do not believe that Sunni Muslim public opinion, as contrasted with Shiite Muslim public opinion, truly nourishes any strong hatred against Salman Rushdie and his novel. Nevertheless, it is under great pressure on account of its own current waves of extremism and terrorism, the threats of which it experiences almost weekly; and thus it prefers simply to remain silent as far as the media are concerned —and as far as the general expression of thought and opinion is concerned, for that matter. There are honorable exceptions, of course, notably a number of articles written in defense of Salman Rushdie and his right to life and to speak out. There have even been acts of no little courage, such as the Cairo periodical *Ibda* that openly took up the defense of this writer in one of its issues.

I would add, though, that Naguib Mahfouz, in writing *The Son of Medina*, and in publishing this novel as a serial in Arabic in *Al-Ahram* in Beirut (the book has gone into twenty editions as of this date), showed himself to be a hundred times wiser than Salman Rushdie in treating a subject that was a hundred times more sensitive and even dangerous than the subject of *The Satanic Verses*. It is true that all of this took place in a different era—more than thirty years ago—when a greater degree of liberty, as well as a greater measure of respect for the rights of man, prevailed in the Arab and Muslim worlds. At that time Khomeini and his version of Shiite Islam had not yet appeared on the scene; nor had there yet appeared that new version of Islam exemplified today by bedouins of the desert using oil money to defend their tottering thrones, thus helping (among other things) to establish in the Land of the Two Rivers a regressive regime prepared to suppress all freedom of thought and expression whatsoever.

For Rushdie

by the Ayatollah Djalal Gandjeih

"The author of *The Satanic Verses*, a text written, edited, and published against Islam, against the Prophet of Islam, and against the Koran, along with all the editors and publishers aware of its contents, are condemned to capital punishment. I call on all valiant Muslims wherever they may be in the world to execute this sentence without delay, so that no one henceforth will dare insult the sacred beliefs of Muslims."

This is, essentially, the text of the famous *fatwa* of the Ayatollah Khomeini dated February 14, 1988. Even a hasty reading reveals that the sentence was not issued merely against a single person, but against an indefinite number of persons. A second, more careful reading reveals the deliberate blurring, or fuzziness, of the "sentence" itself, which no one knowledgeable in Islamic jurisprudence would fail to be cognizant of or fail to note. With the exception of "the author," Mr. Salman Rushdie himself, no precise details are given concerning the identity, nationality, or even the number of persons condemned by this document. To put it another way, what we have here is a blanket order for collective murder. In addition, in order to be competent to carry out the extermination of all those "aware of" the contents of Rushdie's book (who are considered accomplices in its publication and propagation), it is sufficient for someone to be merely a "valiant Muslim."

Ayatollah, Iran. Originally written in Persian.

In the *fatwa*, the aim of its issuance is the only thing clearly spelled out, namely, "so that no one henceforth will dare insult the sacred beliefs of Muslims." Even then, however, neither the term "sacred" not the term "insult" are precisely defined. Thus it is left to the "valiant Muslims" themselves to decide, arbitrarily, what might be meant by "sacred" and what they might consider to be an "insult" to their "sacred beliefs." Unfortunately, this demagogic and deliberately imprecise sentence is only too worthy of Khomeini; in addressing himself as he did to fanatical populist elements, who had already been shamelessly manipulated, he merely succeeded in bringing the religious beliefs of Muslims into even greater disrepute.

Many observers noticed immediately the essentially antireligious and even inhuman nature of this incitement to murder, and they quite properly denounced the blind terrorism of the author of the *fatwa*. Indeed, the anti-Islamic character of the *fatwa* cannot be minimized, any more than the seriousness of the collective murder it enjoins can be minimized. As far as we are concerned, we will not dwell upon the contents of the book of the British writer, which are stated to be the pretext of the issuance of this blanket order to proceed to murder. Anyway, can the content of any literary work, and particularly of any work of fiction, really be cited as proof of the belief or unbelief of its author in any way whatsoever? The answer to this question would involve a whole area of reflection that would extend beyond the range of this particular paper. Similarly, I will not go into what I know, however complete or incomplete it might be, concerning the true teachings of Islam and the markedly tolerant attitude of the Prophet toward thinkers and ideologues of all kinds, whether atheists, religious critics, polemicists, rebels, or even outright enemies of Islam. On the other hand, I can affirm without any ambiguity whatsoever that such an order to carry out an assassination has neither value nor justification in the light of what Khomeini's coreligionists generally understand by "the pillars of Islam" (or principal duties of every Muslim), the *Sharia* (Islamic law), and the *fiqh* (Islamic jurisprudence, the collection of Islamic laws and decrees). In the light of all these things, the absurdity of the assertion of the successors of Khomeini that his order is irrevocable becomes instantly apparent. On the contrary, the issuance of such an order in the first place constituted an unpardonable crime, especially in view of the fact that the one who issued it was holding himself out as "the guide" of the Shiite community at the same time that he was making extraordinary efforts to represent himself as the leader of all Muslims everywhere.

In order to establish the true religious status of the order of Khomeini, several points need to be brought out and elucidated: was the crime, if there was a crime, one that merited capital punishment? In other words, what was the nature of the crime? Who were the ones guilty of the crime? Before what tribunal administering the *Sharia* were these guilty ones brought? Was a proper judicial inquiry ever conducted establishing proof of any kind of guilt? What are the exact conditions and criteria of any Islamic legal judgment? How are sentences properly carried out if guilt of a crime is established?

Then there is the further point we are obliged to bring out, namely, that the only case in Islam in which capital punishment would ever be justified in the absence of a proper court judgment in accordance with the legal procedures we have been enumerating would be legitimate self-defense in war, that is to say, when the lives, security, honor, or goods of Muslims are violated *by force of arms*. And even in this case, fugitives and those who have been taken prisoner are no longer considered enemies.

According to the holy Koran, specifically Sura 60:8, concerning "She Who Is Tested": "God does not forbid you from beneficence and equity toward those who have neither fought against you nor banished you from your homes. He loves justice." Verse 9 specifies that God "forbids any liaison with those who have fought against you and driven you from your homes and who have tried to abolish your religion. The same defense is prescribed for you against those who have assisted them. Anyone who showed beneficence to them would be unjust."

With this one exception of self-defense in war, then, any act that would merit capital punishment would have to be formally recognized as a crime and adjudicated as such. The juridical procedures mentioned above that would have to be followed guarantee the legitimacy only of punishments that fit the crime. As far as can be determined, Khomeini never imagined that Rushdie's book constituted any actual act of warfare; if he had, he would surely not have hesitated to employ the term *muharib*, "belligerent," "enemy in war," to designate the author. Instead, he knowingly employed much more imprecise phraseology; he merely spoke of the book entitled *The Satanic Verses* as being "against Islam, against the Prophet of Islam, and against the Koran"; he certainly did not speak of any arm of warfare being brandished by any belligerent. His own words therefore condemn him. He has in fact ordered a collective murder. This is absolutely illegitimate from the Islamic point of view, and to go on to confide the execution of an order that is thus illegitimate in the first place to any "valiant Muslims" prepared to become assassins on Khomeini's own mistaken word is simply to make *him* doubly guilty and, by rights, himself liable to prosecution.

By his act Khomeini really lost all religious authority. A religious guide must be a just man, free of all crimes. More than that, he abused both the name of Islam and the good faith and confidence of Muslims. He was himself guilty of the major crime of infidelity to the fundamental principles of the holy religion which he in fact betrayed. As a result of his unpardonable aberrations, he exposed both Islam and Muslims to the worst kinds of affronts. It is well known that the Prophet himself stigmatized every kind of action that would lead believers into error or disseminate disorder among the community. According to the Koran (Sura 2:256), there should be "no constraint where religion is concerned; uprightness is very different from insanity." Similarly, those who use religion as a means of trickery or manipulation are not even to be recognized as "believers," even though they are commonly recognized to be Muslims: "the Arabs of the desert have declared, 'We have believed.' Say, rather, 'We have embraced Islam,' for the faith has not yet penetrated your hearts" (Sura 49:14). Finally, those who feign belief out of opportunism, fear, or indifference are firmly reprimanded by the Koran, and held to be "hypocrites" and, as such, dangerous. This Koranic insistence proves the necessity of liberty in religious matters. Whether one believes or not goes back to one's free will; faith cannot be validated by mere sincerity, although it is a quality highly recommended for both believers and unbelievers alike. The *Sunna* (the collection of acts and words of the Prophet) is quite eloquent on this subject: a sincere unbeliever is worth more than a false believer.

For Khomeini and his adherents, however, anyone who appears to renounce Islam is thereby considered an apostate; and all apostates are liable to capital punishment (especially someone born a Muslim). What is worse, though, is that even according to their own criteria for apostasy—criteria not recognizable as authentic teachings of Islam— they are at least supposed to recognize that the crime must be proved beyond any shadow of a doubt. But only a properly constituted Islamic tribunal can establish that the person suspected of apostasy has in fact formally renounced the religion as a whole and in its essence. We should also recall that such actions as criticizing, expressing doubts, asking questions, adopting various contradictory or novel interpretations concerning exegesis on this or that point of Islam, or otherwise having confused ideas concerning the basic teachings of Islam cannot be considered as apostasy. Apostasy consists of a total and irrevocable renunciation of the essence of Islam as a religion and a faith; this is the only thing that can properly be recognized as apostasy. The fact that various sects and schisms exist within Islam is proof of this. Moreover, the renunciation (denigration) of Islam cannot be, properly speaking, considered apostasy either, unless it is consciously issued and proclaimed without any ambiguity, with both force and conviction, by an adult of sound mind. In other words, a fuzzy, elliptical, or sibylline type of statement, one reported by a third party, or even a blasphemous-type statement by someone unaware of its blasphemous character—none of these suffices to establish apostasy in the true sense. It was precisely because of all these considerations, criteria, and restrictions that the mullahs of Iran were unable to find a precise terminology that was acceptable, even to those who were demanding the death of Rushdie.

With regard to the elements of the Rushdie book, which was said to be filled with various "allusions" and "indications," there have been mentioned up to now only certain terms that are themselves highly ambiguous, such as *muhin* ("offensive," "insulting"), but not *munkar* ("unbelieving," "denier of the faith"); *kufr amiz* ("blasphemous"), but not *kufr* ("blasphemy"). Even though some have explicitly spoken of apostasy, Khomeini himself was satisfied to speak only of the content of the book as "against Islam" or "anti-Islam"—but such characterizations provide no basis in Islamic law for establishing a crime.

All of this explains some of the tergiversations and aberrant attitudes exhibited by some of the Iranian mullahs with regard to this whole affair. Not one of them—although for them the book is an offense and its author an apostate—was willing to issue the order that Rushdie should be put to death. Ali Khamenei, who was president at the time and is now "the guide" of the Iranian government, stated on February 17, 1988, three days after the issuance of the *fatwa* of Khomeini, that "if Salman Rushdie apologizes to Muslims, the revocation of his sentence could be considered." But two days later Khomeini put this presumptuous president in his place and reaffirmed that "even if the author of *The Satanic Verses* repents and becomes an ascetic, it remains the duty of every Muslim to send him to the devil."

Neither the teachings of Islam, then, nor the pretended Islamic criteria of Khomeini and his like, in any way suffice for the issuance of a sentence of death against the writer, nor, a fortiori against an indefinite number of other persons supposedly involved. To have issued such a command was automatically to have forfeited any religious legitimacy whatsoever. As a very experienced politician, Khomeini was not ignorant of the fact that his irresponsible decision would seriously compromise the credit of a religion of freedom and peace. Neither Islam itself, nor the teachings of the Prophet, nor the juridical system of the Shiite clergy—of whom he prided himself on being "the supreme guide"—prevented Khomeini from creating the entire Rushdie affair out of whole cloth; it surely amounted to a shameful scandal serving no religious or ethnic ends but purely his own ambitions. Did he not himself declare that "the interests of the regime are more important than religious theories and principles"? The bloody events in Mecca in 1987 and then this order to commit murder represent two graphic examples among many others that could be cited that at no point was Khomeini ever joking. We should recall that the sentence issued against Rushdie came just a few months after the defeat by Iraq, after eight years of war. Khomeini himself had characterized this defeat as "a cup of poison" and as "the loss of honor before God."

In conclusion, I can only repeat the declaration I made on the occasion of the issuance of the *fatwa*; this was on February 20, 1988, at a press conference held in London: "This illegitimate order on the part of Khomeini is a politician's maneuver; it is an attempt to create a new international crisis. He hopes thereby to mask the contradictions of his regime and the innumerable problems without solutions which he faces, following his bitter defeat by Iraq." I added on that occasion: "By the religious authority I possess and in the name of Islam and the Iranian resistance, and in the cause of freedom and peace, I declare that the name of Khomeini is excised forever from membership in the Muslim community. This reactionary politician has abused the name of Islam in order to reach power and he continues today to ill serve and indeed betray the cause of Islam in order to maintain at all costs his intolerable regime."

The heirs of Khomeini have followed the same logic as before in declaring the *fatwa* "irrevocable." What applies to Khomeini applies all the more to them.

Personally, I welcome with gratitude the explanations Mr. Salman Rushdie has offered. He has said that he "in no way had any intention of insulting either Muslims or Islam." This represents a most eloquent statement on the part of a hunted man pursued by a horde of terrorists incited by a regime of false prophets. He is a man whom every true Muslim should endeavor to help and whose rights those same true Muslims should endeavor to secure and defend.

I call to the attention of all observers, intellectuals, defenders of the rights of man and of liberty in all its forms, and upholders of international order the fact that the Iranian political leaders currently in power are promoting, purely and simply, a regime of shameful state terrorism. It would be a grave error to confuse the inadmissible attitudes they exhibit with any kind of fidelity whatsoever to any kind of true religious principles or any other kind of cultural considerations.

Behiya

by Moncef Ghachem

I have heard the groans, heard
the cries, and I have seen the
waves of tears that went along
with them.
> —Tamin Ibn Al-Mu'izz
> Fatimi, Funeral oration
> for his brother Abdallah, A.D. 975

The crime took place on the morrow of the action of the coalition against Iraq in my native town of El-Mahdia, which in the tenth century was the capital of the "intermediary" Fatimid dynasty of Ismai'ili Shiites in North Africa. In those days the town was called "the Invincible" and "the Conqueror," but in our day it is a very traditionalist backwater kind of place. The crime I mention concerned Behiya. She was twenty-two years old, a young housewife, married only four months to one of her neighbors, a worker in the local soap factory; then one night she was stabbed to death in her sleep by her husband.

A crime of passion? Some doubt concerning the question cannot be excluded.

In the factory where the husband worked an "Islamist" network had been implanted roughly from the time labor union action had

Writer, Tunisia. Originally written in French.

been eliminated. Is it possible that this man became contaminated by some of the misogynist and macho (actually fascist) rhetoric of certain of his enlightened Muslim brothers? Did the man not reveal, through such an odious crime, his own incapacity to live any normal conjugal life with a pretty young woman? Had he or had he not for some time been afflicted with a form of schizophrenia, without, however, his immediate entourage ever being able to notice that anything was wrong with him, or to be concerned about it? This particular crime raised many such questions as these. The women of this old town trembled and waited and wept with their whole bodies over the whole tragedy. I myself have to confess, not without some discomfort, that I found myself entirely on the side of the women; their wails echoed the horrible cry in the night of Behiya herself, a cry against violence, tyranny, and barbarism.

Before she was finally killed by him, Behiya had complained of repeated abuse from this husband of hers who had no doubt been forced upon her. Terrible in its deafness to all such appeals, the power in place of the dominant males did not even deign to listen to her. Then one day I happened to be fishing at the side of the father of the young victim, who was also preoccupied with fishing at that particular moment. Two of my friends were also with me. One of them asked, almost jokingly, "When are you going to write something about Behiya?" Then the other friend instantly broke in. "Watch out!" he said. "You could easily be taken for another Salman Rushdie."

"How so?" I asked.

"If you disinter the frightful story about Behiya, you will inevitably raise questions about the morals of this town. And the townspeople won't thank you for it. You may even upset them greatly. They are very susceptible, as you well know, to anything that touches upon the honor of their daughters. The imams, from their tribunals, will denounce you. You will be put on the index and very severely judged. What else?"

"Hey, wait!" I rejoined. "I don't attempt to hide my true ideas and opinions. I was revolted by that crime. Anyway, as you well know, El-Mahdia is neither Mecca nor Medina. These two cities are more undercover. And unlike the character in *The Satanic Verses* who entrenched himself behind closed doors in public houses, I live out in the open. Salman Rushdie lives in Great Britain, after all. He is British. For my part I fish here for Mediterranean bream under your very own eyes."

"But the connection will quickly be made. Let the dead bury the dead."

"I don't agree," I said. "I don't agree for the sake of all the Behiyas both below and above ground. For all the women of El-Mahdia and elsewhere. Precisely because the connection will quickly be made, and the ayatollahs and mullahs condemning creative artists in all sorts of countries will be hanging over our heads, I do intend to speak out about that young woman!"

Salah Al-Bahri also rests here in a cemetery of El-Mahdia; he too came from this town. He was an assistant to the rector of the mosque in Brussels, and he was shot dead along with the rector on March 29, 1989. Just a little while before that, the two of them had declared in an interview that Salman Rushdie should be afforded a trial and should be allowed to repent. According to the media, this double assassination was carried out on orders from the intelligence service in Teheran.

For the funeral of Salah Al-Bahri, a huge crowd assembled. There had been many fewer at the funeral of Behiya.

Our Neighbor Salman Rushdie

by *Karim Ghassim*

He is our neighbor in more that one respect. His mother lives in Pakistan, to the southwest of Iran. Also, he himself is in exile, living clandestinely. Culturally speaking we are brothers as well. It frequently happens that, in the process of fleeing tyranny, neighbors whom one had lost track of come together again, sometimes without knowing it, sometimes without actually meeting. Nevertheless, one way or another, they are all on the same journey, searching for the same lost motherland.

With regard to Salman Rushdie, we are not only linked to him by the experience of loss and of searching; we are linked to him in a common defense against the regime of Khomeini. When we learned of the death sentence issued against Rushdie, we understood what it was that the weakened tyrant was attempting to achieve. He had to give heart to his demoralized partisans, after an eight-year war lost to Iraq—a loss that called into question his own despotic power. But how could he ever give up his monopoly of power and authority? "It is not a question of Islam or of anything like that. The issue is total power." He himself had stated it thusly in the past. And in order to assure this power, he never ceased engaging in terror and inflicting death; he raised murder to the dignity of a "divine grace."

The issuance of the *fatwa* produced for him precisely the crisis he needed; he was able to count on the hysteria of the masses. This

---

Sociologist, Iran. Originally written in Arabic.

was the psychological mechanism that drove the entire politics of the *fatwa*. If there was a disagreement or difference of opinion with the temporal authorities, it had to be interpreted as a conflict with God; every heresy, every dissidence had to be diabolized. In addition, it was imperative to respond to every challenge with maximum decisiveness and rigor. The tyrant understood only too well how cowardly the great powers and great centers of economic decisions would all turn out to be when faced with his decision. How could the so-called "free world" tolerate the reality of a *fatwa* such as this remaining in force year after year? Why did the United Nations fail to see in this act an act of international terrorism and react accordingly? Why did Amnesty International not stigmatize this new form of enforced detention? (The whole world suddenly turns out to be a prison!) Why? Why?

Salman Rushdie has now had ample experience of the cowardice of the powerful. Over long years he has continued to receive counsels of prudence and patience; things will work out somehow, it has been repeated. Actually they have gotten worse; he himself has had to declare that "to remain silent is the most dangerous thing of all to do," as he recently said in Germany. Yes, dear neighbor, you are right. If the silence continues and forgetfulness finally sets in, the enemy will then be able to realize that everything has come at that point in his favor. That is why we do not wish to remain silent; that is why we wish to fight for as long as our neighbor—and our country—have not regained their liberty.

Hope to see you soon in Teheran!

Sheikh Bedreddin

by Nidim Gürsel

Sheikh Bedreddin Mahmud (1358–1416), also known as Simavna Kadisioglu, is one of the most interesting figures in the history of the Ottoman Empire, if not one of the most important. He comes to our notice as much because of his work as a mystic as because of his quality as the ideological leader of a popular revolt that took place during a period of reorganization of the Ottoman state, following a period of disarray that itself was the consequence of the Ottoman defeat by the armies of Tamerlane. The insurrection in question was fomented at Karaburun by two adherents of Bedreddin, Börklüce Mustafa and Torlak Kemal. In addition to Muslim Turks, Jews and Greeks also rallied to the cause of the insurrection, which, so far as the orthodox Muslim sunna are concerned, has been decidedly considered to be heresy by historians. Sheikh Bedreddin, who had been the supreme judge with the armies of Musa Celebi, and had carried out very high responsibilities in the hierarchy of the Ottoman state, was judged to be responsible for this insurrection, and, following a trial, he was executed in the marketplace of Serez, which today is in Greece. Sheikh Bedreddin was the first Turkish intellectual ever condemned to death by government power for his ideas.

The insurrection of Karaburun was put down only with difficulty by Bayezid Pasha. It represents an event that must be classified among the more important popular movements in the history of Anatolia. There were a number of such movements of a religious and ideological character that emerged between the Seljuk period and the beginning

Writer, Turkey. Originally written in Turkish.

of the nineteenth century (when the Westernizing of the Ottoman Empire began). These popular movements also had an economic dimension; they stemmed from contradictions in the landholding system known as the *timar*.[1] In the thirteenth century, the insurrection of the nomadic Turkomans headed by Baba Ishak against the Seljuk state enjoyed, through poets and philosophers such as Sheikh Bedreddin, Pir Sultan Abdal, and Dadaloglu,[2] direct historical continuity with the insurrection at Karaburun. One of the principal links in this particular chain of historical continuity was the movement of Bedreddin, which was founded on the principles of tolerance and equality.

Sheikh Bedreddin wanted to suppress private property; he considered that all wealth ought to be shared for the common good. He also defended the absolute equality of all men, as he did of all religions. It is probable that his ideas, which were far ahead of his times, did not grow out of his philosophical work known as *Varidat* but out of other works we no longer have. The so-called *Manakibdname*, written by Khalil bin Ismail, grandson of Bedreddin, informs us that the latter was the author of no less than forty-eight books, of which only four have come down to us.

In order to understand the kind of regime Bedreddin wished to install, we are mostly obliged to have recourse to some of the criticisms of him formulated by certain contemporary historians of the Ottoman Empire. Some indications, nevertheless, may also be found in his *Varidat*; his views may be considered to represent an extreme example of materialist conceptions combined with the pantheistic dispositions of Anatolian mysticism. Thus, the notion of the oneness of being as conceived by Bedreddin becomes shorn of its metaphysical character and becomes narrowly associated with the idea of a regime free of antago-

---

1   Ottoman system of landholding in common which consisted in grants of land to the beys in exchange for soldiers which the latter were obliged to furnish to the central government, in numbers proportional to the area and quality of the lands granted.

2   A popular poet of the nineteenth century. He was a spokesman for the Turkoman tribes which had resisted the settlement efforts imposed by the Ottoman government.

nisms which, according to Bedreddin, must inevitably be installed one day here below. It is certain that this kind of firm conviction, according to which a day will come when a society without antagonisms will actually be founded on the basis of absolute equality, resembles the same kind of messianism that has been encountered in other societies.

From the point of view of historical materialism, the religious character of the insurrection of Sheikh Bedreddin would have to be considered a specific instance of class warfare. In this perspective, it would represent the natural outcome of the interplay of certain economic and social conditions in a given historical period. Throughout the entire history of Anatolia—or, for that matter, throughout the entire history of Islam—the aspirations of the popular masses toward social equality have generally taken the form of messianism. Thus, the condemnation of Sheikh Bedreddin to die on the gallows at Serez and, a century later, that of the popular poet Pir Sultan Abdal to die a similar death at Sivas represent two closely linked historical events.

The Peasant Wars in Germany and the ideas of Thomas Münzer provide many analogies with the case of Sheikh Bedreddin and the insurrection at Karaburun. We know that Bedreddin, like Münzer, did not believe in another world, and that he was seeking both a Heaven and a Hell here below (the former he considered the symbol of the good and the latter the symbol of the evil in this world); nevertheless he did try to base his ideas on the *hadiths* (the traditions of the Prophet). While Münzer developed a pantheistic conception, the mysticism of Bedreddin denied the resurrection and hence issued in a kind of materialism. Although it also originated in a pantheistic-type conception affirming the unity of God and of the universe, the corollary belief of the oneness of being found in the *Varidat* ended up, in a direct line of development, by affirming a kind of materialism. The method chosen by Bedreddin to explain natural phenomena accorded great importance to the role of reason, as did the theological doctrine of Münzer. In addition, Münzer's interpretation of the New Testament Book of Revelation overlapped with the messianic conceptions of Bedreddin. Both men were very anxious to abolish social inequalities and antagonisms. Influenced by the Italian mystic Joachim of Floris (twelfth century), who was prophesying the imminent end of a decadent world, Münzer concluded, looking at the tumultuous events of his own day, that the end was indeed near. It was for this reason that he called upon the peasantry to rise up against the clergy and the aristocracy, in order to build a new egalitarian society in which conflicts could be ended and wealth could be distributed among the people. Bedreddin underlined exactly the same ideas in his *Varidat*, especially in his interpretation of paragraph 105 of the Sura Ta'ha.

When Börklüce Mustafa and Torlak Kemal launched the insurrection in the Aybin region, Bedreddin secretly left the city of Iznik where he had been exiled and went into the Beylik of Isfandiyariglu, then on to Deliorman in Thrace. His objective was to organize a revolt of the inhabitants of that region, but he was captured and brought before the Padishah Mehmet Celebi instead. He was given to understand that he would be spared if he were willing to abjure his views. But Bedreddin had already decided by then that he was prepared to die for his ideas.

In the end, it is undeniable that in the movement of Bedreddin, as in that of Münzer, aspirations toward a primitive communal-type society were very important. Considering the level of development of the means of production, however, these aspirations existed only in rudimentary form in both cases. In order for such ideas to flourish, the development of a division of labor and the formation of social classes were required. Nevertheless the model envisaged by Münzer, tortured to death at the age of twenty-eight, like the one envisaged by Sheikh Bedreddin, condemned to death on the gallows at Serez, would both have to await a later day and another society. Certainly we cannot deny that the movement of Bedreddin was in many respects strongly oriented toward the future. Indeed, the influence of Sheikh Bedreddin persisted in various ways throughout the whole history of the Ottoman Empire, and a number of sects continued to remain faithful to his teaching. When the Turkish Republic finally arrived, and, especially, after the appearance in 1936 of *The Epic of Sheikh Bedreddin* by Nazim Hikmet, the whole subject of this early visionary came back into vogue, and since then a number of important studies have been done on various hitherto unknown aspects of his revolt.

No One Among Us Can Wash His Hands of This Friend's Blood

by Émile Habibi

The reason I have avoided clarifying my opinion on the Iranian government's decision sanctioning the assassination of British Muslim writer Salman Rushdie could be considered a hereditary reason, if I may say so. Indeed, I find myself among those creatures of God about whom Arab-Islamic history's most renowned free-thinking philosopher, Abou-l-'Ala al-Maarri, said:

> They have lived as their fathers before them lived
> And they have passed on the religion as they found it, without changing anything.

As for the following distich, taken from the same poem, from my childhood until today, I have always been wary of applying it:

> They pay no attention to what they say or hear
> And they, the lost ones, are indifferent to he before whom they bow down.

These recent years, I also all but suffered the same fate as Salman Rushdie does today, but the priests of my ancient church were quite incapable of sanctioning my death; they who lived—and

---

Writer, Palestine/Israel. Originally written in Arabic.

still live—in a time when their own lives are threatened, even though their decision of excommunication, made several times on my behalf, to my eyes resembles our proverbial "dance in the darkness."

It is there that they differ from the priests who authorized Salman Rushdie's assassination (and one would be wrong not to take the latter's threats seriously); but they resemble each other in that those who today stalk Salman Rushdie belong to a community, the Shiites, or the followers of Ali, who, since the beginning of Islamic history, have always been the object of bloody persecutions. I have discovered, to my chagrin, that those who are the targets of such persecution are most ready to spill the blood of others, who, according to them, have distanced themselves from the principles of their original "church." And even if Salman Rushdie isn't of Shiite origin, it is enough that he was born Muslim to find himself incorporated into that most persecuted of communities, that of Islam.

The incitement to spill the blood of Muslims is old indeed, even older than the trials of the Inquisition; and the accusation of deviation from religious principles is as old as religion itself, be it Islam or other beliefs. The Shiites, who lead Iran today and who sanctioned Salman Rushdie's assassination, throughout history have been the primary victims of this accusation; they have suffered even more than the Protestants in the history of Christianity. Moreover, the history of free thought does not differ too greatly in the evolutions of Islam and Christianity; it is after all the Christians who drew lessons of courage from the Muslims' example.

What is tragic and truly appalling is that we find ourselves still, today, in this last decade of the twentieth century, forced to combat this form of excommunication! It seems to me that a deficiency, a crack exists in our civilization as a whole; this deficiency is embodied in the broad gulf separating politics from morality, a gulf no one among us (however sublime the principles he may profess) has found a way to bridge or even reduce.

The content of *The Satanic Verses* is thus less important than the following observation: the vast majority of those who have called for the Iranian leaders to reverse their decision has ceased presenting the image of good faith to the people. From that point on, this "good faith" was perceived as selective. Indeed, the vast majority of Salman Rushdie's defenders has chosen only to defend a cause that is convenient for them and that doesn't cost them anything. But how many among them have heard of the Egyptian secular writer Farag Foda, assassinated in Cairo by religious fundamentalists in early 1992? If our civilization were resolutely honest and of good faith, it would have immortalized the name of Farag Foda beside those of Galileo Galilei and Giordano Bruno.

The whole of European civilization is based on the teachings of the sage Socrates, who preferred drinking poison over making concessions to rationality. There, in truth, is the essence of all civilization, be it Western or Eastern. But how many educated Europeans know the name of Abou-l-'Ala al-Maarri, who also died of poison, having never compromised his own beliefs: "I have no other imam than my reason."

Another deficiency of contemporary global civilization is precisely that it has not yet become truly global, at least not in content. It is rather a question of cultures closed upon themselves, each refusing to understand the others, refusing to recognize how they participate in one another.

It is this deficiency that explains—without justifying it—the inhuman, irreligious, and non-Shiite attitude the leaders obstinately maintain toward the writer Salman Rushdie. And in doing so they bear the stigma of this plague, the Inquisition, passed from Europe to the Islamic Orient. But if we fail to save Salman Rushdie—God forbid!—from this absurd decree of excommunication, the shame will haunt global civilization as a whole, and particularly European culture, since it is to them that Salman Rushdie has turned for protection.

I most certainly do not wish for Salman Rushdie to join that group of great men who chose death over recantation, such as Abou-l-'Ala al-Maarri, Giordano Bruno, or Farag Foda. I fear that then our faith in human civilization would waver, this civilization that has accomplished so much in these last thousand years. No, it is impossible that it should all go to waste.

I only wish that all of us understand, as laypeople or religious, and particularly the former—that today we cannot wash our hands of the blood of this "friend," whether he is one or not.

For Rushdie

by Mohammed Harbi

We are thousands of intellectuals, writers, artists, opponents having fled our countries, some by force, others by conscious decision, because the powers in place left us no choice but silence or compromise and life in disgrace, the splitting of the personality, permanent schizophrenia.

Rushdie is one of our own. Exiled, the feelings he experienced in his society haven't eliminated this connection. The possibility of freely manifesting his aspirations in England didn't make him forget his own people, didn't anesthetize his revolt.

With Rushdie we recognize the disrespect, the principle of pleasure, that is, freedom in culture and the arts, as a source of fruitful examination of our past and present. Otherwise, the specificity of the imaginary cannot be affirmed if a tradition is made sacred, if the fascination of a mythical past remains unshattered.

Like Rushdie, we hold the conviction that to try to fashion a future by constantly referring to "pious ancestors" is illusory. This form of clinging to the past kills all curiosity and all initiative to innovate. The Islamists position themselves on a permanent denial of realities: the falsification of history, negation of the gap between ideas and social practices, narrow-minded triumphalism, and so on. The denial of reality is translated in relationships with followers by an indoctrination aimed at destroying all possibility of individual

---

Historian, Algeria. Originally written in French.

thought. In the end there is only room for idolaters.

Do not misunderstand us. Without free thought, spiritual liberation cannot exist. The failure of the educational systems in Islamic countries is blindingly obvious. These systems that generate closure and intolerance are an important source of the backwardness. In the seventies the Egyptian philosopher, Abdurrahman Badawi, noted that "if an Islamic Renan wrote the history of the origins of Islam, he would not be tolerated because of his admission of his need for an editor!"

Falsehood and censure reign over our history in the name of moral order. Where the principle of authority reigns unshared, there is room for neither freedom nor intellectual pursuit.

And Also for Them

by Jamil Hatmal

This time the emotion seems clearer: on the one hand there is a writer of considerable merit, living in hiding for several years, encircled by a halo of terror and distrust, surrounded by sympathy and hatred. In equal quantities, on the other hand, one finds a power that, reactivating the guillotines, the murderous *fatwas*, and bloody representations, justifies the massacres with a so-called sacred legitimacy. The religion takes on a form contrary to its ordinary purpose; it becomes a text of execution, of suppression of the other, an act destroying anything different.

This time his name is Salman Rushdie. His only crime is having described a certain scene: thus he has found himself attacked by priests, Pharisees, turban-wearers, jailers who, not content to lay the blame on his writings, have lanced him with their sharpened claws, more for pure sadistic delight than for the religious concern attributed to them.

His name is Salman Rushdie and they incarnate the powers, the powers of the sacred, of the supposed morality, of oppression, tyranny, and censorship, powers of the most closed-minded ideology of those who call themselves the heirs of God. His name is Salman Rushdie; it's a well-known name. He is crushed by fear, but he can rely on a semblance of support, the support of the media, that of the voices of conscience, the upholders of justice, and, some-

---

Writer, Syria. Originally written in Arabic.

times, that of certain powers who believe it in their best interest, at least temporarily, to oppose the *fatwas* of murder.

Today his name is Salman Rushdie. But so he doesn't appear as a rare or exceptional case, I imagine him beside Khosrow Jalsorkhi, the poet who died in the jails of Savak, or Faraj Bayraqdar, the poet who spoke out for Jalsorkhi and for whom the equivalent of Savak reserved a similar treatment: his fate remains obscure. Along with him I will name Haytam al-Khoja, a Syrian novelist who wrote about destitution and who in turn became victim of the miserable squalor of prison.

This is why I stand on their side, facing the other camp, that of oppression, physical elimination, and orders of arrest. This is why I choose Salman Rushdie over the murderous turbans, or Mansour Amhad Rajeh, a guest in the Yemenite prison of Taiz, over the turbans of tribalism, and yet, that is not all. I prefer the scars of torture on the face of Muhammad Afifi Matar, the Egyptian poet who whispered "no" and was answered with whips and electric shocks. And I choose Farag Foda, the Egyptian writer who was answered with death.

Should Salman Rushdie remain alone while he is surrounded by the names of the dead and prisoners of political or religious oppression? Should he remain alone while the body of Lebanese thinker Hussein Mroué is still warm from the bullet wounds possibly inflicted by the very same people who issued the *fatwa* against Salman Rushdie? Is he truly alone while Mroué's compatriot, the thinker Mahdi Amil, was assassinated and is today prisoner in his own tomb?

So we stand on the side of Rushdie because he is himself, we believe, on their side, and because we are trying, with our weak and trembling fingers, to reconstruct the message of these scattered voices that come to us from the hangman's scaffold. It is not only for him that we take sides—even if he does deserve it—but also for all those like him and like them, and for life itself.

Twilight on the City Wall

by Ahmed Hegazi

The man's blood spilt in the suburb is a rose
arisen from the sand that rained down on the country
it is the blood of the tortured silt, laid bare to the storm's
breath
it is our final cry
our open wound in the heart of this blackness
it is a blood come from the captive sun like a lock of
its hair
twilight bleeding over the city wall
Where do the shadows of Gog and Magog return . . .
The sparkling of this carbuncle
will shine in the ash
until the end of all this ruin
until the Day of Resurrection

These are the barbarians thrown there, into this paradise,
by the deserts
where their dogs growl, where their immense flocks bleat,
where they walk, encircled by locusts.
One would say they have faces of crows
eyes of wolves
legs of bull.

Poet, Egypt. Originally written in Arabic.

They trudge over the country
And scatter their desolation everywhere.

This is how this country's houses have covered with sand,
and the gardens that offered green shadows
that sheltered the dove at calm dawn,
and sprouted lilies and daisies,
have turned into ruins, salted expanses where vapors of
sulfur and bitumen rise.
The sand covers the roads, the cafes, women's breasts, the
morning papers—
a strange sand has seized the city
whose innumerable grains gnaw at the country and its
people like as many worms
the towns and villages have turned to sand
and the River born of the steps of Spring on virgin hills
of a rainbow come to rest on Earth's bed
of a divine prayer descended onto the lips of the creatures,
the River of this country
celestial mare, arc of alliance,
which steals the earth's green to provide for men,
even the River has withdrawn, surrounded by the sand,
stagnant on the arid plain
This country's half moons and minarets, the stars of its sky
have turned to sand
and the people, made similar to the desert,
have become marionettes stuffed with sand, wandering the
sterile space,
traveling the expanses where they lose their way . . .
Who will buy these marionettes?
Who will buy them?

Sons of Osiris!
No tree of broad shade exists that hasn't retained some
quivering hint of its father

No bread bowl or ewer exists that doesn't have a trace, a
curve of its home coast . . .
But the sons of Osiris have given themselves over to
sterility.
Their faces, the palms of their hands
their eyelashes, their fingers, their beards
their bread, their gait, everything of theirs is sand
and their sons and daughters are also held by lawful sand . .
.

And I who since my youth have darkened my eyes with
kohl
I cast my eyes upon all this in sadness
and I weep, although the tears won't be of any help.
In each corner of the land I find a souvenir and many
reasons to cry;
beneath each rosebush, I held a tender rose
and drank a glass overflowing with spirits;
I walked, glorious, with a docile companion.
Leaving the foam of the nights in my wake,
I penetrated the brilliance of dawn.
Ah! if I could
I would build in place of these fragile brick buildings and
balconies
a new coast, well adjusted, from my own ribs . . .

Iram was, and is no longer, something no one could build
the likes of.
It was a city, offered to the peasants, the seamen, the
builders, the singers, the harbingers of prayer, but not to
the destructive tyrants. It was like a poem, brought forth
from its stanzas and made city, a river embracing the hill,
whose abundant foam came from the gardens planted with
vine; it had homes with vaulted rooms,
a universe of dreams and desire,

of rhythmic movements of lively bodies floating in the
evenings of summer
the summer, when it was good to watch over
cries of birth, wedding songs,
a magical dance which led the living and the dead and the
newborn, the adolescents, the vigorous blacks, together . . .
Iram, something no one could build the likes of,
who will save it today, now crushed beneath the sand,
who will give their arms to the mistress of the land, who
will save it?

The blood of this man spilt in the city,
is the end of those who killed him, and who killed the city,
it is a new birth for the city, a cry,
spread like a call throughout Iram, erasing all its ruins and
the ruins of its sons.
The message in his spilt blood, a true and spiritual
message, has become a rejection glowing red from the
inkwell's bottom.
Sand, go away!
Sand, go away!
Locusts, be on your way!
The new Iram of writers' blood is born,
of the word of the poet exiled far from the city to chase
away the tyrants' corruption and domination . . .
From now on the message can flow on all lips and
the pride of facades be humbled!

Practices of Another Time

by Fereydoun Hoveida

I do not admire Salman Rushdie's novel. But the single fact that a writer continues to be threatened because of his book constitutes an inadmissible scandal during this fin de siècle. These are practices of the Middle Ages which have no place in our time. I have said it several times—and I will repeat it as long as necessary: no person, public or private, be he a political or religious authority, has the right to decree the death of another person. The penal codes of all nations, including those of Iran, condemn incitement to murder. All Islamic countries are, to my knowledge, members of the United Nations. By signing the UN Charter, they have agreed to apply its principles which include the right of writers to express their opinions and publish what they see fit. A work can be publicly criticized, but the country that commits the crime of condemning a writer to death becomes outlawed by the international community. The last time books were burned was in Berlin in 1933. The last time writers were burned was in the Middle Ages!

Writer, Iran. Originally written in French.

For Rushdie

by Sonallah Ibrahim

Without freedom of the imaginary, there can be no authentic artistic creation. The best expression of this freedom is irony which translates a healthy attitude toward life and history. We all use irony in our daily commentaries and in our wit, in mocking ourselves, our traditions, our habits, even our most sacred values, without scorning them. Salman Rushdie has done nothing more serious than what we all do each day, and what can be found in droves throughout the heritage of Islam, at the time of its cultural flourishing, in all kinds of anecdotes, stories, poems of Abu Nuwwas, Omar Khayyam, al-Maarri, or even the Sufi mystics.

Rushdie's drama is having published in a very particular political context: on the one hand is the Iranian regime's attempts to regain the naive adherence of the popular masses and to make them forget the suffering inflicted by a tyranny draped in the folds of religious robes; on the other hand, the echo this affair has found with Muslims embittered both by the hardships Western imperialism has made them endure, and by the denial of permanent justice that reveals the West's attitude toward the Palestinian people. Lacking the power really to confront this situation, many of these Muslims have chosen to withdraw into the past, retaining not those periods of cultural bloom in which reason and thought were respected, but those of decadence and decline, when thought, creation, and even irony were prohibited.

Writer, Egypt. Originally written in Arabic.

Every person of conscience must go to the aid of this great writer in hardship, to multiply the pressure to end the threats on his life, the attack on freedom and right to expression. But before that, every person of conscience—especially in the West—must struggle for justice for the Palestinian people and now for the Bosnian people who are going through their own ordeal. Each day, among the victims falling under the blows of racist hatred, are some of the writers and creators of tomorrow.

For Salman Rushdie

by Adil Jasouli

I don't know Salman Rushdie, I skimmed *The Satanic Verses*, I am not of Indian or Anglo-Saxon heritage. Nevertheless I feel close to this man who finds himself alone, condemned to death, perpetually under guard, due to a criminal *fatwa*, decreed by a dead man for whom it was the last breath of life, and of death.

There is no need, here or elsewhere, to discuss the novelistic value of the work, nor to know how the novel might have shocked the imbeciles and fanatics who speak in the name of Islam, since these are criminals who, like any mafia, do not hesitate to "put a contract out" on a free man.

What troubles me is the place of the words of independent intellectuals in an Arab-Islamic world delivered to the demons of intolerance, regression, and closure on itself. "Domestic" repression being the norm and revealing itself to be insufficient, the Iranian regime has inaugurated repression by remote control against all those in Europe and elsewhere who try to secularize Islam and put it in line with critical modernity.

To stand beside Rushdie today is to bet that in the long term there cannot be a democratic transformation of Arab-Islamic societies without free thought and without necessary and salutary destruction of all taboos.

The current reflux, which greatly exceeds the geography of the

---

Sociologist, Morocco. Originally written in French.

Arab-Islamic world, should not encourage apathy in the face of idiocy and barbarism; quite the contrary. Because we know, better than others, that poets are always right.

The Adam of a Free Liberty

by Salim Jay

The exorbitant demand made on Salman Rushdie—"to die as the price for his freedom"—is well within the tone of a dictatorship that expresses its power by unleashing troops armed with megaphones and with the power to stone its own population.

The novel is the quintessential exercise of freedom in the modern world, from which contemporary Iran accepts technology while refusing to let the flames of the poor human imagination, sovereign, tortured by ghosts, express themselves.

Novelist Salman Rushdie's freedom is costly for the British government in terms of secret agents and bodyguards. Nevertheless, the employment situation in the world being as it is, placing a price on the heads of all novelists and translators, be they British, Finnish, Egyptian, Bulgarian, Nigerian, French, Spanish, Italian, Portuguese, Serbian, Croatian, Danish, American, German, Belgian, Japanese, and so on, would resolve, it seems to me, the problem of unemployment among readers.

Since the books that I write don't guarantee me the means to eat every day, I would happily offer myself as the bodyguard of a brother—or sister—threatened by killers. But the violence done to Salman Rushdie is not, alas, an imaginary hypothesis.

Nevertheless, the only truly free man today is Salman Rushdie. By inventing a story of the imagination in prose, situated between

---

Writer, Morocco/France. Originally written in French.

heaven and earth, between hell and paradise, he has defended the right of us all to be unique, governed by our dreams and audacity. Salman Rushdie is the quintessential hostage in this century of hostages and hostage takers. To salute his freedom is to salute five billion exhausted, scorned, hunted freedoms. He is the Adam of a library to come: one of freedom.

An Open Letter to Salman Rushdie, or 1,001 Reasons to Admire Him

by Kadhim Jihad

Dear Brother,

To begin, more as a homage to your fertile novelist's imagination than as a manifestation of compassion—you are greater and more dignified than all that—here is a little true story.

In April 1979, as Saddam Hussein monopolized power in Iraq and I, a young Iraqi poet fresh off the boat to study in Paris, had just signed a few petitions against this regime and offered a few poems (things about which you know the consequences in our unfortunate Orient), the prefecture of the Paris police (under Valéry Giscard d'Estaing) rejected my application to renew my permit to reside in France. A refusal that meant ejection, an order to leave French territory. Not wanting under any circumstances to return to Iraq, and since no other European country would grant me a visa, the only remaining alternative, which was whispered to me by a few writer and journalist friends, was to hide out somewhere for the time it took for a campaign to be organized on my behalf and for a Parisian lawyer to obtain for me the status of political refugee. A few months later, the idea worked, handled smoothly by a young attorney full of fervor, to whom I could offer no more than a collection of legal philosophy books for his efforts, beautiful, true, and which he said, no doubt to comfort me, he needed badly.

Poet, Iraq. Originally written in French.

Today it is enough, dear brother, to recall those few months in forced hiding to be shaken by two simultaneous feelings: the infinite horror of any limitation on one's freedom and a no less infinite admiration for you. My modest experience of limited confinement, exempt of the danger of immediate death, is by no means comparable to or as tragic as yours. But you know better than anyone that this painful experience never leaves you intact and seizes you again each time someone else has to go through it. Yes, the heaviness during hours and moments, the paranoia that at times engulfs you, great and tangible as your lucidity might be; the constant fear of an unpleasant turn of events, the rampant feeling of the futility of everything; a painful allergy to all ease and lightness, this unbearable gravity of being; the hatred of all hypocrisy, even when it is comforting and in good faith; the decay, even in passing, of the body, suddenly thrown back upon itself, not reconciled with itself; the delirious, floundering spirit that constantly needs to be refreshed and reanimated with readings, poems, children's stories— yes!—that you tell to yourself, becoming at once the author, the storyteller and the listener; the neighbor's steps and the noise (is it music? is music still possible?) of the tenant in front that take on other shades, fill with other meanings, or are suddenly devoid of sense; the regard (suspicious?) of the local baker when you venture out to buy bread one morning, against the advice of friends and lawyers, and who is surprised (does he know something?) that you haven't come out in so long. All this and a thousand other things that don't come close to what you are living, whose magnitude I imagine, as great as the facilities, these poor and useless substitutes for freedom that surround you, all this demands admiration. Add to this your talent—this work that hasn't ceased to establish itself as firmly as possible in spite of everything—and above all the clarity I see in your purpose, when others see in it quick judgments dictated by anguish and impatience. When, for example, you remind the West that by defending you against the arbitrary decision with which you were stricken, an arbitrary decision no true system of beliefs could tolerate (we speak out here against those who threaten to kill in the name of one monotheism or another), it is doing nothing more than defending its own principles: the freedom of expression, the right of the circulation of people and ideas, as well as the art of the novel. I have never suspected you, dear brother, of naïveté, far from it. I know, I am sure that in recalling it, you would also say to the West, with the art of allusion and innuendo that is your own, that it continues to fail, often seriously, these principles and values it believes and proclaims to be its own.

You, dear bother, must undoubtedly think, as I do, that we are part of a great farce. A tragicomedy whose actors, or rather, participants, are whispering lines and replies to each other and whose supposed adversaries, engaged in an apparently unrelenting battle, are objectively united and allied. It is the same West that showers its writers with laurels and beats down the blacks in California or makes secret deals with ayatollahs in order to win votes, and arms Saddam Hussein to the teeth against his own people under the pretext of destroying his power. You must subscribe, as I do, to the idea of two philosophers (Gilles Deleuze and the late, lamented Félix Guattari), according to which we can no longer accept human rights without criticizing Western democracies that show themselves to be tolerant internally but, more often than not, are accomplices of the most sordid dictatorships abroad.

There also, in recalling the weaknesses and breaches in your own way, you are an essential force in pioneering the struggle for a more tolerant Orient and a more coherent West.

Ballad, or the *Fatwa* of the Masters

by Hélène Kafi

He told us, in fact, Attar, the purest of the Sufis, the humblest of the poets: "Thirty phoenix fashioned my Simurgh. Mythical bird, it alone can ensure your mystical flight. Am I on the way to Mount Qaf? Pretext for evasion, summit of perfection . . ." The storyteller then fell silent. His blood was spread around.

THIS WAS IN THE YEAR . . .

A devil called a "holy man" proclaimed himself imam and laid siege to Iran. Attar trembled on his couch. The Simurgh flew away from Nishapur. The throngs deserted the seven villages of love. "It is the return of darkness," the dervishes of Balkh declared. And the imam cut out tongues. The response, however, had already been announced and spread around in the mosques. Mawlana Jalal al-Din thus recited: "Ma Ze Qor'an maghz rabardachtim, ostokhan bahr sagan bogzachtim—we have taken my marrow from the Koran so as to leave the bones to the dogs."

And the echo carried the prayers from the Diwan of Jalal al-Din Mawlana. And the echo implored Shams Tabriz, "the master, the reflection of the Creator."

"Cupolas, minarets, and mihrabs are stamped with his secrets. There is neither deaf nor blind who claims Osmosis. No imam will be satisfied with mere bones. Only the initiate will find Shams Tabriz; dazzling truth, he will be revealed to you."

Writer, Iran. Originally written in French.

And the imam pursued Mawlana, and he cut Shams off. The sun was henceforth dull; thick and somber were the draped arabesques that pressed down on the crowd; the chains were heavy, the swords deadly. Captured disciples were executed, those who wept stoned.

Let us consult "the oracle," whispered the faithful about Hafiz Shirazi. Does he not know the Book by heart? And pilgrims invaded Shiraz, a devastated city, where the taverns were burned down. The faithful gathered at the Musalla; the mausoleum of the poet was abandoned. The WOMAN breathed the dust of withering roses; silent nightingales, all in a daze, she consoled; with bittersweet tears she watered fading orange trees. The cup of wine, crucible to the burning breath of Layla and Majnun, Shireen and Farhat, Rameen and Vayce, was spread about.

Pilgrims chanted: "Glory to the martyrs of love. To the muse now returned. To the one who keeps you. Khawaja Hafiz Shirazi, enlighten us with your light." The BELOVED WOMAN with a thousand faces—including faces of women loved, women dreamed about, women whose praises have been sung by the country's greatest poets—was stretched out on the flagstones of the mausoleum. And the crowd listened to the Poet, speaking by the very mouth of the Prophet:

> What say lutes and harps? Listen. They forewarn you: O you who drink, drink in secret, or your life will no longer be yours. With Love they will drag you in the mud, you, the Lover. They will outrage both older people and youth, each in their turn. Of Love you must not speak; its delights are forbidden. This rule so hard to follow—how many times have I heard it spoken? We are rejected, shamed; we are birds caught in traps; but what about them, behind their curtains, how many duplicities assail them? They use us ill, they go too far! Our old master is besieged by the rigors of travelers who have come in order to dislodge him. To some it is said with great seriousness: "The desired union

will come about through zeal." To others: "It is fate!" Then, everybody's wings are clipped. Where, then, lies the truth? The world is both changing and unchanging; it goes one way, then another; you are lost through false hopes and false appearances. O you who serve the "black heart" with the secrets of alchemists, what is your gold worth beside the hearts of those whom Love alone assists? Drink then, *hafiz*! All things considered, mufti and sheikh, provost and qadi, are all impostors! And do you want to know about some other impostors? They are the *hafiz* themselves, those who know the Koran by heart!

And so the Noble Scribes too have all thus written "in chorus," as it were, that imams, sheikhs, and muftis are all impostors.

THIS WAS IN THE YEAR . . .

The imam-sorcerer howled from the height of his perch: "Break all the pens!" So both the pens and the fingers that held them were crushed; the writers, poets, and storytellers were all poisoned.

For the last of the nightingales, stuck on a branch of an orange tree, there danced the shadow of the dreamed-about WOMAN whom the Angel asked "what sort of ideas" her shadow was made out of.

"It was made out of intolerance and obscurantism. The imam lives on 'absence.' He drinks in 'nonexistence.'"

To the Rushdies who already know the verses by heart I say, in honest truth: "Imam and mufti, provost and *qadi*, are all impostors!"

The Words of Poets and Wandering Minstrels

by Ahmed Kalouaz

There are hackneyed words, so questionable in the end, such as "live free," or "rather die standing than live on one's knees"—phrases written on walls, chanted, screamed at the top of one's lungs. And some die because of them here and there, known or unknown, draped in silence or showered with praise: celebrated but dead. Words today can always come back tomorrow against their authors—what are the words of a poet, a minstrel worth?

Let's move, change seats to ask ourselves other questions, even if they have no answers. Is freedom of expression the right to say everything, show everything under the pretext of being a writer, filmmaker, or journalist? In this world of ratings, where often, to be credible, one has to shock, where is the line to be drawn? I don't know the man who wrote *The Satanic Verses* nor those who judged him and condemned him to death. If I loathe the latter, I don't necessarily agree with the opinions of the former. If I concede that his writings could bother some people, I find the judgment they pronounce—in the name of God?—inconceivable.

The problem with God is that he isn't familiar with electoral balloting and even less so with democracy. He lets people name themselves, proclaim themselves, seize the scepters of megalomaniacs claimed by peddlers or ignoble impostors. The God I

Writer, Algeria/France. Originally written in French.

imagine would be rather tolerant, less hateful, too busy to keep a record of censures. He already has so much to do.

And if one has to risk one's life for a few words, that wouldn't be new, or voluntary. Those who cut the tongues and hands of singers can be reassured, there will always be words that will make them shudder. Those who burn books worry, however, that there is still a book they forgot to destroy, a book that will hound them and keep them from sleeping the sleep of the unjust.

The Hidden Side of the Rushdie Affair

by Ramine Kamrane

The international repercussions of Khomeini's *fatwa* have had the effect of making certain aspects of the Rushdie affair obvious while hiding others. This distortion, which is primarily due to the silence of Islamic artists and intellectuals, has been reinforced by the media's domination of the event. Among the accepted ideas, three merit careful attention.

It is often said that the Rushdie affair symbolizes the confrontation of Islam and the West, without always going to the trouble of specifying which Islam and which West are involved, when neither is monolithic nor without contradictions. Fundamentalist Islam revitalized by the Iranian revolution is a politicized, Bolshevist, totalitarian variant of the religion. It prospers throughout "the land of Islam" where real problems can coexist with imaginary solutions of culturalist inspiration. It is at once an aspiration for power, a mode of government, and an ideological justification. What this particular Islam rejects from Western civilization is the modernity that distinguishes it from so-called "traditional" societies, but which exhausts neither its wealth nor its history. Fundamentalist Islam has also always been quick to borrow, imitate, and assimilate as rapidly as possible all kinds of relativist and culturalist antimodern discourse and ideas developed in the West itself. And this has hardly prohibited it from strongly proclaiming its cultural other-

Sociologist, Iran. Originally written in French.

ness. One too often forgets that Rushdie could be considered Muslim, his agnosticism as well as his British citizenship hardly upsetting those who proclaim a borderless, religious *internationale*. The Fundamentalists wage war on modernity; they are hunting down the man they consider the Muslim artist who incarnates it.

We usually hear about how the Rushdie affair is a hateful attack by Fundamentalist vandals on a talented artist. Such a presentation of the situation is capable of seducing artists and especially writers. Nevertheless, the attack led by the Fundamentalists targets modernity as a whole, far from a simple aesthetic affair. Their strategy is founded on the lack of distinction between religion and politics, which corrupts both of them. This strategy's supreme weapon remains physical as well as intellectual terrorism. By making each object of contention sacred it allows intellectual terrorism. Rushdie is not the object of this attack because of his talent, and it is not only as a talented artist that he should be defended. He dared to treat a sacred object in a profane manner and secularized it. The Fundamentalists want to prohibit the demystification of the "Islamic world" by condemning a writer to death and discouraging future challengers.

Finally, the Rushdie affair is presented to us as an international crisis that should be managed and resolved by Western governments. Westerners defend Rushdie, who resides in Europe. So far they have avoided imposing significant sanctions against the Iranian government and other branches of Fundamentalism spreading the call to murder. Suppose the Western governments manage to force the mullahs to yield in the case of Rushdie (which is hard to imagine given the indolence of some and the arrogance of others); the conditions of this crisis will remain unchanged and will still produce new effects. Let us not forget that Fundamentalism's first concern is the "Islamic world" and the affair can be resolved only in the heart of this world. Criticism of the religion conducted over several centuries by the West will remain ineffective until it finds proponents in "Islamic land," because the ideas, universal as they may be, require incarnation. Only "Muslims" can perform this task.

The Rushdie case is the international side of a crisis that has shaken the Muslim world for decades, if not longer. At its core, it can be resolved only by modernist, secular, humanist "Muslims."

Letter to Salman Rushdie

by Khemaïs Khayati

Dear Sir,

1,408 days of detention!

Such a long exclusion for a book? Just yesterday, I saw myself demonstrating for your right to expression and against the *fatwa* hung over your head like the sword of Damocles. This *fatwa* is not targeted at you exclusively. Through you it touches other Arabs and Muslims who, if they don't think as you do, share your spirit. It is for this reason and after having read *The Satanic Verses*—which I rather appreciated for reasons other than religious—that I publicly express my support for you.

1,408 days of detention!

What could I have done during these three years? I certainly loved, traveled, read, hung around, spoke unhindered, unafraid of the emergence of the glacial shadow of uncertain death, the somber mouth of the cold weapon, and the loaded glare of the sponsored criminal. But it is also certain that no discussion, no caress, no travel between Tunis, Paris, and elsewhere takes place without impacting you who are forced to live far away from your child, travel in anonymity, love far from the light of day, read with the heart and spirit of one who could lose track of the pages, wander around counting your steps, trust the person you want to talk to about the rain and beautiful weather.

When life becomes a prison, then injustice is great in this

Journalist, Tunisia. Originally written in French.

world. And in my Arab and Muslim world, this prison is growing by the day. The Egyptian Farag Foda leaves his home; death awaits him without anyone speaking out against this crime, apart from a few timid voices quickly silenced. A Somali child wants to eat; death is in his bowl. Another child, Palestinian, stops at the doorstep of Khan-Younis; death snatches at his life. A Bosnian woman walks down her lane; death does violence to her womb.

You, Farag Foda, Somali and Palestinian children, and the Bosnian woman, what crime have you committed? A book, some articles, the search for a bowl of rice, for a country or an identity. What could be simpler than what you have asked for? You shouldn't die for having wanted to live, nor be raped for a crime of identity, nor be banished for a country.

I know I am not alone in thinking this way.

The day we demonstrated our support against this villainous *fatwa*, we were a handful of journalists, writers, psychoanalysts, filmmakers, musicians, painters, and students raising our banners over the Place du Trocadéro, banner of human rights, stating clearly, without ambiguity, "as Arabs and Muslims," that a religion that calls for death is not our own, that this Islam is not the one my mother raised me on. One day in my Tunisian adolescence, when I denied the existence of God and refused to keep Ramadan, she told me in a grave tone: "This is between you and Allah, I cannot interfere." Nevertheless, she is Muslim, believes in God, prays five times a day, fulfills her acts of charity, fasts, dreamed and still dreams of making her pilgrimage. It was my first lesson in tolerance, which I haven't been able to find in the temple merchants, Khomeini, Tourabi, Madani, and Ghannouchi, who mix the affairs of Allah with those of men.

To love or hate *The Satanic Verses*, that question is secondary when a man's life can be swapped for a postage stamp. To agree or disagree with Farag Foda's ideas is an absurd question when, after his life has been taken, his writings are prohibited. It is true that you have the right to imagine, think, write, and say what you please without necessarily drawing the fires of death upon you. If a religion is afraid of a book, it deserves to be shunned. If the religion of the most beautiful book that has been given to me to study since my childhood, the Koran, makes groundless accusations and creates a terrible fate for another book, this religion is suffering from amnesia. It has quickly forgotten that many times it has been called into question and many times it has managed to shine forth even more brilliantly. How does it forget the doubts of al-Maarri and al-Hallaj, the splendors of the Alhambra and the Taj Mahal, the glimmerings of al-Wasiti and al-Hariri, the rationalism of Ibn Rushd (Averroès), the positivism of Ibn Khaldoun, the curiosity of Ibn Battouta, the voluptuous poetry of Layla al-Akhialiyya, the banter of Ibn Abi Rabia in Mecca during the season of pilgrimage? They are Muslims all the same, and their Islam has never flirted with intolerance, hypocrisy, hatred, bigotry, prudishness, and the gloom of the smooth talkers of Islam today who are financed by the dollars of Wahhabism and encouraged by the murderous *fatwas* of Khomeinism. Don't tell me this religion is responding to attacks made on it by the West. This is a bad reaction to a false accusation.

Nasser, Bourguiba, Boumédiene are no longer; there only remains little chiefs who take themselves for big ones. In the absence of all freedom, all democracy, they are faced only with other little chiefs who want to become big themselves. And that is the civil war declared in Algeria or latent in Egypt, in Tunisia and even in Palestine. Faced with the *hijab*, the acid, and a *charia* eaten away by *yajouz* (taboos), there are denouncement, inquisition, torture, trials, and prisons. This is how a civilization loses the sense of true grandeur, pleasure, and the feeling of "good living." All Muslims are not attacked by this "idleness of spirit," by atrophy of the imagination, by this castrating Puritanism. Not all submit to the dictates of adorers of a past, prestigious as it may be, even if it was that of the prophet Muhammad.

Believe it, you are not the only Salman Rushdie. Others like you have scattered in Arab and Muslim lands. And it is not the sickening literature of Ibn Baz or Metwalli Chaarawi, nor the inflammatory sermons of Sheik Kichk Belhadj, nor the crimes of the

"Afghanis" that are going to prevent my children, nieces, and cousins from raising the standard of revolt and crying: "An end to the masquerade! May sensitive Islam submit to the *ijtihad* of any sincerely Muslim individual or may it be stacked in the attic of forgetfulness so that we may taste life."

Is it lack of faith that, having loosened the reins on the imagination, has come to deserve a *fatwa* accompanied by a murderous bullet? You have one of the characters in *Midnight's Children* say: "I admit it: above all things, I fear absurdity." Aren't we faced with this absurdity that gnaws away at the product of thought, that sends millions of teenagers to certain death, that teaches at the end of the twentieth century that "the world is flat" and deprives all Arabs and Muslims of their reason for being, that of loving this world of here and now as if savoring eternity and working for the hereafter as if one were to die tomorrow?

Sooner or later (optimism makes me write that sooner would be better), the reason for freedom of thought, writing, imagination, and action within the framework of the law, and nothing but the law, will come to the fore. Certainly, at the pace these waves of gloom unfurl over the Arab-Muslim world, I fear that individuals cannot sustain a solid resistance when civil society abdicates to the reason of the state. There also, we must be armed against the pessimism of reason, that of the individual as well as that of the state, which makes us surrender under the weight of the absurd for which you and Farag Foda have paid the price. It is vital that we demonstrate our solidarity with you and share your exile, because it has to do with the freedom of us all, Arabs and Muslims, who want the Arab world to be born again through free and rigorous criticism of the terms upon which it is based.

So Be It

by Michel Khleifi

It was without any hesitation that I agreed to write on the Salman Rushdie affair, as if writing had become an act synonymous with courage, challenging fear and murder. At the moment I decided to do it an image of infinite complexity came to mind: a double image made up of cries, abuse, insults, threats, protests, ignorance, negligence, "fear of tomorrow," hypocrisy; but also of joy, extreme excitement, personal satisfaction, and all the other politico-strategic combinations camouflaged behind this affair, since the day the Ayatollah Khomeini declared his famous *fatwa* (an irrevocable legal act under Islamic law).

I myself had become, in my own eyes, a "dirty affair," torn between, on the one hand, the heartbreak, analyses, apprehensions, autobiographical confessions of Salman Rushdie and, on the other hand, the need to adopt a simple position of principle: to know that every person has the right to express his ideas in the manner and by the means he sees fit (I say this without forgetting that, in certain Islamic and Arab countries, dozens of writers and thinkers are executed without anyone lifting a finger in protest). But the Rushdie affair has exceeded its simple position of principle to seize and push us into the waves of contradiction that shake this little world: a world ever more constrained to accept only a single master, a single empire to impose its will.

Filmaker, Palestine. Originally written in Arabic.

How can one take a position that is not oversimplified? Is there only one clear line of demarcation between the protagonists? The affair is not simple: For Salman Rushdie/Against Islam, or Against Salman Rushdie/Against the West, or even With Salman Rushdie/With the West. This position, which draws a border between good and evil, between the democratic, civilized West and the rest of the world, including the Arab and Islamic world, considered tyrannical and reactionary, is too simplistic. Just one condition: do not touch Israel, which remains for them a moral and humanitarian country. I do not find myself on their side, however; I know that when I think and rally around the cause of the people's emancipation—and the Palestinian people also have the right to dignity—then I think and am rallied to join the cause of Salman Rushdie, of the legitimacy of his right to complete and absolute freedom of expression, to dignity.

And I am against the politics of double standards.

And I think that justice is nothing more than a sausage that is sliced and distributed unequally according to merits and interests.

Reading the works of Salman Rushdie dazzled me and allowed me to discover his immense creative talents. His ability to express the reality of India and the Muslim world and juxtapose it with the concrete reality of these Third World children, born in cultural confusion which affects them in the very depths of their villages and pushes them onto the hazardous paths of emigration, armed only with their will and their thin bodies, is fascinating. All dangers await them: racism, hunger, police, as well as all kinds of psychological poverty. And they still come in search of an honorable life in "democratic countries" which I don't think are the best example of good morality for the people.

But wouldn't it have been more profitable if the Iranians dedicated the two million dollars earmarked for Rushdie's eventual assassin to paying an "army of writers" to respond to the author of *The Satanic Verses*, in literary, historic, or scientific research—if there had been material to respond to, because, of course, there is no possible response to an artist's imagination? He has the right to touch on subjects and deal with them in the manner, style, and language he chooses and desires. He has this right because he struggles alone for the unity of the elements that make up his cultural personality, alone against dislocation, the risk of creating within himself a confusion of diverse and contradictory influences. This is how the children of the Third World live each day. What is the problem if certain among them, blessed with formidable creative abilities, manage to blend so many dreams and realities in their souls?

As if being against the Gulf War meant supporting Saddam Hussein; as if taking a position in favor of the reigning Arab families and company induced an identical position vis-à-vis the imperialist West; or even as if siding with the Palestinian people in their struggle for rights against the Zionists in power placed one suddenly on the side of the anti-Semites, Nazis, and such.

Always the same breakdown: Them/Us, Us and Them.

Again I hear the voice of Saleem Sinai, hero of Salman Rushdie's *Midnight's Children*, throw his cry of intelligence in the face of the world: "Brothers, sisters. . . . Do not let this happen! Do not permit the endless duality . . . to come between us." But what shouldn't have happened has happened, and here we are faced with a new situation.

And I, like the horse in *A Wedding in Galilee*, wander in a wheat field mined by Israeli soldiers to keep the Palestinian peasants from working there. And like this horse I am surrounded, threatened by mines everywhere, mines on the verge of exploding at a single touch and tearing me to pieces. But it is a question of getting out alive: I have to because I have a right to this world, and I deserve to be able to enjoy this life.

For example, does my taking a position in support of Salman Rushdie's freedom oblige me to go along with Parisian intellectuals who have at the same time taken a position for the destruction of Iraq and Lebanon? It is these very people who viscerally reject the Palestinian people and who have recently adopted a "postmodern" attitude, declaring themselves the champions of democracy for all the causes of the world, except the Palestinian cause. There, we see them dig in their heels in a determination that has since become archaic, and which shows that they have remained inalienable to their original tribe which must seem to them, in the end, the only plausible (possible?) truth since the Second World War. And it is as if this truth should be erected as the cardinal law of all humanity!

It is they who gave the West the right of humanitarian intervention which it uses and abuses where it pleases, when it pleases. They have freed the voice that leads to the new world order.

Will this new modern monster be insensitive to these dreaming children?

Once again, it obliges them to make a painful decision: either the plunge into the obscurantism of ancient beliefs, or the controlled integration by the programs of modern technology.

The most beautiful childhood memories are those where epic and religious worlds blend, dream and reality, especially for us, children born in towns and countries where several religions, legends, ideologies, cultures exist side by side. If the religious could know what we spent our time dreaming about and how we imagined the heroes of sacrosanct stories, their only option would be to kill all the children in the country and pay millions of dollars to liquidate the rest, those who emigrated or went into hiding. So we, children of Nazareth, Muslims, Christians, and even Jews, have made a narrow escape. It is clear that our sexual life has blossomed in part through what we have imagined or deduced from the Bible, the Gospels, and the Koran. Was the Angel who visited Sarah, Abraham's wife, sent from God or a story told by an adulterous wife to camouflage guilty relations? These are the realities we live each day.

One question bothers me: these politicians, religious leaders, these men who hold the power, have they forgotten that they were once young, that they had dreams and doubts and all other kinds of problems with the outside world? Have they forgotten forever how they discovered love and the body?

I laugh thinking about the passage in *Midnight's Children* where the hero, Saleem Sinai, is showing off in front of his friends, and especially in front of Evie Burnes, his ability to ride a bike; how, furious, Evie pushes him down a hill and, losing control of the bike, he hurtles into the middle of a political demonstration where a mass of excited people shout out their politico-linguistic protests. How, finally, he is saved from the chaos by a song in Gujarati that his nanny taught him.

And there is the dreamer Salman Rushdie, once again on his bike, showing off his immense literary talent before the world and his skill in juggling with the art of writing. And there one hand pushes him violently in the back into the center of a political free-for-all and takes us with him, surrounded by hostile faces which mix up smiles and grimaces. Taken by fear, we struggle with each other as we can, gesticulating to clear a path for dialogue. Can we hope to be saved again by Saleem Sinai's Gujarati song?

Ah, if we could hum it again as an emblem of our freedom!

It is undeniable that Salman Rushdie's song is at home in our midst. Only our cowardice turns it away, pushes it out of our circle, thus dooming it to certain death.

All that remains is our struggle to force a dialogue. Whatever the issue, Salman Rushdie remains, with his works, the most vital and most shining element of our cultural heritage: by defending freedom, we will protect "the seas of stories . . . so the origins of creation are never polluted."

And that is the example we need for the Third World to emerge from its poverty.

The Writer and the Story

by Elias Khoury

I see Salman Rushdie in solitude, a writer living alone and hunted, who lacks words while he no longer knows the anguish of writing but only that of heroes of novels. Living within a fictional text, the writer has himself become a story. And with him we discover once again, one of the truths of our times: the imaginary leads to the real and reality exceeds fiction. Did Rushdie knowingly take this path? Is *The Satanic Verses* one of the hazards of this fin de siècle in distress?

In our world the writer participates in the game of his heroes, and the relationship with freedom has become more ambiguous. This ambiguity is explained by the encounter of two factors: it is the failure of the projects of modernity and modernization under the blows of Western savagery allowing the protection of dictatorial and terrorist regimes which pushes people to desperation. It is also the crisis of values in a world divided, as in the days of antiquity, into Romans and "barbarians." In his writing Rushdie has tried to say that there is another choice, that of freedom, capable of confronting this earthly hell and designing something new. He challenges death of the spirit and that is why he has been repressed in his world of origin as in that to which he has turned. And it is this double repression that is the object of his story.

So he follows the path of those who have questioned authority, from Ibn al-Muqaffa' to the victims of the Inquisition, those who in

Writer, Libya. Originally written in Arabic.

our times have become foreign—whether they leave their countries or remain there. From Taha Hussein in the thirties to Salman Rushdie, it is still a long journey in the quest for freedom, and in terror. Could writing have become a crime when crime, repression, famine, and poverty have overtaken three quarters of the earth?

An Indian writer lives his story, and before him we have the obligation to tell him that he personifies our solitude and that this story is our own.

The Clock

by Abdellatif Laabi

Seconds fall like pebbles
from the sterile belly of the clock
The pendulum drips
clot by clot
into the mouth of a black cat
half Aztec, half Chaldean
In the hearth
fire celebrates its archaic mass
and when it comes to the episode of the Imam
killed by treachery in Iraq
a sharp tongue emerges, dripping with blood
as long as the dagger of the crime
Seconds fall like pebbles
from the sterile belly of the clock
The pendulum drips
clot by clot
The cat has disappeared
A door left open
bangs in the wind
breaks into its litany of vengeance
Why have they imposed this clock on me
What do they want of me
That I go to take it down
and crucify myself on the wall
until the return of the Imam?

Writer, Morocco. Originally written in French.

Chaos

by Bahauddeen Latif

And what had once been God were just your guard
attempting with a dirty eye to fill
the last hole up. And yet you lived on still.
                                        —Rainer Maria Rilke

West Germans could not say why they so passionately wanted to be reunited with East Germany. They were sure it was not motivated by nationalism. A much more noble idea informed their yearning. They reassured us again and again that it was for the sake of Europe that Germany must be reunited, and they would make no claims on lands lost to surviving countries. And yet there was trepidation on the faces of Jews interviewed on the night the Berlin Wall finally came down, and the triumphant post-Nazi flag of West Germany flew everywhere, held high by so many young hands, even by some black ones. At the time few would have questioned the German pan-European sentiments.

All too soon alarm bells began ringing. The Jews and Gypsies had been decimated and culturally obliterated, and yet the word "Jew" was on the lips of Germans who had apparently no experience of the past. We were informed repeatedly that all was good and healthy with the new Germany, whose active citizens were keen on the environment (dumping pollutants in foreign countries), human

---

Writer, Bangladesh. Originally written in English.

rights (elsewhere), the Amazon rain forests, and so on. In fact, the bile was lurking all the time and gathered momentum once they gained their objective of a reunited Germany.

Jews were thin on the ground (having been the lifeblood of the commercial and intellectual life of the urban German landscape only fifty years ago), but their graves were still around and still were desecrated. "Foreigners," anyone of any number of generations not of the *Volk* stock, were set upon in the streets, on trains, in their homes, shops, and workplaces. And all the time the police looked on, the citizens encouraged and incited, and the politicians looked the other way as the new post-Nazi generation burned, kicked, slashed, and killed women, men, and even babies.

And then appalling excuses were made by concerned Germans, who claimed the incidents were isolated in the eastern part of Germany. And so all the reassurances were in tatters. The bizarre thing is that Germans became more and more obsessed with their image abroad than with tackling the rise of German fundamentalism.

There are very urgent lessons in the German experience in our century, in that it was, as some assess, the apogee of trends established by the Enlightenment. The Western obsession with eugenics was but an expression of such an inclination, say undisdainful critics.

One wonders what would have happened to Salman Rushdie if he had been a resident of Germany. He would almost certainly have been a "guest worker" with limited rights. As an Indian immigrant he would have faced deportation or been silenced, especially if international relations or trade was affected in any way. By contrast, Britain has granted Salman all the protection of the state. Also, in Britain, we have thankfully avoided victimization of Muslims, at least in the serious media.

The worldwide threat of Islamic fundamentalism is largely a figment of the imagination of the Arab countries, as well as the Zionists. Lets face it, the Islamic fundamentalism of the Kingdom of Saudi Arabia, which makes no pretense to being a democracy, is a very close ally of the U.S. Saudi Arabia (and also the neighboring Gulf states) is a benefactor of all the best Islamic institutions, whether in education, media, or printing and publishing in all corners of the globe, in Britain, Italy, Egypt, Bangladesh, France, Malaysia—a fact openly acknowledged by all. Saudi Arabia is also home to the largest Muslim database in the world. The real menace the world faces is the gross disparity and despotism reigning in much of the Arab world, which gets filtered as an Islamic phenomenon.

One wants to avoid generalizations, but they are impossible in the Arab world. Most of the brutal, murderous, corrupt oligarchies have been in power for an average of twenty years! In Egypt's case the oligarchy has been in power ever since Nassar took power in a coup. Even the Palestinian nation, the most democratically organized Arab government, continues to be headed by the same man who renewed the nationhood of the Palestinians. Arab states have good laws in the statutes, but most do not apply even to mild critics of the regimes. The result is some of the best Arab (for the benefit of Indians, Bengalis, and other Muslims and Europeans who assume all Arabs to be Muslims, I must shock them by pointing out that some 20 percent are Copts, Maronites, Catholics, Druzes, Alawis, Jews—excluding Burbia or Kurdish ethnic groups. Faud Khuoi's *Imam and Emirs* provides an excellent overview of the Arab religious milieu) and Muslim minds have to seek refuge in Europe, and even then their safety is not assured. The bold and beautiful Arab intellect is in exile, and all the world knows of is the ugliness of Arab regimes.

Recently, the unelected oligarchy that has ruled Algeria since defeating the French colonialists canceled the only free elections to prevent the certain victory of the Islamist FIS. The FLN regime boldly announced to a grateful world that it was safeguarding the region from Islamic fundamentalist clutches. Soon the regime unleashed a violent pogrom against FIS supporters constituting a substantial majority of Algeria's population. Habits die hard in the Arab world; the liberals have joined hands with the FLN in trying to flush out the FIS. Eat you heart out, Israel!

The policymakers in the U.S. must be all too aware that Islam does not pose a threat to Western interests. Certainly the numbers are large, but the technological base is pea-sized and littered all over Afro-Asia like patchwork, with no center to hold. The love affair between the fundamentalist Saudis and the U.S. is such that a Saudi prince was a very noticeable presence at the Super Bowl, a pinnacle of the American way.

If the truth be known, Islamists are a threat to fellow ideologues, since the scene is riddled with fractiousness. In a democratic environment Islamists would have to fish in the same seas as the Saudis, at the very least, or even tip over in the way of Turkey, Malaysia, Bangladesh, or Palestine, where women have taken to decision making and state power without misogynist terror, so much a part of the testament of experts in the Islamic mind.

One can do no better than to look at the plight of the Palestinians to see where this collective menace of a billion Muslims is leading. Despite the enormous amount of poetry, tears, and sympathy for the Palestinian people and their demand for a homeland, they remain dispossessed, unwanted and distrusted refugees in every land. Palestinians were recently "ethnically cleansed" out of Kuwait. In an issue like Kashmir, the P.L.O. and Egypt sympathize with the Indian position and indeed have warned outsiders not to interfere in India's internal affairs.

During the eight years of unjust war against Iran (a war in which untold millions of people were killed and wounded), the U.S. and its allies poured huge amounts of arms and billions of dollars into Pakistani and Islamic Afghan coffers. Unbelievably, the infidel U.S. lionized and fed the Islamic fighters and rejoiced in their victory.

In Britain we have been living through the consequences of unresolved enmity between two Christian religions for several decades, some would say 350, at least to Oliver Cromwell's era. Every day the din of the Irish war of religions comes closer and closer to our cities. The British knew something about homegrown forms of religious fundamentalism, even if quite a few feign otherwise, which drives men to kill and wound. Sharing the same island, human beings discriminate against each other and cannot bear the shadow of another because he is a Catholic or a Protestant.

Someone asks a puzzling question: is it not convenient to blame religious fundamentalism alone; surely there must be a deeper hurt somewhere else too? And I pout, of course, and ask Mr. Kelly why he writes so conspiratorially about Islam. Some kindly person nods and shouts in Mr. Kelly's direction: obfuscation!

The Jonestown mass suicide was an aspect of Christian practice. The recent happening in Waco, Texas, is also associated with Christian fundamentalist trends. The pro-life Catholics' murderous campaign in the U.S. is soon to be installed around the globe; and many more such groups have spread around the Christian world. Do these occurrences justify putting forward a thesis about the "Christian mentality" or "Jewish mentality"? Of course not. And yet 150 million Bengalis, 130 million Arabs, 90 million Turks, and 25 million European Muslims are made to endure such generalizations.

In our century slavery has been made illegal everywhere; sovereignty of nations, large and very small, is recognized; there is a United Nations; peoples of diverse origins co-exist in almost every city; diverse religions and cultural groups emerge thousands of miles away from their origins; eating habits acquired over hundreds of years gain new ones with the introduction of hybrid African, Chinese, Italian, Polish, or south Asian restaurants; areas of cities gain a Chinatown, a Banglatown, or a festival like the Notting Hill Carnival—all these transformations have come about without war or conquest. Today's settlers have no desire to dominate the natives, as so often in the past, even within living memory in Australia and New Zealand.

Complacency can easily sink all our achievements. To keep the gains from sinking into another bout of European chaos, a disdainful, irreverent, dissenting firmament needs to keep vigil over the landscape, to keep arguments raging about art, religion, culture, race, nation; to keep plurality from being annihilated, as happened in the Holocaust.

Salman Rushdie is a product of post-Holocaust plurality in which his own Hindu-Muslim heritage of Asia is welded to the irreverent, disdainful, even playful challenging atmosphere of

Western Europe. This dangerous cocktail was imbibed under dominant imperialist ethos and then through free choice as an immigrant to European shores.

In Salman Rushdie's writings all the tensions of this hybrid are present, even in the Indian vocabulary he so richly exploits. He made the first generation of English-south Asians visible as a cultural entity in British life and literature (until Salman, in literature, British Asians were invisible except for occasional appearances as illegal immigrants). The recent history of south Asia, filled with hate, fear, and deceit, was somehow less tinged with divisiveness in his novels. It became possible to see brimming chaos as part of our collective past. I speak from experience when I say that Salman spoke to both Muslims and Hindus of our generation, not experienced since Nehru. Alas, the pity is all the gems of south Asian lives in *The Satanic Verses* will remain undiscovered for another decade.

If only our media had had the foresight to engage in the controversy in a different light, it would probably have been resolved by now. The national aspiration of one nation became entangled in ambitions on behalf of the faith. And so the root set in. So often potentates glower at the amount of attention *Time* editorials give to their latest perorations. In this way an unread novel became a savior and cudgel to hang the frayed and tattered banner upon. Suddenly an entire nation began to feel proud after a cruel defeat at the hands of the Arabs. Even the dissenters began to sense the world's eyes upon them—the world acknowledges their destiny, they the sons of Cyrus. Some at least gloated at finding a generalized Islamic menace. An ex-Labor minister even regretted that Muslim migrants were not barred from entering Britain (Salman would have been among the barred category).

The facts are indeed stranger than fiction. Penguin Group's publications have not faced destruction or removal from libraries in the Muslim world. In fact, it is doubtful that their titles are in any less demand. The Islamists I have encountered still have the Robinson book on the Prophet along with hundreds of other titles. But there is no doubt that Salman's *Satanic Verses* will remain an area of contention, for most Muslim's are unlikely to overcome their objection to the book.

Since the affair Muslims have begun to see for themselves how little of the Christian tradition holds any barrier to the irreverent artist. Religious authority is much eroded in Western European countries dominated by the Protestant ethos. In England some Anglican church leaders doubt many of the central tenants of Christianity, like the trinity or the resurrection, and yet continue in their vocation (of course such individuals face great hostility and opposition). Like Muslims, Catholics and Orthodox Jews cannot always comprehend the Protestant ways of the Anglicans.

Except for a few exceptions, Muslim organizations have concentrated on lobbying, demonstrations, and the law courts—all the means available to individuals and groups in a free society—to seek the banning of *The Satanic Verses*. Despite such noise there is no known instance where local Muslims have carried out any serious unlawful acts. With hindsight, even the much hyped book-burning incident was really less alarming and certainly incomparable to the menace of French peasants destroying and burning truckloads of English animal carcasses in Parisian streets, often depicted in newspapers and on TV in England. The Muslim Briton is all too aware that another religious minority has been remarkably successful in its lobbying and legal initiatives. The Jewish community through intense lobbying and demonstrations was able to get a theater to withdraw a play. And more recently, a novel was banned by the authorities as the book dealt with matters sensitive to a section of the Jewish community (the writer was himself of Jewish origin).

Salman is an irascible iconoclast who finds his opinions irresistible. And sometimes he can be really irritating. He told Paris *Match* that he wanted to challenge and reform Islam. Well, he must really be excused for such a plonkish, silly throwaway remark. Lest we forget, despite all the degradedness of the Muslim condition, in an earlier era, even three centuries ago, a Voltaire would have been at home in the caliphates' cities of Baghdad, Cordoba, Cairo, Istanbul, or Sarajevo. It is well recorded that during the reign of

Harun al-Rashid (786–809) "the scholar and the poet could live at ease, for there was no shortage of patrons, and learning was valued more highly than wealth or noble blood."

Friends, we can all bask in the glory that is the past, but the future beckons us. Most of the Muslim world's children are without shoes and malnourished. The U.S. is flying in food parcels for the people of Gaza, Bosnia, and Arakan. From Bombay, the columnist A. M. Rosenthal of *The New York Times* is filing a report from Salman Rushdie's beloved place of birth. He writes: "Hindu hate literature against Indian Muslims [it would have included Salman too if he were still living there] is almost exactly the same in manufactured paranoia as the protocols of the Elders of Zion, Hitler's favorite. . . .

"So in Bombay the recipe for the alchemy that changes prejudice into murder can be known—history, contempt, poison, cowardice.

"Knowing will not prevent it from happening again (as in the Weimar period). But it might help, and that is the best that can be said."

For Rushdie

by Amin Maalouf

To condemn a man to death for his writings is unacceptable, and the threats against Salman Rushdie have and will continue to tarnish the image of Islam for a long time. Those who endeavor to put forward another image of this great world religion, those who insist on the humanistic values it contains, on its long tradition of tolerance, on its significant contribution to humanity's moral and scientific progress, on its irreplaceable position in any universal perspective, in a word the friends—Muslim or otherwise—of Islamic civilization see their work sabotaged, compromised, partially destroyed. Overstatement is always to the advantage of the fanatics on both sides, and the true victims are invariably those who are trying to build bridges.

It is true that the Muslim world is going through a period of profound disarray. After centuries of grandeur, it has seen a long decline, and to its own internal crises has been added a traumatizing confrontation with the rapidly expanding West. All those who are concerned by this situation cannot help but wonder "each morning," as Jamal al-din al-Afghani said, how to escape this historic impasse, how to return the Islamic situation to the place it deserves, how to rid it of this inferiority complex, of its hypersensitivity, how to rid it of the mentalities and states of mind of the age of decadence and push it into the world of today. So it plays the role it should be

---

Writer, Libya. Originally written in French.

playing, that of a religion in constant pursuit of knowledge, ratio-nality, and universality. The worst way to "defend" Islam is to drive the Muslim world into this syndrome of the perpetually attacked, the perpetually humiliated, the eternal loser, and through some sort of pathetic, sterile bravado, make it resemble the worst caricature its detractors could wish for.

That numerous Muslims felt offended by the content of a book, and that they wanted to demonstrate their indignation is an attitude that cannot be contested. I suppose many Christians must have had a similar feeling when Renan attempted to demystify the life of Jesus. And more globally, when the French Revolution, anticlerical-ism, and Marxism targeted the religion of the Europeans. Nevertheless, in retrospect, these attacks, far from weakening Christianity over the long term, since they allowed it to sharpen its arguments, actually served to articulate a social vision, to help Christianity rethink itself and thus refind its place in a constantly changing world. No doctrine dies from being criticized, or even attacked; but it can die from being made impermeable to criticism.

The essential problem remains, that which makes a Rushdie affair possible in our days. I want to talk about the fact that a billion Muslims have the impression of living in a foreign, hostile, indeci-pherable universe. They no longer even dare hope for a better life, in freedom and dignity; they wonder how they can be integrated into the modern world without losing their souls. For them it is an anguishing dilemma indeed, but also for the whole of humanity, because it brings with it heartbreak and violence. Until it is resolved, other dramas await us, before which we will also be impotent.

Returning to a State of Law

by Camille Mansour

I haven't read *The Satanic Verses* and I don't think I ever will. In the end, what Salman Rushdie has written doesn't interest me at all. But to shake an effigy of Rushdie in order to mobilize forces of an intolerant Islam is atrocious (as is using the issue to suggest that Islam as well as Muslim society as a whole is intolerant). I find it inadmissible that any authority—a state, a tribunal, a religious leader, a party—declare his death sentence or call for his assassination for what he wrote. It is reprehensible to prohibit that he think, imagine, or write as he pleases. This is as true for moderates as it is for extremists, for atheists and believers, liberals and fundamentalists, libertarians and moralists, universalists and, dare I say it, racists.

I willingly believe that every society imposes limits on the public expression of this freedom when it leaves the private domain to enter into the public. I am not a censor and I wouldn't want to be in the censor's place, but I would like to recall a few simple legal truths:

—Public freedom of expression should be the rule, and its limits, the exception;

—Only the law of the state (the positive law, not the religious law) can define these limits, not executive authority, and even less religious authority or fluctuations of public opinion;

Political Scientist, Palestine. Originally written in French.

—Only tribunals of the state can, in accordance with the law, following an action initiated by a public ministry or by ethical or private individuals admitted as strictly involved civil parties, pronounce judgments limiting the public exercise of an individual or group's freedom of expression;

—The limits that the law can impose on the public exercise of freedom of expression must not in any case affect the person of the author, his or her freedom being a fortiori his or her life! They can only affect the work, and more precisely, by decision of justice, the incriminated work, which can be dealt with in a moderate fashion in the following ways: correction of a defamatory paragraph, seizure of regulated sales;

—The case of the application of limits on the public exercise of freedom of expression should be defined in the most restrictive manner: slander, attack on public order, humiliating and degrading attacks on the human being (such as child pornography), incitement to racial hatred. Slander, for example, can concern only the honor of the slandered individuals and should not be identified with criticism, even caustic or mocking, of the validity of systems of ideas or religious beliefs. The accusation of attack on public order should not be used as a pretext to silence opponents or free thinkers, to protect an authoritarian regime at bay, or to allow demagogic overstatement.

For my part, I think the only criterion that can legitimize legal limits on the public exercise of freedom of expression is the incitement to the offense of the dignity of individuals or groups. Obviously, Rushdie's book, according to the commentaries and debates it has inspired, escapes this criterion. I do, however, find it normal, also in the name of freedom of expression, that certain Muslims have declared their dislike for *The Satanic Verses* because they see in it a mockery of their religion. The only reproach I would make of this book is of a political order: it has unintentionally reinforced what I would qualify as the atrocious in the attitudes of its enemies as well as in those of its defenders.

Waiting for Another Community

by Abdelwahab Meddeb

Rushdie, you have written what no man has written. One must be grateful to you because with you Islam has entered into a territory that was forbidden to it. Instead of condemning you, in the name of Islam I congratulate you. Your book and the rumblings it has inspired are the sign of a vitality that had for centuries deserted this space.

You wrote your novel with the books of the *Sirah* (the canonical biography of Muhammad) open before you. You haven't subverted the slightest detail of this sacred and venerated biography with the spirit or freedom of the novel. Novelistic technique leads deep into fantasy, and the slightest fact belonging to the source can be unmade and remade according to a perspective that carries the event (or its image) in the lands of imagination, ignoring the constraints of space and time.

Does desecration begin when a writer decides to use mythical figures as imaginary material? Such mythic images are fixed in abstract space and time which makes them untouchable, irremovable. Their capture by the imaginary gives them an animation that liberates them from their fixed state. And the distance that protected the sacred characters is abolished. Is it with this abolition that desecration and blasphemy begin?

The imaginary challenges temporal coherence; telescoping periods, it provokes diversions and reversals. This game of move-

---

Writer, Tunisia. Originally written in French.

ments perverts the mythical figures since virtue and vice are simply two sides of the same coin. Is it in this returning that the representation of belief collapses, that the metamorphosis of the scenes ruins the landscape of faith?

Never in Islam has the imagination seized these figures to feed a fiction that manhandles the myth. Indeed, the catalog of divergences, deviations, blasphemies, audacities, interpretations that transform the text would be dense. The cultures associated with Islam would not have breadth without their rebellious and disobedient authors. It is enough to recall the innovations, interrogations, irreverences, or liberties of Abu Nuwwas, Hallaj, Bistami, Tawhidi, Maarri, Ibn Arabi, Rumi, Omar Khayyam, of *The Thousand and One Nights*, to perceive the expanse of the corpus. Moreover, these authors and their works (all from the Middle Ages) do not have the favor of our contemporary fundamentalists who, returning to the letter of the Koran, impose a shady moral order. Aren't they conspiring against the joyous, carnal tradition, the cult of beauty and pleasure that long ago made the reputation of Islam and inspired fascination abroad?

I set apart Ibn al-Rawandi and Azdi, the two authors who stepped even farther into the realm of desecration and disbelief. Ibn al-Rawandi (early tenth century) is probably Islam's only out-and-out atheist. Educated in the Mutazilite school (theological rationalism creating an abstraction of God detached from the world and men), he denies prophecy in general and that of Muhammad in particular. He paints ferocious portraits of prophets, denouncing their faults, their weaknesses, their trickery. He reduces the figures and symbols of the religion to illusions. He scoffs at the dogma of the inimitability of the Koran, revealing the incoherence of the images and connections, pointing out insufficiencies and entropy in a discourse that abuses the allusions to the point of confusion.

Azdi (early eleventh century) wrote in his *Stories of Abu-l-Qasim of Baghdad* the most spectacular desecration of the sacred scene. The almost sadistic call to sexual excess is interrupted by a scatological, coprophagic language that sullies the Kaaba, the

Zemzem wells, the Tomb of Medina, and the Pulpit, which for him is shared.

Hallaj uttered: "I am God," and was decapitated following a trial that lasted nine years; Sohrawardi was executed in 1191 for having denied the end of the Prophecy. But neither Ibn al-Rawandi nor Azdi was disturbed. In a theocentric city, in an era when religious law was the rule, they escaped the doctors' condemnation. Chroniclers who report on the extracts of Ibn al-Rawandi are astonished that he didn't die hanged.

I offer this brief recollection to place Rushdie's novel in an Islamic context and to insist on its extraordinary turbulence. In ancient Islamic culture writers went against the norm by means of poetry and speculation, never with recourse to fiction. Even the extreme passages of Azdi's story do not constitute facts; the blasphemy and desecration are brought about through abuse. They recall the duels of Medina hoodlums. They belong to aims permitted by the oral tradition that are not transcribed. While Rushdie's characters are not content with words alone, they act out the inversion desired by their creator, take it to term, and change the glory of their models into turpitude.

The expatriate status of the writer and the exile of his characters engender a destruction more radical than his own origin. The Islamic tradition is shaken because the writer has been informed by Western irreverence before belief in general. Refusing the duality that would have led him to find refuge in his roots, closing the gap of the internal division, Rushdie returns to the original scene in order to dismantle it and reconstruct its unity while participating in the Western adventure of the death of God.

In his Western assimilation, Rushdie takes responsibility for the anti-Islamic polemic carried like a banner in the name of Mahound, which appeared in medieval Christian works to designate Islam's prophet as a heretic and enemy. It would be laughable to see in this adoption the pledge of an integration founded on treason. I willingly see in it the sign of a sovereignty that seizes any instrument of its creation to do away with its origin. Thus he repeats the discourse of disbelief on a ground where faith is still alive, fascinating those in the West who continue to dream of a return to the center of their relegated faith.

Within Islam, Rushdie's aims therefore concern everyone. He deals with origin and belief in general and their exacerbation in a situation of exile. In spite of the autonomy of classicisms and traditions, in spite of their reciprocal ignorance, the borders are no longer solid and the space of autarky is diminished. Islam has been secularized by one of its own in a European language—that of the Empire, with which the world deals with its affairs. The message was instantly deciphered by the first concerned, in search of material to feed a bellicose polemic confronting two logics, two irreconcilable principles. The opportunity was dreamed of. It was seized on the run. This was the condemnation to death. This disastrous *fatwa* is in itself scandalous, and even more so for those who have gone beyond the primacy of the religion for two centuries and who have instituted a project founded on the distinction among the man, the citizen, and the believer. Must it be recalled that the freedom to write and to create stem from the rights of the person wherever he comes from? Those who stir up political competition between the logics go astray; in truth, throughout history, the principles follow from abolition to abrogation. When the dismissed principle manages to survive, then triumph, regression is introduced. It is appropriate to remind those who claim Islam for themselves that these issues were already theorized by Averroès in the twelfth century.

The mullahs mislead themselves; they ignore that their condemnation of Rushdie is only a situational response that sacrifices a man without any way to dispel the effects of his work, which are already immense. Hasn't *The Satanic Verses* confronted the extremes that Islam has always hidden? Hasn't this work urgently actualized the aporia that has held this same Islam back since Averroès? It is time that the concept of separation, introducing the autonomy of political and religious fields, be reflected and put into practice. Undoubtedly, transforming and surviving this offense, Islam will erect a statue to Rushdie: for having made it undergo the test of reform, the test of adventure, and the ordeal of disenchant-ment. Isn't it true that in confronting attacks without succumbing to them one achieves the potentiality of one's eternity?

But one question remains unanswered. Would I have the right to temper my adhesion to the radical aim of Europe, to the "Western mortgage," if it intended for me the inhuman, the disas-trous, the severing of the community pact, the difficulty of setting it up again? Waiting for another community, I would not like to remain prisoner of an alternative, reducing me to practicing sense-less cruelty or tinkering for survival on the margin of a gregarious world faithful to the point of idiocy in its myths and its rites.

Traps

by Misska

W hy this collection of testimonies four years later? Why so late? And yet the issue seems so simple! An Indian of Muslim origin living in Great Britain writes a novel. One of the characters in this novel, Gibreel Farishta, dreams of Mahound, a businessman in the city of Jahilia who, ready to do anything to succeed, goes so far as to claim that Satan whispered to him a verse to the glory of polytheistic goddesses; he also kept, in a brothel called The Curtain or the Hidjab, prostitutes who answered to the names of the wives of the Prophet of Islam. For the clique of leaders savagely condemning this writer, this text is an offense: a death sentence is addressed to all the planet's Muslims or the community of believers, giving them the responsibility of executing him. The order is given for them to "kill [the writer and the editors] immediately wherever they are, so that no one will ever again profane Islamic society."

My intellectual community throughout the world "naturally" expresses their indignation in the name of writers' inalienable rights, freedom of imagination, secularism, and the defense of human rights. And this reaction, in the name of principles, seems to be evidence in itself. But of which principals is it really a question? Of Western principles, it has been said, of Enlightenment, of a clear, universal, paradigmatic reference: there, that's the evidence. But what is that for Islam? Why does the intellectual community of

Journalist, Algeria/France. Originally written in French.

Muslim origin seem to have taken so long to make themselves heard collectively? Are these categories of thought unknown to us, unrecognized, forgotten? Of course one can always, as our ideologues do, "modernize" Islam "by making Allah's light shine on the West," speak of Islam as a "precursor to human rights," pathetically force a rivalry with Europe regarding the origin of these values. This will never be anything but a mimetic discourse that, in reality, colonizes our history, a history that is now read only through an identical reproduction, the height of it being that this discourse is maintained by the very same people who are declaring a merciless war on the West.

But is it possible to defend Rushdie in the name of these great principles while the very idea of their universality is called into question?

How important really is the destruction of a country (such as Iraq, Palestine, Lebanon) next to the manna of black gold? How important is a people's integrity next to the market? How important is the creative freedom of a Rushdie, or even his captivity, next to the strategic potential of Iran, a Muslim country, yes, but dictatorial and terrorist? It is as if the Gulf War had shaken in us the structure of these values built through pain, at the price of a rupture with the social order, as if in joy, thanks to the discovery of a singular, sovereign thought. Now the issues are clouded.

But to refuse to invoke them to express our solidarity with Rushdie is to take him hostage a second time. There is a trap in which to defend the author would suddenly come to mean an allegiance with the West, with a deceitful God. How can we avoid what can appear as just another manipulation? Can we even avoid it? Hasn't the Islamic defense campaign organized by the imam paradoxically given rise to this religion's most violent attack in ages on the West? How can we find, coming from our point of view, nourishment for the indignation necessary to defend a writer, a blasphemous writer at that, against a death sentence? What recourse can we find within our culture when it is not a question of pronouncing a moral condemnation: how can a religion really not blame those who "play" with its most sacred symbols, like the sacred enclosure of women? One cannot manipulate the revealed Scriptures, the Prophet and his wives whom the tradition designates as the "mothers of all believers," and expect to get away with it. It is rather against intolerance that one stands up, against a *fatwa* issued by an old man struggling with his power, whose legitimacy is questioned by many religious personalities. Isn't this Rushdie affair actually a Khomeini affair; isn't this religious question rather a political question; isn't Rushdie first and foremost a political prisoner? The sacrilege is having restored to life—though still with the distance dream implies—the characters who people our prophetic Truth, like a reconquest of our memory inhabited by their presence, haunted by what our tradition tells us, what it hides. Doesn't the force of Salman Rushdie's novel reveal an imagination and a poetry that delights in unveiling the intimate figures hidden by all-powerful dogma? Isn't there any other way to think of reading the founding Book?

Just one final question: what is the fate reserved for those in Algeria who circulate falsified Korans throughout the country?

The Prey

by Abdel Rahman Mounif

Salman Rushdie is the symbol of a double tragedy: the first facet of this tragedy is its backwardness, and the second, the complicity of the West; because the impasse at which this writer currently finds himself—and which we all risk, today or tomorrow, knowing in turn—is the natural consequence of the absence of civil society, freedom of expression, and human rights. It originates in the historical heritage of the West's relationship with the peoples of the Third World. And note, finally, that this tragedy has been exploited by certain forces.

The Arab and Islamic societies, which were victims of the West's colonization and exploitation, once freed from direct colonization, found themselves at the bottom of the social scale, deprived of the most fundamental conditions for the establishment of civil society. They are characterized by the absence of law and by the domination of patriarchal relations and traditional institutions.

Moreover, the fundamentalist wave that currently holds sway is the result of the organized, merciless, often even savage destruction of the forces that one could hope would play an illuminating role, and would contribute to creating a climate favorable to dialogue, interaction, and in the end, change. But the West has preferred to give its favor and support to a group of regimes that were, for the most part, directly or indirectly, at the root of religious movements,

---

Writer, Syria. Originally written in Arabic.

in the name of the fight against communism, and in order to guarantee certain economic interests, especially oil. The raison d'être of these religious movements is opposition to enlightenment, rationalism, and democracy. The regimes supported by the West devoted themselves to assuring all possibilities for action, financing these movements, and handling all kinds of overtures. There are numerous examples of this, especially in Arab and Islamic countries, and it will suffice to evoke a few of them here.

The Shah of Iran, after the failure of the Mossadegh revolution in 1953, had as his essential goal the suppression of all elements and manifestations of rationalist and democratic forces in Iranian society. His position had the effect of giving the traditional and notably the religious forces the necessary latitude to dominate public opinion. An intellectual and psychological climate was thus created which in turn contributed to these forces' rise to power.

Saudi Arabia, a country under a traditional and backward regime, was for a long time the primary source of support for the fundamentalist movements. This support, which took different forms—political and financial support, protection—far from being confined to the Arabian peninsula, had a worldwide range. It is a secret to no one that fundamentalist forces like those of the Afghani Mujahidin received direct financial aid from Saudi Arabia.

Anwar el-Sadat rose to power in 1970 and he did his best to link Egypt to the West organically, to the point of transforming this relationship with the West into pure and simple dependence. He also had the task of finishing off the liberating, rationalist current that existed at the heart of Egyptian society, and that is why he made "faith" the emblem of his "new" state. He gave free rein to the activities of the fundamentalist forces; moreover, he used them for support to combat and weaken other movements. It didn't take long before fundamentalism became all-powerful on the Egyptian public scene and even threatened its future.

These three regimes just mentioned are creations of the West and are used as models for their relations with other states, notably in the Third World, and especially with Arab and Islamic states. It is thus the West that holds primary responsibility for the policies implemented by these vassal regimes.

The fundamentalist movement left as a legacy by the shah is the fruit of his own policy and consequently that of the West. The revolt of the Great Mosque of Mecca in 1979 was the logical result of a government that had prohibited all political activity other than that of the fundamentalist forces. And the current growth of the fundamentalist movement in this same country is one of the consequences of its West-inspired policy. In the same fashion, when Sadat tightened his grip on all the emancipating and democratic forces, then threw their leaders into prison, he rolled out a red carpet to the fundamentalist forces who were going to take advantage of it to extend their domination and prepare themselves to seize power.

An ancient Arab poet said: "He who makes a lion his falcon's prey/will be chased by the lion during the hunt." This applies to the majority of the West's vassal regimes in their willingness to turn to fundamentalist forces to counter progress and democracy.

This region of the world has known long periods during which law remained the frame of reference. Tolerance characterized social and political relations; dialogue was the means of arriving at mutual understanding; the ultimate arbiter against the spirit of hatred and rejection was logic and public opinion.

Let it suffice to evoke here the trial of Taha Hussein during the first quarter of this century, a trial from which he emerged justified and stronger to continue his mission and spread ideas of civil society: the sovereignty of the law, equality, freedom of opinion and belief. Today, in this century's final decade, we bear witness to an unbridled "campaign" aiming to burn a book that isn't even recent, *The Thousand and One Nights*. One notes that religious fervor has almost become the only judge empowered to authorize the release of books. It is these circles who, for the future, hold the right to pull from circulation works nevertheless written by men of enlightened faith, with the approval of the competent authorities, and for the simple reason that arguments can be found in them that diverge from the message of fanatic fundamentalist forces.

Moreover, when the prohibition of the book, its confiscation, or its burning aren't enough, these religious forces don't hesitate to pronounce decrees of physical liquidation on the writers themselves. The assassination of Farag Foda is perhaps the most recent example, but one mustn't forget that numerous similar operations preceded it, among which Hussein Mroué was one victim. He was an almost eighty-year-old man whose only crime was to present his interpretations and opinions rationally, and to call for dialogue.

The governments that the West set up and continues to protect have established semblances of tribunals that declare death sentences and carry them out. Let's recall the Sudanese thinker who dealt with certain Islamic issues in a personal way, and whom Nemeiry had hung. The same death sentence was issued, a few months before that, in Saudi Arabia against a young man, decapitated because, it was said, he asked questions about certain religious problems in a way the fundamentalist movement considered impious.

Such a situation is the complex result of a long series of accumulated factors, but the central cause may reside in backwardness and fanaticism, and also in the false idea that perceives this same situation as created by the need to defend one's identity against a West that has not left the slightest latitude for dialogue and mutual understanding.

This is why the case of Salman Rushdie appears today as the extreme point reached through persecution, fanaticism, closure, the loss of all freedom of opinion. If Rushdie finds himself personally concerned, of course, as a writer and thinker, all Third World intellectuals are no less so. This leads us to condemn this type of practice and reaffirm the freedom of belief and expression, which remains out of reach of any Sword of Damocles, and any threat against the existence and well-being of people who are accused only of thinking differently.

All writers of the Third World live with the feeling of being the prey, and often the easy prey, offered to totalitarian or backward regimes that neither accept divergences of opinion nor respect diversity of viewpoints. Confronted with such a situation, intellectuals must stand firm and stick together. The West must also revise its positions and finally recognize all the crimes it has committed with regard to other peoples. For these faults, or at least for some of them, it must, in the future, offer reparation.

How to Read *The Satanic Verses?*

by Sami Naïr

Salman Rushdie must be read. And one day, a systematic analysis of *The Satanic Verses* will have to be undertaken. It will be discovered not only that Rushdie is comparable to Joyce and Dostoyevsky, but also that what makes him famous today—his atheism proclaimed in the heart of the Muslim world—is only an effect of a totally derisory period in the global framework of the book. If Salman Rushdie hadn't been Muslim, or at least of Muslim origin, the issue wouldn't have been raised and the book would have passed unnoticed; it undoubtedly wouldn't have even been read—except by the happy few who read brilliant, obscure authors like Malcolm Lowry or William Faulkner. Only here our reading is invoked and conditioned by the scandal—the scandal of the book in the eyes of some, and the opposing scandal, which is ours, of seeing the book condemned.

There are three possible attitudes in response to this book:

1. One can attempt to show the blasphemy by gleaning this and that from the text, particularly virulent passages on Islam from which one can deduce that the book deserves to be prohibited and its author effectively brought to justice. This is the attitude of those who have proclaimed themselves representatives of Islam in non-Islamic countries.

This manner of looking at things, if it must be recalled, is inad-

---

Political Scientist, France/Algerian origins. Originally written in French. This text was originally published in the magazine *Esprit* in October, 1989.

missible. It is contrary to the freedom of the author, the freedom of the reader, and collective freedom in general. Regarding the author, this attitude is equivalent to reinstating the tragic crime of blasphemy that the West, often at the price of a schematic secularism, managed to eradicate over the course of its history. Because there is blasphemy only where there is belief, and it becomes criminal when the religious belief is the state religion. Thank God, one might say, that this is not the case in democratic countries! Salman Rushdie is also conscious of the fact, and this is why he warns the reader of his concept of free thought. "Where there is no belief," he writes, "there is no blasphemy" (p. 380).

Regarding the reader, the attitude seeking prohibition of the book is (I weigh my words) absolutely despotic and totalitarian: under the pretext (unprovable of course since the book lends itself to various interpretations) that a "community" (to be defined: is one Muslim by origin? by self-definition? by the state in which one lives?) is stigmatized in its faith, one prohibits the reader from judging for him or herself. The first argument by which this way of seeing should be combated is of course that no one can force anyone to believe that this is a book to be or not to be read, and those who feel targeted always have the possibility of responding. But this argument should not overshadow the essential: to know the sovereign freedom (in all senses of the word) that the reader must be the judge. Kant said of the modern era, opened by the Enlightenment, that it is the era of humanity's access to the *majority* of judgment, that is, to responsibility and reason against the arbitrary and despotic. To believe that the reader *cannot* judge is in fact to deny him the *right* to judge—and thus to keep him in a permanent state of minority. This theme, obvious for a society whose subjects are formally equal, is naturally not so obvious in states where the majority of the population—the women—are kept in a legal state of submission: great homage, here, is also due to Salman Rushdie for the passages he devoted in his book to this scandal.

Finally, regarding collective freedom, this attitude comes back to subordinate artistic creation to the imperatives of a particular faith—in this case Islam—a religion that no law has recognized, until proved otherwise, to be superior in relation to other beliefs. That the representatives of certain official Catholic and Jewish institutions have declared themselves "in solidarity with Islam" (again: who represents what?), is their business, but should they be reminded that neither Diderot's *Religieuse*, Feuerbach's *Essence of Christianity*, Spinoza's *Tractatus theologico-politicus*, nor Roth's *Portnoy's Complaint* are prohibited today, and that these works, each in its own way, harbor a far more subversive criticism of religion than *The Satanic Verses?*

2. One can also, in response to the book, undertake an inverse and contradictory reading of it. This would be the way chosen by those who try to show that there is nothing in the text that justifies the anger of good consciences or wrath of potential killers. It is the attitude of poor Salman Rushdie himself, a recluse today between life and death. This will also be the reaction of justice, seized by Muslim associations, which invariably respond as the shepherd to his wife.

On the literary level, to try to show the text's lack of offensiveness is, in the end, not very flattering to the author: true creation adapts poorly to half-measures and blunders. Rushdie's book, in its form and content, is a veritable literary success; in it the author realizes an exceptional prestidigitation by which the most contained lyricism, the most naked poetry, the most dramatic monologue, the most salacious apostrophe, as well as the most profound philosophical meditation cross, intertwine, and merge to end in this pure gem of writing, this *Ulysses*, this *Gargantua*, this *Gulliver's Travels*, which is *The Satanic Verses*. Before such virtuosity, never were Rimbaud's words truer: "it is forbidden to forbid."

3. Finally, one can refuse to participate in the argument and send the censors and defenders back to their obsessions. In the end this is the most just critical attitude, since it sees the debate as a false debate—which it really is. But the weakness of such a reaction is brutally obvious: how can one snatch the book from the networks of meaning surrounding it today? How can one, to use the jargon of

modern literary criticism, abstract the extra-textual and contextual conditions of the interpretation of the text from the text's readability? To ask the question is to answer it: it is impossible to read Rushdie without recalling that he is condemned to death for his book.

The fact remains that these three approaches should not hide, or even inhibit necessary access to *The Satanic Verses*. The whole book is a long and superb allegory of our world, beliefs, myths, desires and frustrations, pains and pleasures, existence and future. A profusion of characters and actions around the two protagonists, Saladin Chamcha and Gibreel Farishta, evidences the Rushdian quest for meaning in a world gnawed away at by evil (cancer, which runs through the novel like a living and agonizing obsession). Saladin Chamcha and Gibreel Farishta miraculously escape from a plane crash (the plane is called Bostan, "garden" in Arabic) on their return from India. They are both actors, one at the height of fame (Farishta), the other more discreet since he specializes in voice-overs. Officially dead, there they are, back on the ground, one more or less an angel (Gabriel), the other a devil, Chamcha (Satan, the Arabic Shaytan of the Koran). Through these two characters, Rushdie actually poses a single and unique problem: that of the quest for the meaning of existence. Chamcha's is the most painful quest for authenticity in an inauthentic world where values are totally degraded; he desires good and becomes—in physical appearance—a devil; he desires integration into an adopted society (England) and ends up with exclusion. A problematic hero, he is torn between a deep need for transcendence and the rejection he feels for the religious response. His uprooting and his rejection of his origins are not a trivial negation: they correspond instead to his conviction that he is making a choice of civilization and that the West is superior to the East. But the same movement by which he escaped his origin brings him back to his roots: he is Indian in England and English in India—although people from both places tell him the opposite. This escape-return to the origin ends in a single existential attitude that assumes heretical experience and embodies itself, in the novel, in the demonization of Chamcha's body.

Gibreel Farishta is the reverse, or the obverse, of Chamcha: he leads an intense intrasocial life that borders on debauchery (in the sense Lucian Goldmann gives this term in his beautiful analyses of Pascal). He unscrupulously pursues and achieves success, notably by personifying, in film, the role of the good prophet in low-budget pictures. In terms of values, his are the opposite of Chamcha's: he is the beautiful soul, Hegel's *schöne Seele*, satisfied with his future and submissive to the world's prosaic order. His existential experience is that of the otherworldliness of success *in* the prose of the world. This is why, if he becomes an angel (which, in a sense, he already is because of his name, mentioned several times, Gibreel, the angel Gabriel who dwells in the New Testament as well as the Koran), it is because he managed to embody the behavior of the heralding prophets, in good as well as bad, which is the condition of success in the world's prose. But the bad is deep; if Chamcha, the devil, is confronted with himself at the end of the novel with no true response, condemned for eternity to doubt, Gibreel Farishta, himself eaten away by cancer (the incurable evil of the world), ends by committing suicide. Obviously, these two characters supply the same system of meanings: they are a single character. But between them, the experience of the writer himself is also profiled: Salman the Persian in the novel. Through his impromptu interventions he intensifies the double quest of Farishta-Chamcha; thus he also undertakes, in his own way, the return to the roots, in his case to *Jahilia*. In Arabic, this name means at once origin, ignorance, savagery. It is, according to Islamic tradition, the anti-Islamic state of the world. Muhammad's prophecy came to save this world, by reciting to him (Koran) the truth of God and demanding submission (*Islam*: to submit).

It would be fascinating to analyze this quest of Salman the Persian in detail, and it could easily be shown that Rushdie the writer is religious here in his own way; but it is enough to emphasize that this search, Dostoyevskian in its demands (the return to original purity), is anti-Dostoyevskian in its content: contrary to the hero of *The Possessed*, to Raskolnikov in *Crime and Punishment*,

Rushdie-Salman the Persian ends up with no forgiveness or pardon from fault or punishment. In truth, neither fault nor pardon exists in Salman Rushdie's universe. At the beginning of the world, the most beautiful prophecies concealed their opposites; there is only power and domination, and all the revealed truths, especially those that assume the sacred aspect of religious monotheism, are manifestations of this power and domination. From that time, the difficult question is posed for the author to know whether or not, behind this radical pessimism, one can move in the order of the world thus reincarnated. Rushdie's response is clear: the preaching of origin must be distinguished from what it becomes in the hands of men in search of power. This is expressed in *The Satanic Verses* by the following observation: "With Mahound, there is always a struggle; with the Imam, slavery" (p. 234). A struggle with Mahound-Muhammad, because he erred himself, since the devil placed the verses in his mouth that weakened and contradicted his monotheistic revelation—but it was corrected and thus confirmed that he was not God but a man in prophecy, thus accepting discussion on the content of his revelation; slavery with the Imam—"Loose robed, frowning, ominous, awake: this is the Imam" (p. 208)—who has only a single word in his mouth: kill. Because the revelation once made, codified, standardized, and institutionalized, is no longer questioning, restlessness but material force, an instrument of battle. It is that which pushed Khomeini to preach Rushdie's assassination: more than Islam, it is the bloody magisterium of the Imam that is in question in Rushdie's novel!

Interpretations of *The Satanic Verses* could be multiplied infinitely; but this novel is so rich that no partial reading could exhaust it of meaning. With Salman Rushdie, the world, Western and Eastern, should assume not only the gesture of a deep-seated anger and profound pessimism in view of the history of the two civilizations, but also admit, against the sounds of the sabres and the vociferations of all the censors and potential assassins, that a great, a very great writer is born.

Affirmation of Being

by Okba Natahi

An ethical imperative pushes us toward the following affirmation: one must resolve, today, to write with Salman Rushdie, that is, with what has opened again—with and in spite of him—as a rupture in the field of Muslim religious belief and its existence within reality. This ethical imperative requires us to think in order to elucidate the structural markers within this field, but it also requires that we refuse to participate in the nonsense of blasphemy and the *fatwa* in which an essential question is enclosed: that of the subject.

How can one think of this non-place into which this call for murder has projected Salman Rushdie? Through the Rushdie affair, as in Bosnia-Herzegovina, where one sees the murderous ravages they generate, two registers can be found, confused: that of the symbolic foundation of an individual, that is, the mythology to which he refers, the memory of his ancestors, and that of his citizenship. Everything is happening as if Rushdie were not a British citizen and one could pass judgment on him independent of the laws of the city where he happens to be. In other words, one would have us believe that being Muslim (which is a symbolic reference) is a citizenship, and consequently an irreparable contradiction-exclusion emerges between these two registers. It must be said that one particular reading (both in the West and on Islamic land) of the genealogical question would have to impose the following idea that

---

Psychoanalyst, Tunisia. Originally written in French.

there would be—within the Muslim symbolic foundation—
inescapable, destructive confusion and trampling of the registers of
subject and citizen.

But that isn't all, because it is the subject, as well as the citizen,
who find themselves threatened. Rushdie seized on the importance
of this when he wrote: "When you let someone else's description of
reality supplant your own, that's as good as being dead." I would
add: if you let that happen, you are already dead; you aren't the subject of your own life.

One can only suffer with Salman Rushdie, and be affected by
the ordeal he is enduring, because how can you live when you are
reduced to a small piece of a reality imposed by another? How are
you going to write, think, when you are refused the possibility of a
singular relationship with reality? Rushdie endeavored to transmit
the reading of a symbolic event that seized and affected him internally. This can be understood as one possible way of telling a tale
within a larger tale that some would like to preserve unchanged and
regard as a fetish.

So, once again, how can one be guilty of writing, dreaming,
imagining? In whose name are you refused the right to use an event
from your own mythology in your work? Why would you let this
event, which you've also been told belongs to you, be taken away? It is
only because the goal of a fundamentalist belief (like the negation of
time and subjectivity) excludes all attempts at an individual relationship with a symbolic foundation, and eradicates all transmission that
is not a priori approved and endorsed by the group. How then can
you exist, be the subject of anything, if human and imaginary authorities prohibit you, through violence, from the portion of subjectivity
that comes to you through confrontation with all forms of reality?

Perhaps this is the role one could assign the exile with regard to
the revision employed in the relationship any subject establishes
with reality. Rushdie finds himself projected into the middle of
nowhere, his life is lived in an individual manner, and one can wonder whether he doesn't pay for the cowardice and fear of people on
Islamic land when questioning the concepts of belief, subjectivity,

and reality (the destructive effects of the Ghazali-Ibn Rushd [Averroès] confrontation have endured). Such a reopening through thought presents itself as an "advancement in civilization."

Salman Rushdie was astonished by the violence of the parents who hung signs on their children's bodies calling for murder. Indeed, that says it all: it will suffice to refer to Freud's developments in *Group Psychology and the Analysis of the Ego* concerning the hypnotic state and the phenomena of identification to make us realize the psychic modifications that a crowd has on an individual. So, perhaps we can propose that it is this same hate toward Rushdie that is found unconsciously directed by these parents under the influence of a crowd, onto their own children. It could even be that a certain bond of alienation, in which one makes the other undergo what one has undergone oneself, has given birth to an insane and murderous passion that, without their knowledge, leads these parents to want to turn their children into murderers of thought, which consequently kills the possibility of thought in their children. But it is known that the child can exist as a separate subject only by going through the mortifying impasses with his parents to become an individual: these may be the same children who will write books on Rushdie's books.

The call to murder indicates the weakness of a system of thought in which those who proclaim it are found petrified; because how can one explain that human beings find themselves passively propelled into a logic of murder if it isn't because they have been controlled, alienated, without recourse, before a wall that confiscates their choice for an individual bond with reality?

The Salman Rushdie Case in Turkey

by Aziz Nesin

Being an opponent not only of Muslim fanaticism, but of all religious or ideological fanaticism, I believe it is incumbent upon all intellectuals to struggle against it wherever it raises its head. The work of Salman Rushdie inspired a scandalous image of Muslim fanaticism. Then it was the West's turn, in Bosnia-Herzegovina, to provide the sad spectacle of Christian fanaticism. There, moreover, it is not a question of an individual fanaticism, as in the case of Salman Rushdie, but a collective fanaticism, rooted in the Christian world's unconscious, which caused the deaths of 200,000 Muslims. Through a latent antipathy with regard to Islam, Europeans and Americans, be they Christians or not, non believers or atheists like myself, but ready to react to the slightest violation of human rights, remain unmoved by the martyrdom of 200,000 Bosnians and by the atrocities that continue to be perpetrated in this region. There we

Writer, Turkey. Originally written in Turkish. Aziz Nesin, whose life was recently threatened, completed in the spring of 1993 his project for the publication of *The Satanic Verses* as a "defense of tolerance and democracy": he presented extracts in the leftist daily *Aydinlik*. The paper was seized, and on July 2, 1993, in Sivas grave incidents occurred, leaving thirty-five dead: Fundamentalists burned the hotel where Nesin was staying. According to them he was guilty of having called "the originality of the Koran" into question and having published fragments of the novel. A polemic ensued between the Turkish writer and Salman Rushdie—the latter deploring the cutting up of a text that is not suited to that kind of treatment and its political use, albeit for lay people.

see the greatest hypocrisy of the Christian world's history and attitude, of which the Armenian attacks in Azerbaijan are another example.

So it is this duplicity I have to denounce before anything: man cannot see an enemy in man, whatever his religion or ideology. I met Salman Rushdie in London, through Harold Pinter, and I was one of the first writers in Turkey actually to protest against the fanatical attitude of Muslims with regard to him, as well as against the death sentence pronounced by Khomeini. At the last meeting of the Turkish Writers Union, I suggested that it take the initiative to publish *The Satanic Verses* in Turkish, a project no publisher would dare take on for fear of signing his own death sentence. I drew attention to the offensive aspect of this attitude for intellectuals while justifying the publishers' reticence, and emphasized that to publish the work would require the union of all Turkish publishers. Almost one hundred Turkish writers signed an agreement to assume responsibility for this publication.

Let's remember this point: no writer has the right to refuse the reprinting of a work he has published. It is well understood in law, as was the case of Sartre regarding *Mains sales*; he objected to the ideas put forth in a previous work, but couldn't prohibit the publication of a work that didn't reflect his current thought. The right to read a published work, once released, no longer belongs to the author, but to the readers of the whole world. He retains only the author's rights, which he can refuse to touch in the case of a work of which he no longer approves.

Salman Rushdie commits the greatest possible error by prohibiting the publication of his book for fear of being overcome by Muslim fanatics. This book is actually no longer his; it is part of the global heritage.

I still haven't had the chance to read *The Satanic Verses*. It is not because of its merit or its usefulness that I wish to see it published in Turkey, but solely because of my opposition to censorship. My reaction would have been exactly the same had it been a question of a work of religious nature. No legal obstacle exists in Turkey to the translation and publication of Salman Rushdie's work, and in my opinion it does damage to Turkey's honor to yield to the pressure of death threats. Only when the book appears in Turkey will we be able to judge its quality. Muslims certainly have the right to criticize the work, place blame on it or even oppose it, but in no way do they have the right to kill Salman Rushdie or those who publish his book in Turkey. In spite of the decision approved by a petition bearing a hundred signatures, two or maybe three years ago, at the Turkish Writers Union, the board has taken no steps to undertake the translation and publication of this work. At each meeting of the board, of which I am a member, I bring up the issue, but my efforts remain in vain. All evidence suggests that the board feigns ignorance of the decision for fear of fanatics, and unfortunately, I can't blame them: our friend Ugur Mumcu, journalist, ardent defender of Atatürk's reforms, today fell victim to a bomb placed in his car by fanatics, and unfortunately, this is not the first of this kind of assassination. Many other intellectuals have paid with their life for their attachment to the ideal of progress desired by the founder of modern Turkey.

At the next meeting of our union in March, in two months, I will again request the start-up of the Turkish publication of Salman Rushdie's book. If I cannot get Turkish writers to sponsor this enterprise together, I will take personal responsibility for its publication.

It is the duty of all of us, intellectuals the world over, to combat Muslim or Christian fanaticism without distinction, however and wherever it manifests itself, not only where the media shines its lights.

Of Salman Rushdie and Fanaticism

by Tahar Ouettar

I don't know where to start: with Arab-Muslim history, or with the current situation of Arabs and Muslims? If we turn to our history, we won't find any case similar to that of Rushdie and Khomeini. All we know is that in the twelfth century under the Abi Zayr, a vizier, not a citizen, a vizier of Jewish origin moreover, wrote a book against Islam, the Prophet, and the Muslims. No sentence was pronounced against this Ibn Al-Nagrala—that was his name—no heavy or light punishment, no imprisonment or exile, no death sentence. Its only result was that the philosopher Ibn Hazm, among other Muslims sure of themselves, their faith, and their ability to respond to the situation, wrote a famous text entitled *Response to Ibn Al-Nagrala*. The poem on this subject by the *faqih* of Granada, al-Albiri, is also known.

Today, Salman Rushdie, a British subject who needs a visa to enter any Arab or Islamic country, especially Iran, and who will wait for hours at customs while the validity of his passport is verified, this British subject, Muslim by birth and perhaps a believer, committed a foolish act—let's admit it was foolish. He attacked the person of the Prophet. And instead of drawing from our confidence in ourselves, our religion, and our Prophet to pay the affair no heed or respond in kind, here we are panic-stricken, declaring that he be put to death and that his voice be snuffed out! A legitimate anger

Writer, Algeria. Originally written in Arabic.

has thus been diverted for evil ends, for political use. Neither international law, nor traditions, nor the *esprit du siècle* allows a citizen, a *faqih*, or a judge of any Islamic region to launch a holy war against whomever commits a foolish act against things sacred to Muslims. Otherwise, an army would be needed to eliminate whomever didn't believe in our faith and cast doubt on the sacred. I must confess my shame with regard to these men of the twelfth century who had more confidence in themselves, showed themselves to be more tolerant than our contemporaries, and had more faith in their Prophet than the majority of our believers today.

For Rushdie

by Orpham Pamuk

Everybody, both as a matter of wisdom in general and out of respect for fundamental rights and liberties, must wish for the withdrawal of the condemnation of Salman Rushdie, and must make appropriate efforts to see this realized. It is not just a matter of an assault on the freedom of a writer being an assault on the freedom of everybody; more than that, we must actively want this talented and courageous author to be free. The media do not sufficiently emphasize this latter reason, but we must place it in the forefront of any defense of Rushdie.

The death sentence that menaces him sets in motion a double mechanism and provides satisfaction for two different interested parties. On the one hand, it establishes the image of a "fanatical Islam" in Western public opinion; on the other hand, in Muslim countries and particularly in those Muslim countries under Iranian influence, it reinforces the judgment that the West sees in Islam nothing but fanaticism. It is thus not difficult to designate the main beneficiaries of the very effective diffusion of current prejudices the media are re-enforcing. In the West the beneficiaries are the conservatives for whom Islam cannot change except through force and violence. And on the other side, there are the Muslim fundamentalists who go on maintaining that democracy is an alien institution, incompatible with their religion. The whole Rushdie affair, we

Writer, Turkey. Originally written in Turkish.

should not forget, is a media phenomenon serving low, vulgar, violent, authoritarian, imperialistic, and antidemocratic interests in both of the two camps. We should not therefore fail to see that the tragedy of this individual writer, intrepid and authentic as he is, is our tragedy too. And since we can neither ignore the catastrophes that affect us nor simply leave their solution to others, the Rushdie case is one of conscience for all those who would like to see the advent of democracy in the Muslim countries.

It was only a short time after the disgraceful reaction of the Turkish government and Turkish public opinion in the Rushdie affair that there came about the assassination of Turan Dursun, a former man of religion who had become an agnostic and had written articles against Islam and the Koran; the assassination of Bahriye üçok, a professor of lay Islamic theology at the University of Ankara; and that of Cetin Emeç who, in articles published in one of the most important journals in the country, had declared open warfare against rising Turkish fundamentalism.[1] The perpetrators of these assassinations still remain unknown. In the month of December 1992, in which I write, it is easy to imagine that all of these assassins still at large, as a result of the incapacity of the Turkish government, have surely been greatly encouraged by the scandalous reactions that were brought out by the Rushdie case in this country. As for the Western media and public opinion, which do not react against terrorism until it reaches their own doorstep, meanwhile ignoring murders being perpetrated right next door to Western Europe itself—they too will only encourage future ayatollahs, just as the present Turkish government and current Turkish public opinion are encouraging them.

---

1   To this series of attacks, we must now add the one that took place on January 24, 1993, against the celebrated journalist and writer Ugur Mumcu, who had devoted several studies of the greatest importance to the phenomenon of Islamic terrorism and its connections with the capital.

Guess Who's Coming to Dinner

by Wassyla Raïs-Ali

The tacit acquiescence or, at least, general indifference of a silent majority who have neither condemned nor supported Salman Rushdie casts a harsh light on the Muslim community. Before this multitude of silence, one can first of all consider that the men and women of this community saw in this global production of the condemnation of a writer by the Iranian ayatollah only a banal government act, used as they are to excess, insolence, the arbitrary nature of those who dictate their lives. They said nothing in the case of Salman Rushdie like they say nothing the multiple times they themselves, their neighbor, sometimes a son or a daughter are the objects of not a death sentence, but one of these little vexations that can turn into veritable reclusion. How many anonymous Rushdies and people in hiding are there in our cities?

But that doesn't explain everything. Four years ago, because he wrote a work of fiction portraying the life of the Prophet, a Muslim writer was accused of apostasy and buried alive, the principal hero of a scenario that gives every Muslim the duty and right to kill. And this man, guilty of writing, little known except among lovers of good literature, a subject of Her Majesty the Queen of Great Britain and perfectly at home in London, one of modernity's Babylons, has become in spite of himself, in spite of us, the emblematic figure of the transgression of God's law. Thus, the fear of God and the indif-

---

Attorney, Algeria/France. Originally written in French.

ference toward one's neighbor are blended and reinforced.

One says nothing because one never feels concerned with what happens to others, and because between a man's freedom and the law of God, for the near majority of Muslims, fate is sealed. It must be said, in defense of the silent who maintain a spiritual and serene relationship with the religion, that the law here has been violently broken: the *Verses* are impious. With regard to the others, those ready to fight for freedoms, it seems to them ill advised to defend a profane act. Faced with the law of an enclosed community, such abstract, new rights as freedom of expression, creative freedom, secularism, all of which have so little importance in the daily rhythm of life, didn't stand up: of course the artist is free, but this time he went too far! In societies where a man's freedom is not ontological, but rather granted, negotiated and constantly renegotiable, this time it was refused—by the silent majority and by the governments of Muslim countries, including those who profess a harshly anti-Islamic attitude: even if they didn't formally support the sentence, they didn't denounce it; by doing so they would have given the Iranians the monopoly on the defense of the sacred.

But voices have risen, breaking this terrible silence—isolated individuals, without access to the media and, in general, living outside their countries of origin, pushed by the fear that Rushdie's condemnation would efficiently update the primacy of God's law they hoped to see fall into disuse, eroded by time and by the freedoms the intellectuals, artists, writers, poets, and women stole and took with the sacred, leading a veritable army of ants to the foot of the mountain. And among them, how many are there who don't consider Rushdie an unwieldy hero?

Rushdie is unwieldy, but the affair has arrived just in time. Our task is to accept him, whatever our sympathy for the person, and not only in the name of these abstract, universal rights we so seldom share. We would thus confuse ourselves with those who make him a hero of freedom of expression against Islamic obscurantism which one also knows tends toward the empire of evil. To defend Rushdie by placing his method in doubt or calling it into question would be a way of diverting the meaning from our rendezvous with history. It is in the name of separation of the sacred, which the writer's blasphemous act unveils, a separation placing our connection with our community in peril, that we must take the defense of Salman Rushdie and accept him at our table as a brother.

For Rushdie: Imagination, Fiction, and Freedom

by Hadi Rizk

Condemnation for "blasphemy" claims to have its roots in the respect for God—or his Prophet—and in the desire to rectify the offense. This is precisely the superstitious attitude of the self-proclaimed upholder of the law who is deeply mistaken about the idea of God. The infinitely infinite being, the being that gave rise to itself, could this being be offended by anything? By the same token, could the infinite being be a person, a desire, a will, that forms so many characteristics of the finite? Indeed this *delirium* (which all who have understood that servitude is attained only by those who lead men to desire their own submission and powerlessness, as if it came from their own freedom, have known how to exploit in order to dominate) has belittled the gods rather than making them share in human delirium.

"God's warrior" resembles a finite speck of dust that wants to massacre another speck of dust under the pretext of safeguarding and restoring the infinite! Cruel derision recalls the urgency of *an atheism of the idea of God*: religions' right to appropriate, to reduce the idea of God must be contested and one must prefer the coherence of this idea to the gloomy realizations of the desire for belief.

But there is something more serious, because the imagination, which leads people to picture the ideas they create according to the

---

Philosopher, Libya/France. Originally written in French.

order of their desires and bodies, constitutes, by its power of connection and representation, the most beneficial of abilities. It is a condition, however, that accompanies the recognition of the nonexistence of its objects. Thus this power of synthesis expresses a virtue, a force of spirit, and an ability to invent ideas, feelings, and passions capable of uniting individuals.

Literary fiction thus presents this essential vocation: through the signs of common language, it exhibits that which it poses as a true lie, according to an intuition, which belongs to the creators, the limits of our imagination, in that opaque zone where illusion is constituted through beliefs, prejudices, and images born of frustration of desire and resentment of impotence. The illusion is timeless and fixed, no longer recognizing itself as a sign to decipher, as a cause to investigate. It is up to the writer to dissolve these limits, where the mythology of powerlessness orders subjectivity to withdraw into its idiosyncrasy, into its fantasies and resentments. For this the artist invents a new regime of words, an unbound language that expresses the truth of individuality.

Thus the artist has the intuition of the ideas that make up the imagination of one individual, along with that of all other individuals: the particularity thus made the test of a judgment of common sense, which could be shared by all, to the precise degree that the fiction intervenes with a *second-degree* imagination, a reflected imagination, deconstructed and reduced.

In this sense and beyond a simple defense of tolerance— because the fanatic, who is never more than a powerless lover of tyranny, would sooner turn tolerance to his advantage by claiming respect for his resentment, passivity, and his "right" to demand the hatred of the other, by taking pride in an injured "identity"—it must be reaffirmed that to condemn a writer is to threaten the idea itself of society as a union of free men. Individuals do not live together to constrain each other by building fortresses supposedly to protect the square meadow of their asphyxiated differences: the social bond implies the increase of each person's power to live through his relationship with everyone else.

This is why the condemnation of a writer signifies death for the life itself of the collective, which cannot be founded on the forceful blow of a particular, sad passion, erected as a standard of thought, of life, of conformity to a preestablished model. This negation of the imagination, of desires, and of the feelings of others is an *antisocial violence*, which refuses the liberty of the artist all the more since it appears linked to a social relationship whose cohesion can be assured only through freedom.

To sentence a writer to death—because no form of justice is compatible with such a regression—comes back to identify the peace of the city with the order of the cemeteries. This invalidates any chance that this reflexive expression of the imagination through art can contribute to creating, without recourse to a transcendent order, a common space in which a universal, which merges with the affirmation itself of the *individual*, can be formed in the heart of an *open*, *offered* reciprocity of meaning, image, and fiction.

The Hole Left By God

by Nourredine Saadi

It isn't a mystery if, from the point
of view of the level of consciousness, Muslim societies are less creative than the individuals who
make them up.

—M. Harbi

January 14—February 1989: Begun in Bradford (England),
Muslim demonstrations against the publication of *The Satanic
Verses* continue in Paris, India, Pakistan, Iran, the Maghreb. Five
dead and a hundred injured in Pakistan, people who couldn't have
read the banned book, any more than the thousands who burned it
in Assiout, Tunis, Algiers . . .

February 14, 1989: In a *fatwa*, the Ayatollah Khomeini
"announces to the fervent Muslims of the world that the author of *The
Satanic Verses* is condemned to death." A price is put on his head.

February 16, 1989: The author, Salman Rushdie, expresses his
"profound regrets for the trouble caused for true believers in Islam."

February 18, 1989: Thirty Arab, Turkish, and Iranian writers
sign a petition: "We are all Salman Rushdies."

The thirty were followed briefly, but the renown of the signatories would never overshadow the silence of the others. Hundreds of

---

Attorney, Algeria. Originally written in French.

others refused this battle so as "not to cut themselves off from their people." The intellectuals of what is still called, for lack of a better term, the Arab-Islamic world will have once again missed their chance. In this case, it is nothing more than what is unfortunately so common in our countries: a "banal" political repression detrimental to human rights, well-known territory where one knows that, except for its never-ending cowardice, it freely gathers up the names of authors like so many cards in a library catalog. Here the affair felt the sulfur of scandal, of limitations; it breached this invisible border, the impassable line that barricades our "authenticity"—the religious, the sacred.

In his response to the zealots, Rushdie lucidly set the stakes: "Dr. Aadam Aziz, the patriarch of my novel *Midnight's Children*, loses his faith and is left with 'a hole in him, a vacancy in a vital inner chamber.' I also have this same hole left by God within me. Incapable of accepting the indisputable absolutes of religion, I have tried to fill the hole with literature."[1]

What good is it to linger over the terrain of the theological argument regarding *The Satanic Verses* or over an appeal for the freedom of expression, when the "crime" attributed to Rushdie actually rests on this metaphor, this unspeakable relationship between the void left by God and its filling by the word? Transgressing the taboos, the writer is irremediably captivated, led to "walk in the forbidden spaces."

From "still, she turns," the momentum of all free imagination seems to continue by "still, I write." Such is the lesson of *The Satanic Verses* and the battle proposed to our intellectuals by the Rushdie affair: the duty to live and consider its truth in relation to the reference; a writer, he uses it in his domain: the infinite fiction of writing.

It is the old conflict between writing and its censors, always armed with "realism." Yesterday it was "socialist realism," today the construction of an "Islamist realism." What have they done,

---

1   *Sou'al*, no. 9–10, July 1989.

those who have kept silent during this affair, "so as not to shock the people," if not act "under the dictates of realism?" In another sense of the word, it is "circumstances", but the impact is the same because their evasion, the extinguishing of their own words, leads to the sacrifice of their status as writers.

But between Khomeini and Rushdie, the issue is not about a critical debate on writing. The ayatollah's recourse to armed criticism is totally in keeping with his political thought: a displacement of the terrain of freedom of expression as a human right to an eschatology of rights of God to which every believer would be answerable.

The true "scandal" of the Rushdie affair, its symbolic importance, stems as much from this inquisitorial process of apostasy as it does from the foundations that legitimize it: prohibitions for the individual in the name of the community's beliefs, existence beyond the sacred myth of unitary, indivisible origin. Permanently charged with self-repudiation to exist only for the community's cohesion. For having understood the tragedy of this infernal cycle and considered the possibilities for its opening, Farag Foda fell to fundamentalist bullets. Against the Islamist *universitas*, this unacceptable spiritual terrorism, he waged war in the very heart of the theological dispute for the separation of Umur ad-din and Umur ad-dunya. In *Qabl as-suqut* he wrote: "The first order is a divine message and the second an attribute of the human," words that led their author to his death. So let us not miss this sentence; it is a question that demands an answer, one of the stakes of our history. At its turning point, what is taking place today—here in Algiers we undoubtedly resent it more dramatically—is a valuable example. As necessary as it may be to battle fanaticism with arms, it would be illusory to believe that this battle can be won by the police and the state of exception alone. More important is the "war of words" to bring Rushdie back. In this area, as Foda shouted, "the Arab world's elite holds a great responsibility." He paid the price for the right to think and write that there could not be democracy in the city while theological and political orders were mixed. The word is placed in our home under terror, and the rare politics that become aware of it prefer to resort to understatement and euphemism. It is a question of lay people, and the experience of our predecessors in modernity has shown how bloody the history of the emergence of civil society was, which only allows the rupture with holism and the liberation of the individual, responsible for his own consciousness.

While I write these lines, on November 25, 1992, the writer Rachid Boudjedra has had his life threatened by fundamentalists for having denounced the "FIS of hatred."

Postscript, December 1992: At the time when the Egyptian state affirms its determination to combat fundamentalism, notably by condemning Foda's assassins, his complete works, republished in homage, have just been banned and removed from bookstores on the order of Al Azhar "in the name of Islam, state religion." Once again, against the religious state, politics activate the state religion "in the name of realism," thus symbolically justifying the act of the killers who, moreover, were condemned to death. It is a sad tragedy that the infernal circle of this intellectual, in the image of all who have the courage to proclaim themselves as such in the Arab world, is reduced to silent desperation, even after his death.

January 3, 1993: Here is the text of an article published today in the Algerian daily *L'Opinion*:

The Cairo international fair will host, beginning next January 26, a series of lectures on terrorism and extremism under the title "The Decisive Confrontation," announced the president of the Egyptian Book Association.

Some one hundred researchers, thinkers, members of security, and information teams will participate, as well as former Egyptian Ministers of the Interior. In the same series, current Egyptian Minister of the Interior, Major General Abdel-Halim Moussa, will give a lecture on the "antiterrorist struggle."

The president of the Egyptian Book Association said that a dozen lectures will be organized on the topics of security, sociopolitical and economic questions as well as information issues.

He specified that during these lectures the subject of the origin of extremism will be addressed as well as its socio-psychological repercussions and the role of the struggle against terrorism.

Of note, the last Cairo fair, in which some 25,000 people took part, included a conference on the concept of the Religious State and the Civil State. It was led, among others, by the Imam Ghazali, Islamic thinker Muhammed Amara, and Councillor Mamoun Amara, spokesman for the Muslim Brotherhood.

No comment, because there are indications that, elsewhere, one already knows where the alliance of the sword and the church will lead.

Against the Orthodoxies

Edward W. Said

It is not only a "case," but a man and a book. Salman Rushdie has suffered unconscionably as a human being. In hiding for four years, he has lost his personal life and all personal tranquillity. Forced constantly to move, unable to be with family or friends, he has been a hunted man, ironically in full view of the world, for whom the dreadful Iranian *fatwa*—as vengefully obdurate as it has been stupidly murderous in intent—is an occasional item on the news. No person, no matter what the circumstances, should have to live this way.

But we must also remember the book itself, *The Satanic Verses*. An epic of migration, instability, and volatility, it challenges all conceptions of fixed identity, with a wit and originality that appreciate in time. Why do readers find it hard to accept its energy? Because it overturns not just religious orthodoxies, but national and cultural ones as well. *The Satanic Verses* is a great novel and a great challenge to settled habits, to lazy authority, to unthinking, unconscious assent. Were it the loathsome curse against Islam that it is portrayed as being, readers could set it aside and ignore it. It is attractive, engaging, funny: it offers not a dour unsmiling sermon, but a riotous carnival, and is much more humane than a counterdoctrine or new dogma. So the author *is* the book.

Lastly, Salman Rushdie is a cause for writers as well as for ordinary men and women who live in the formerly colonized world, in

Writer, literary critic, Palestine/The United States of America. Originally written in English.

Islamic or Arab countries and in many other parts of the Third World.

Rushdie is everyone who dares to speak out against power, to say that we are entitled to think and express forbidden thoughts, to argue for democracy and freedom of opinion. The time has come for those of us who come from his part of the world to say that we are against this *fatwa* and all *fatwas* that silence, beat, imprison, or intimidate people and ban, burn, or anathematize books. Rushdie, his book, and his life stand at the frontier where tyranny dares to pronounce and exact its appalling decrees. His case is not really about offense to Islam, but a spur to go on struggling for democracy that has been denied us, and the courage not to stop. Rushdie is the *intifada* of the imagination.

Regarding Rushdie

by Tayeb Salih

I hasten to say that, as a Muslim, I strongly disapprove of the death sentence passed by Iran on Mr. Salman Rushdie for his notorious novel *The Satanic Verses*. I do not know why the Iranians thought it necessary to resort to such a harsh measure, for it is obvious that their decision, notwithstanding their understandable anger, does not do Islam any good, and only brings wide-ranging condemnation upon Iran and raises a tedious novel and its author to the status of a cause célèbre. Mr. Rushdie has, wittingly or unwittingly, become a latter-day Dreyfus.

For one thing, Islam does not need this kind of protection. It is an established religion, some fourteen centuries old, in which over one billion human beings, from all races and religions of the world, believe. It has managed through its long history to withstand attacks and heresies compared to which Mr. Rushdie's contribution looks trivial. Indeed, it can be argued that Islam has always thrived on controversy, and has actively sought to combat ridicule and skepticism with reason and enlightened dialogue. Mr. Rushdie's novel would have passed unnoticed if it had not been for the notoriety given it by the Iranian decision.

It must be remembered that, in the majority of Muslim countries, most people, if they have at all heard of Mr. Rushdie or his novel, have reacted with contemptuous indifference. No governments

Writer, Sudan. Originally written in English.

or religious authorities in countries like Egypt, Saudi Arabia, Syria, or Morocco have gone so far in their condemnation as to pass a death sentence on the writer. Why, then, has Iran reacted so violently? It seems to me that Iran, being a militant revolutionary state, more than any other Muslim state feeds upon and suffers from the age-old fears and prejudices current in the West about Islam. Mr. Rushdie claims that he did not intend deliberately to slander Islam, but wanted merely to be "playful" and "fanciful" within the artistic license allowed by the form of the novel. It is all fiction, he says, not history.

That may very well be so, and the argument would be more convincing if his fictional playfulness had taken place in an environment of understanding and tolerance, or at least an atmosphere of benign curiosity. As these conditions obviously do not exist in the West, it can be said that the novel can only further confirm the prejudices and misconceptions already prevalent. The Iranian Muslims, in their overwrought state, were in no mood to laugh. They could not see the playfulness. They could see only the insults.

Mr. Rushdie is a Muslim, even if only nominally; somehow it hurts more, this kind of thing coming from a Muslim. If it had been a truly English writer, or a French writer or American writer, people might have shrugged their shoulders and said, "Oh, well. What else do you expect from them? It is the usual rubbish." But here you have it from the horse's mouth, so to speak, and indeed that is how quite a few Islam-haters in the West took it and immediately proceeded to use it as yet another stick with which to beat Islam.

Add to this the fact that the book is not a history, comparative study of religion, pretended objective refutation of the truth of Islam, or a travelogue. You have quite a few of these books at any given time. Nobody takes any notice of them. Nobody wanted to pass the death sentence on Naipaul for his book *Among the Believers*. No, Mr. Rushdie's book is a novel. It is fiction, yet in some ways it is more real. You have actual characters, especially when they are thinly disguised, of the Prophet and his followers. You have the wives of the Prophet given their proper names and meant to act as courtesans in a brothel. You have situations, incidents, and dialogue. Very fanciful, Mr. Rushdie might think, but if you do not happen to share his joke, you could become very angry. Indeed, you could become murderously angry. No Iranian—indeed, no Muslim—could have been amused by Mr. Rushdie's portrayal of Salman-al-Farisi-Salman the Persian—one of the earliest and most venerable companions of the Prophet–or of the Prophet's daughter, the revered Fatima-al-Zahra.

It all goes to show that writing fiction is a very serious business. No matter how much of a joke you want it to be, you cannot be certain that somebody, somewhere, will not take it seriously and proceed to act on the assumption that it is dead serious. What does a writer do then? Does he not say what he wants to say out of fear? Or should he insist on saying exactly what he wants to say and accept the consequences?

In Mr. Rushdie's case, the consequences have turned out to be too tragic. His joke has turned into a nightmare. Nobody, Muslim, or otherwise, above all a fellow writer, should fail to feel genuine sympathy and sorrow for him in his predicament. I am sure that the Prophet himself would have let him go free, for it is authoritatively told that when he conquered Mecca, the last and most formidable bastion of resistance to Islam in Arabia, he looked at its frightened inhabitants, among whom were many who had done him great injury personally in word and deed. He said to them, "What do you expect I shall do with you now?" "Nothing but good," they answered, "because you are a generous brother and the son of a generous brother." He looked at them awhile, then said, "Go in peace."

Our Iranian brothers no doubt are aware of the saying in the Koran "Whoever chooses to believe, let him believe, and whoever chooses to disbelieve, let him disbelieve." I hope they will do as the Prophet did, reaffirm the noble and tolerant nature of Islam, and let Mr. Rushdie go in peace. Let him conduct his spiritual and intellectual dilemmas freely and without coercion. If he willingly embraces Islam, then they will have reason to rejoice. And if he freely rejects Islam, that can only be like a tiny pebble slipping away from the side of a mighty mountain range.

Islam and the End of History

by Joseph Samaha

Two writers have shaken the world these last few years: Salman
Rushdie and Francis Fukayama, and both have revealed an intellectual tendency toward the planetary level. *The Satanic Verses*, indeed,
could have gone unnoticed if the Imam Khomeini, who, in his own
words, had swallowed the poison of defeat on the threshold of the
tomb, had not felt the need for young, fresh blood allowing him to
continue his battle. In the same fashion, *The End of History* might
not have caused so much noise if the crumbling of the Berlin Wall
and the dismantling of the Soviet Union had not, after the fact,
transformed this thesis into a sort of prophecy.

When the imam issued his *fatwa* without having read Rushdie's
book, a strange thing happened: a broad current of opinion in the
Islamic world became identified not with the victim, but with the
executioner, inverting the roles. Hundreds of thousands of people
demonstrated and dozens among them died in solidarity with
Khomeini, who appeared as a victim of a Western-Christian plot
aimed at Islam and Muslims. They called for the execution of a man
of the Third World left, making him one of the tools of the plot.
Perhaps it was normal that demonstrations took place, and that they
were violent in regions like India and Pakistan, where an Islam in
crisis finds itself opposed, in a long battle for identity, with an even
more miserable and fanatic Hinduism. The nationality of the writer

Journalist, Libya. Originally written in Arabic.

also undoubtedly explains the exasperation of this very special sensitivity. But the breadth of the reaction and the direction it took didn't cease to grow: the rational formulation of the North-South conflict, taking hold of the industrialized West and the Third World, yielded to another form of opposition centered on identity, giving priority to religious and cultural difference and going back to the theses of the famous Pakistani-Indian Islamist Abu-l-'Ala al-Mawdudi. This is why the widely noticed appearance of Fukayama's article, preceding the book, favored indifference with regard to incitement to murder in the Islamic world; one saw only noise there outside the walls of civilization, while history was coming to an end: why this hubbub? said Fukayama, your backwardness can't trouble the definitive triumph of democratic and liberal values. Nevertheless, this is for us the time of an ennui, which the tumult of people implicated in an end that overtakes them cannot disturb.

In this drowsiness of history, there is no place for the "dawning of Islam." And it is perhaps Khomeini's *fatwa* that best sums up this new "period." The promise of paradise made by Khomeini to the potential assassins, this arm of Islam emerging from hibernation, is undoubtedly insufficient. A few dollars have to be added to that to cover the path to Eden, providing the power to adhere to post-history and enjoy the values of triumphant democratic liberalism. To this sum is added the cost of the operation according to the prices in effect in a market so powerful that it could provoke the collapse of a great empire and announce, with this fall, the end of history. It may not be coincidental that the amount promised by Khomeini to Rushdie's eventual assassin approaches that which the United States offered to whomever could identify one of Khomeini's agents who participated in the taking of American hostages.

When Jean-Claude Barrault writes, in *De l'islam en général et du monde contemporain en particulier*, that "an end of History is hardly possible with the resurgence of Islam"; and as Jean-François Revel explains, in *Le Resurgissement démocratique*, how democracy stops at the walls of Arab and Muslim worlds, one finds the point of convergence between the Rushdie affair and the Fukayama phenomenon.

But the latter makes fun of those who see an obstacle to the end of history in the flux revealed by the Rushdie affair, or an attempt to make it start up again, at the source of the danger, oil; those who weigh the fact that "the young German girls don't wear *chadors* or pray facing Mecca" won't worry about this at all.

There is, once again, an obvious relationship between the Islamic world's discovery of its spiritual mission, on the occasion of the Rushdie affair, and the Western world's celebration, with Francis Fukayama, of its own victory. Both participated in the destruction of what Rushdie represents: the hazy yet rational, leftist expression of the relationships between developing countries and the industrialized West.

Both the defense of the right of freedom of writing and the condemnation of the *fatwa* are obvious. But many among those who took the opposing position knocked as much as they could, within the limits of their regressing conscience, at the doors of the "emerging new world." And none among them can find an excuse within this backward conscience, and that is the sign of a failure to formulate the problems clearly and find adequate solutions.

Hundreds of thousands of people would have had to demonstrate for the defense of Salman Rushdie, even if dozens had to fall. If this had taken place, one would have had a sufficient proof of the "realization of backwardness," of the escape from the "retarded conscience." And that would have served neither Khomeini nor many of those in the West who, in 1989, observed Islamic reactions with irony, then supported the armies in 1990.

Letter to an Inquisitor

by Elias Sanbar

Dear Friend,

Allow me to begin with a reproach. You close your letter with "your faithful and loving disciple." Besides the fact that it is too honorific for an old man who has made the search for the supremacy of the Good the goal of his life, and not some quest for ephemeral honors, it seems to me that you don't do yourself justice at all.

The last trial you judged is a primary example. And I find myself at a loss to answer your request and set forth, in your own words, "the fundamental rules that should govern our battle to serve Morality and the Good."

But I like you and admire you too much to deny your request. So please accept that a humble old man, now at peace with himself, and who no longer fears anyone, addresses to you from his Castilian retreat the essential principles that have ordered his judgment and guided his modest but relentless labor to save his brothers from their blindness and to show them the Good as it must be seen.

Ah! if only those I condemned had known how much I really loved them; if they had only known to what point I tirelessly searched for their salvation; if they had only imagined the suffering I felt when I saw them tortured.

Some of the terms I am going to use will seem inappropriate, others, shocking, even offensive. You will ask yourself how can such

---

Historian, Palestine. Originally written in French.

procedures be used to serve the holy Cause we defend. But it is not you I will teach that Evil is combated with Evil and that, in the mission entrusted to us, no place should be left for that which only perverse souls invoke under the appellation of "acceptable rules" or "reign of law" or even "respect for the physical integrity of the accused." All that matters is overcoming the tentacular Beast who takes possession of souls and blinds the spirits of men by cloaking itself in the robes of "free arbiter," "freedom of opinion," and other travesties of chaos and perdition.

Here is my advice:

Know that only the ignorant and the least skillful among us have recourse to lies to consolidate their accusation. The first directive I will give you—but do you really need it?—is always to make the distinction between the liar and the forger. The first fabricates falsehoods with falsehoods while the second creates falsehoods from the truth. Be a forger, never a liar.

Take good care of the people who support you. They will always ask you to do more. Glorify them for that, and engrave in their spirits, naturally inclined to offense, the idea that they are the living and collective expression not of the good in general, but of the absolute Good. Reduce your role to be only the voice of the people and the spokesman not of a caste, a group, or an order of society, but of Good itself. Thus, any opposition you encounter will appear as the expression of an Evil just as absolute, with which no compromise is possible.

Your action targets the future. To dominate the future, fix the past. Never evoke the old days to back up your arguments; instead, reduce them to a sort of lost paradise, for which there is nothing but glorifications of origins and regrets about the perversity of the present. Guard against men's temptation to want to rethink their past, reduce the time to an idyllic instant, and make your battle a relentless quest for the original purity nonexistent today.

Words are formidable because each person can fill them with his own desire. Be economical with words, which doesn't mean stingy with discourse. But always use the same terms; hammer instead of speaking. Practice and teach the use of the single word to indicate multiple and various situations. Always use the word "unicity" to say "unity" or "uniformity"; your audience will always be inclined to prefer their collective integrity to diversity, because that will reassure them regarding their fate and will spare them from wondering.

Your task is gigantic and you must be sure to play an active role in it. To this end, seek favor among the repentant, renegades, former slaves today converted from the ideas you are battling. They still hold the feeling of having to redeem themselves and will look for redemption by relentlessly attacking your enemies.

Always opt for simple ideas. Their simplicity will appear as the herald of their force, their obvious truth. For this, you will be able to count on men's natural tendencies to be lazy in judgment and tired when faced with difficulties. And your audience will be only more satisfied to be guided by he who thinks for them.

Combat the power to associate words, ideas, and things, because in spite of what I've already told you, your partisans may succumb to this temptation. To do so you must never ignore this train of thought—it can rise before you when you least expect it—but precede it by spreading your own associations and reasoning. Leave no void in the spirits of those who surround you and anticipate their questions.

Finally, distrust deceived crowds. They always have a natural tendency to come back to reality and demand fulfillment of your countless promises. You cannot keep them eternally occupied with trials; you will have to alternate by offering them compensation and material improvements. By giving satisfaction to the animal instincts of our poor natural condition, you will also buy the time necessary to uncover new enemies.

I was tempted to write you ten rules; no one is sheltered from the workings of the Devil. But the Spirit is there that immediately made me anticipate the sacrilege I was preparing to commit. My letter has only nine; you will state nevertheless that I express only eight. Because the last is the one you will formulate yourself and destine for your exclusive use. Take guard, it is the most terrible. It bears on what you will say when, your mission completed, you are alone, faced with yourself.

Lamentation

by Leïla Sebbar

I am dead. I led an exemplary life of unconditional and daily obedience to Allah. I led an endless and heroic battle at home and abroad. Allah pardons me this journey onto impious land, it was profitable, I have returned to my city, and I have pursued the glorious battle, merciless. I have succeeded, in the name of Allah, that his name be praised, the Merciful, the Persevering. I have hunted out evil everywhere, without respite. I have vanquished the demon wherever he hid, in the most indecent languages, in the most inaccessible regions, in the least suspect homes. I commanded, in the name of Allah, and I conquered where I carried weapons, leading the way, with the most faithful companions and warriors.

I am dead.

I deserved to be at the right hand of Allah.

And here I am in Satan's chamber for eternity, on the dark journey of the most miserable of the miserable. Allah is just. What I did in my life on earth, in the final pious and sickly years, I would do again, I shout it out, but no one is there to here me, I am alone in the Darkness pursued night and day, there is no longer night and day, by the laughter of Shaytan, alone with me alone.

I am dead and Allah is just.

What I did to deserve such a fate, no one wants to tell me. The Devil repeats to me, through the length of hell, that this punish-

Writer, Algeria/France. Originally written in French.

ment is as exemplary as my life itself.

I am dead and I am not in paradise. Punished for having proclaimed in the face of the earthly and celestial world a *fatwa* against a blasphemous writer. Me, punished. And he will not go to hell. Allah is just.

But he didn't receive me on his right. I am not admitted next to Him whom I loved, defended, imposed on all men and women.

So, He didn't love me.

He preferred the Other. He whom I condemned for Him alone. For his glory. Allah doesn't love me. Does he love the one who doesn't know Him? The one He doesn't know?

Allah has condemned me to wander eternally in black solitude. Allah is just.

A Test of Humanity

by Youssef Seddik

Ancient Muslim historians and chroniclers, beyond all suspicion as to their "fidelity to the message of Islamic faith," reported these facts: "A companion of the Prophet, Abdallah Ibn Abi Sarh, was one of the Prophet's secretaries; he recorded the revealed verses from Mohammed's dictation. At a certain point he renounced his commitments toward the new religion and returned to Mecca to rejoin his family. He confessed to them having often tricked the Messenger *by writing something completely different than what Mohammed had ordered him to inscribe.* On taking Mecca the Prophet condemned him to death, but 'Othman, his illustrious companion and future caliph, interceded on his behalf and Mohammed pardoned him. Later, the same 'Othman, entrusted with the caliphate, would name him governor of Egypt!" (See, among other chronicles, the Baladhun's classic *Futuh al-Buldan*, in particular the appendix entitled "The Question of Writing.")

The time has not yet come to defend the cause of a writer against fanatics of the all-religious in the name of human rights and individual freedoms. Let's continue to draw arguments from the spaces of forgetfulness and deletions these people have carefully constructed around the events, characters and texts. A Muslim able to read the founding Texts of his religion would be blind if he didn't see that the Koran's originality is to be found essentially in this

---

Writer, Tunisia. Originally written in French.

vulnerability of the prophets faced with the divine: Abraham doubted God's ability to bring the dead back to life, Joseph coveted his benefactor's wife, Mohammed allowed himself to be caught in the snares of satanic discourse, the time for a test of humanity. And all that is stated clearly in the sacred Text. Egyptian Naguib Mahfouz prolonged the tale of all these "prophetic deviations" through the novelistic imagination in his famous *Children of Gebelawi (Awlad Haratina)*. Salman Rushdie, seized by the "devil of poetry," as the Arabs said in the times of Mohammed, did the same thing. And Mohammed would have surely pardoned him, as he pardoned Kaab who opened the poem about his conversion to Islam with a long evocation of his profane loves, and read it before the Prophet.

For Rushdie

by Habib Selmi

Arab culture does not constitute a monolithic whole: following the example of the other great cultures of the so-called Third World, it remains diversified and plural and shelters well-differentiated movements. And contrary to what one might be led to believe by numerous contemporary writings, one can find in it, notably since the beginning of the century, many luminous moments associated for me with the names of several bold thinkers such as Taha Hussein, Taher Haddad, Farah Antoun, Shibli Shmayyel, Adonis, Sadik Jalal al-Azm, and others. Let us not forget the no less determining role played by several poets and film and theater directors. The problems they expose are fundamental, narrowly linked to reality: the separation between religion and the state, the relationship between the present and the "glorious" past, the condition of the individual in modern society, the importance of freedom and reason, East-West relations, the attitude of the intellectual vis-à-vis power.

In the past, the visions were coherent and the goals pursued fairly clear. It was often the West (rationalist, secular, humanist, in love with freedom) that served as the model and ideal for the sought after evolution. The ideas spread by Arab thinkers—for which some of them suffered—provoked visible changes in the mental and cultural structure of society. That of Taha Hussein, for example,

Writer, Tunisia. Originally written in Arabic.

who was condemned for his work on anti-Islamic poetry, inspired a long echo in cultivated circles.

Thus, the Arab intellectual had, especially in the first half of this century, a certain presence and influence. But these have diminished considerably over the course of this decade, before the fundamentalist and obscurantist wave invading the Arab world from Sudan to Tunisia, from Egypt to Algeria (it seems intellectual influence in general is diminishing all over the world at the end of this century). What happened to Salman Rushdie because of his novel—which I read with interest and enjoyed greatly—is only a new symptom of this phenomenon. What did Arab intellectuals do to support Rushdie? Nothing but a manifesto in the newspaper *Libération* (which wasn't reprinted in any Arab paper or magazine), signed by a few intellectuals living in France. Other than that, there was a small gathering on the Trocadéro esplanade; and one notes that the majority of people mobilized were of Maghrebi origin.

The fact is that the intellectuals who defended and still defend Rushdie are for the most part Western, even if some are doubtful about this appellation. So what should Arab intellectuals do today in societies where the forces in power are working to marginalize them? One must, I believe, above all, keep from despairing; there is really nothing worse that discouragement, despair, the chronic feeling of impotence. So we must remain attentive to the beat of real life, avoid falling into the trap of self-censorship, and not be afraid of dealing with subjects held as taboos like religion or sexuality (my last novel, *Photograph of a Dead Bedouin*, was banned in certain Arab countries on the pretext that it was "licentious"). Finally, we must write with all the sincerity and freedom we are capable of to express clearly our rejection of Arab regimes that refuse to see change in the world and that seem to have taken, despite what their propaganda machines affirm, the side opposed to human rights, freedom, and democracy.

Is that being idealistic? Perhaps, but what is an intellectual worth, from the Third World in particular, if he isn't attached to ideals?

Farag Foda Was Assassinated

by Antoine Sfeir

Farag Foda was assassinated. On a Cairo street one day in June 1992, this Egyptian intellectual who wielded humor and sarcasm was felled by the bullets of an Islamist commando. He who carried the attack to the heart of these groups of sorcerer's apprentices, denouncing their methods, their dress and dietary codes, their actions, had to fall to the blows of these men in black who use Islam for the strictly political ends of seizing power.

Farag Foda was assassinated. His voice was silenced.

What could be more simple for the Islamists than deciding and proclaiming who are the good and bad Muslims? "If you're not with me, you're against me." Farag Foda was a bad Muslim who had pushed presumptuousness to the point of extolling, in this Egypt inhabited by 40 million Muslims, the radical separation between religion and the state with all that it implies in terms of freedom and belief. His voice had become bothersome, like that of Mahfouz, or even that of Salman Rushdie. After the failure of their strategy of violence adopted in the seventies and eighties, the Islamists renounced the taking of power by armed force. They chose to make local attacks on different domains of public life (focusing on legal, economic, medical, judicial, journalistic, and publishing institutions), with the goal of Islamizing society at its base. Thus these Savonarolas of Islam were able to play the role of censor not only on

Historian, Libya/France. Originally written in French.

the religious level, but in every sector in daily life. And with the bothersome voices multiplying, they wanted do something to slow it down: this was Rushdie, then the Creil schoolgirl's veil affair, and then Mahfouz and Foda.

And this strategy is working: how many Western editors are afraid—the word is not too strong—to publish Rushdie? The strength of the Islamists is that—a blessing of imperialism and colonialism?—they know our culture perfectly while we are completely ignorant of theirs. Once again, they play on the terrain of knowledge. And when some of their associations snatch up *The Satanic Verses* to create a scandal, they know perfectly well that, being totally ignorant of Islam, of its vision of man, society, and the world, no Western judge could make a judgment in the end.

Foda's assassination did not shock his Egyptian compatriots. The Orient's turbulent history has been throughout the centuries and remains today a string of massacres, assassinations, attacks, crimes, and murders.

It will never be repeated enough: to blame the Islamists, to denounce their actions and lies is not an attack on Islam. On the contrary, it is to take up the defense of Muslims themselves, the Islamists' first if not only victims. It is to protect them against those who above all don't want to hear any voices but their own and who, wanting to make Islam a taboo subject, would be happy for this religion to be the object of rejection. Their will to control intellectual life and all that is said, written, or has anything to do with Islam, their relentless attempts to impose a single morality indifferently draws religious and political barriers, which, if overstepped, they say, gives them the right to punish. They set themselves up as judges like the Pharisees of the temple, to capture the power, assure it, and protect it.

Salman Rushdie calls himself a nonbeliever and there is the renegade! He proclaims himself a British citizen and here is the rigging of an antiquated neocolonialism. To be silent is to accept that the voices of Mahfouz, Foda, and Rushdie be silenced, and that Rushdie become a living dead man obliged to hide to stay alive. To be silent is to become a consenting accomplice of the Islamists and their methods! To be silent is to cover up all the murders committed one day in the name of the Most High, he who tells us in his commandments: "Thou shalt not kill!"

To be silent is to resign oneself to the suppression of life in the name of the religion that is supposed to be love, supposed to be life. To be silent, finally, is to accept that the horror begin again.

And this time you won't be able to say you didn't know!

The Glowing Ember

Anton Shammas

1. The translator of *Kitab Kalila wa Dimna* from Persian into Arabic, in the middle of the eighth century, was a Zoroastrian, or a "fire worshipper" as the Arabs then would say, who had translated himself into Islam and became Abdullah Ibn Al-Muqaffa'.

Ibn Al-Muqaffa' brought into Arabic literature, besides one of the finest Arabic styles ever, something that was never there: fictional narratives and fire of the imagination. The Islamic, Abbasid establishment of his time, still jittery over the enormous power that had fallen into its hands, was preparing itself for the lofty mission that new rulers—caliphs or otherwise—often tend to revel in: stifling the imagination, monopolizing memory, and inventing the past. His *Kalila wa Dimna*, questioning the conduct of tyrants and rulers, drew the attention of Al-Mansur, the second Abbasid caliph, it would seem not because of its subversive constructs but, rather, because it had released the genie of the imagination from the sealed bottle of the memory-oriented Arabic literature.

Lured by the flames of power, he chose to put his magical style at the service of an oppositional voice. Then he found himself, in his midthirties, on the perilous side of the political map. And when he went to see Al-Mansur's new governor of Basra, his employers worst enemy, many people saw him enter the governor's palace, but no one saw him come out.

Writer, Palestine/Israel. Originally written in English.

The sordid details of his execution are often omitted from Arabic literary histories, though the Governor promised him, according to certain accounts, "a death whose details would be circulated by caravans." But we know that the limbs of Ibn Al-Muqaffa' were consumed by the same element that he had brought into Arabic literature.

2. In one of the most captivating tales of *Alf Layla wa Layla*, a book without which Salman Rushdie would be hard to imagine, King Yunan orders the execution of the sage Duban, whose magical powers have triggered the envy of the grand Vizier. The sage, rendered powerless now in the face of the lethal *fatwa*, asks the king's permission to go home in order to leave instructions for his burial, to donate his medical books to one who deserves them and, in particular, to bring the king a book entitled *The Secret of Secrets*, for safekeeping in the royal library.

"What's the secret of this book?" the curious king asks. "It contains countless secrets," the sage says, "but the chief one is that if your Majesty has my head struck off, opens the book on the sixth leaf, reads three lines from the left page, and speaks to me, my head will speak and answer whatever you ask."

When the sage, faithful to his promise, returned to the palace, his head was struck off and placed on a platter. Then it told the king to open the book. The king opened the book and found the pages stuck. He put his finger in his mouth and—some thousand years before *The Name of the Rose*—wetted it with his saliva and opened the first page, then the second, until he turned seven leaves. "I see nothing in this book," he exclaimed at the sage's head. "Keep opening," the head told the king. And he did, and the poison of the blank pages spread through his body.

But these things seem to happen only in tales, and modern writers, unlike the sage Duban, have lost the two-way relationship with power and can no longer strike back. And those who have the power are not affected anymore by the deadly glare of the blank page; instead they order the erasing of a written page, the de-writing of a book, the execution of an author, without leaving their courts.

Salman Rushdie's book is full of words. Almost as may words as Shahrazad's. However, Shahrazad's king was willing at least to listen. Rushdie's is a king who does not listen *in principle*. The voices he hears are not of this world. He lives in a monophonic, monobiblic world; a world that has a single voice and a single Word.

It's a sad set-up, and there nothing much we can do about it. Except for one thing: speak back. Otherwise we will all become self-poisoning, silent blank pages.

3. A certain *hadith*, attributed to the Prophet, speaks of a time that will come when the believer will have to cling to his faith as he would to a glowing ember in his hand.

Abraham's Guest

by Salah Stétié

I will undoubtedly never read a line of Salman Rushdie. Scandal isn't my cup of tea, as one might say across the Channel. Well, what a detestable title: *The Satanic Verses*, tenacious yet profit-minded at the same time! Today, in spite of its appearance, Islam has become so fragmented throughout the world—whether on the political, economic, or sociocultural level—that there is not, in my opinion, any kind of audacity capable of dealing it a death blow from a great European capital.

But that isn't, nor ever has it been, the problem. It is that of people's freedom, the freedom that all prophets, one after the other, have—or will—come to guarantee. It was Omar, the great caliph sage, one of the closest of the close to Allah's Messenger, who affirmed it. This indignant question to one of the officials in the grip of his caliphate is, in fact, attributed to him: "How did you make slaves of men whose mothers raised them free?" Among the recognized rights of the free man inevitably figures the freedom to express oneself. Islamic society, in the great moments of its history, was, as is known, open and tolerant. "Tolerance?" said Paul Claudel. "There are houses for that." Paul Claudel is as deeply mistaken as all those whom fundamentalism threatens internally: tolerance has no house; it is a space: a space the size of man's freedom.

Man can be victim or oppressor. He can be so by action of the

---

Writer, Libya. Originally written in French.

sword and by action of language. One who persecutes by language ends up being persecuted by the sword. And that is intolerable.

And that is rejected, it seems to me, by Muhammad himself. One knows the famous *hadith*: "Help your brother," said the Prophet, "be he persecutor or persecuted." And as he was asked how to come to terms with eventually helping an oppressor: "It is up to you," he said, "to prohibit him from persevering in his opinion." It is first compassion that speaks: "Help your brother."

But here—which goes just as far in this direction—is an admirable story taken from the *Bustan*, the prestigious work of Saadi, a Persian poet and marvelous Sufi mystic of the twelfth and thirteenth centuries:

It is told that for a whole week no guest appeared in the dwelling of Khalil (the friend of God, a nickname given to Abraham by the Muslims). Waiting impatiently for the arrival of a pauper, the blessed Prophet neglected to take his meals. He went out one day, to look into the distance: his eyes perceived, at the end of a wadi, an isolated traveler, like a willow in the middle of the plain; the snow of the years had whitened his head. Abraham ran joyously to meet him and offer him hospitality. "Stranger," he said, "you, who are worth more to me than the light of day, consent to share bread and salt with me." The traveler accepted and entered into the host's dwelling, where he came to know generosity. The servants lavished the humble old man with attention; the table was set and all took their places; but at the moment of reciting the *bismillah*, only he remained silent. Abraham said to him: "Stranger, you who have lived long days, I do not find in you the feelings of piety that adorn old age. Before taking your daily meal, shouldn't you invoke He who provided it?"

The old man responded: "I would not know how to adopt a rite that the fire worshiping priests didn't teach me."

The august Prophet understood that his guest professed the hateful faith of the Magi. He chased him like a scoundrel whose presence sullied the purity of his home. But Serosh, the angel of the Most High, appeared to him and said in a voice full of menace:

"Khalil, for a century I have given this man life and subsistence, and it takes you only one hour to curse him! Because he prostrates himself before the fire, do you have the right to refuse him the shelter of your arms?"

Serosh, help!

Reading Rushdie

by Nadia Tazi

Salman Rushdie has undoubtedly been unique in the annals of literature. His sharp originality working at the meeting point of several different worlds, eras, and conflicts points to a certain eccentricity, or rather, a quite exceptional position, which he occupies, and which was not really properly appreciated before the "Rushdie affair" itself came along. It is more a matter of art—an art of living as much as an art of writing—than of something merely given. One does not easily just happen to get born a British citizen of Indian origin and of Muslim faith, all at one and the same time. However, one does not simply become such, either, in the sense that one would ever attempt to construct such an identity out of some sort of eclecticism and a more or less accomplished cosmopolitanism; rather, an identity such as this is unclassifiable a *priori*. It is neither truly Indian nor is it Muslim in the proper sense of the word; it is English only by adoption; and it is actually of Kashmiri-origin, Pakistani in spite of itself... Or, according to various other points of view, this same identity of Rushdie's is too oriental for some, not Islamic enough for others; it comes out of the secularized Bombay school with all of its imperial style; it is overloaded with dialectics, flesh, gods, and History with a capital "H," not to speak of the various postmodern myths which attach to it. Or again, if one wants to diminish its strangeness in a negative kind of way, it can be called

---

Writer, Morocco/Spain. Originally written in French.

external to everywhere and to nowhere at the same time; it is hope-
lessly dissociated and unable to base itself either on any binding
attribute or any assured meaning; it is even unlike its own self—or
any other selves as well—and yet it cannot for all that remain the
same without somehow exalting itself as another at the same
time...To say all this, in a word: it is not able to renounce or discard
any part of what it is, and so it is obliged to fall back on the art of
writing fiction capable of effecting its liberation and bringing it glory.

Rushdie willingly presents himself as a "translated man," and it
would be wrong to read alienation into this, making an obligatory
appeal to the dominant culture. Actually the formula refers to
something else entirely: to an immediate tendency which does not
correspond to any existing type or archetype and which signifies the
impossibility of persisting in adhering to any single identity, even
one's own original identity. The divergence is there from the start,
and something of it always subsists which cannot be properly represented and which is not exhausted by the one common name. It
only converges in the need for a leap beyond the logic of belonging;
it is necessarily overwhelmed, profaned, and then inserted into
another relationship—all in all, its very pertinence is called into
question: according to one's point of view, Rushdie appears now as
an orphan, now as the son of several mothers like his character in
Shame; indeed, he appears as a minority member of the most
restricted of minorities, as if he were enclosed in a system of
Chinese boxes, one inside the other, as he himself has said. And all
this becomes even more complicated by the various disconnections
that are inherent in any exile. With regard to the English language,
for example, far from being a foreign language "corrupted by its
colonial origin," it is, on the one hand, the common language or lin-
gua franca of polyglot India as well as of the world's "global village"; and, on the other hand, it is the very fluid, transitive material
of a Joyce and a Pynchon, eminently capable of modulation. Finally,
though, if it is absolutely necessary to link the character we are concerned with to an origin, it must be linked to a threshold: to "the
Gate of India," the cosmopolitan metropolis of Bombay at the first

moment of its independence, itself heir of an old and mixed tradition, itself "translating," even as it absorbed even the British stratum and harnessed its own very ductile type of syncretism to modernity...

Rushdie comes to us, then. Certain people say he is obscure; all of him imposes itself at one and the same time, inappropriately. There is a multiplicity, or, better, a multitude, which one senses is maintained in a certain disorder and lively incongruity and which extends itself in loose and floating threads, cheerfully exerting itself in order to express at great cost the excesses, whether inscribed or engraved, of *The Satanic Verses*, that whole series of hardships that are exposed; and in order to express a growing discordance as well as a rare solitude. In a certain sense—by some stroke of fate, of force, or of genius—an identity such as this proves itself (it is not so much multiple as it has willed to be multiple; it is never simply something given; it is always renewable, always able to become something else). "'I' is a word of order," a performative act. More exactly, this wandering constellation has found its place, and has given rise to a sovereign work (itself invulnerable, untouchable). Last name: Rushdie, from the Arabic *rashid*, which essentially means coming to maturity. First name: Salman. Naturalized writer, novelist, short-story writer, and, occasionally, essayist. Not one of the least of his qualities is the substitution of another form of fidelity in place of a quest for identity which is essentialist, purist, and, in a word, integralist. This other form of fidelity of his is a commitment to writing which assumes the risks of plurality and multiplicity at the same time that it reflects and expresses an authentic intimacy with the culture of Islam. (In this sense, Rushdie has not only infringed upon religious law by his blasphemy. What cannot be pardoned him by many is his withdrawing from the *Umma;* his refusing to be one whom the community forms; his maintaining of a singularity on the margins of that fraternity; and his challenging of the basic meanings on which it is based. Moreover, he does all this without even appearing before this same community or addressing himself to it in particular; and he does it at a time, moreover, when the collective mind of this community is more closed than ever before, and also at a time when its great resentment is joined to the further fact that his origins, after all, do lie within it.)

The truth is, according to Rushdie, that at the outset his work profited from the germinal power of exile; his life was interrupted twice (once in Pakistan and then in England). He has had to be assimilated to the Fall, so much does the loss of home, in its radical and irrevocable nature, seem to affect the self and to undermine the foundations of certainty. It is joined to the loss of faith, and that in turn only aggravates the original uprooting, compounds the dissociation, and brings about a definitive crossing of a line and a making of a definitive commitment to something else: if God is dead, exile is then to be wholly consummated as far as the Umma or Transcendence are concerned. Trying to cauterize the wound left by the absence of God simply means that, henceforth, writing itself becomes one's great Cause; it becomes an end in itself which is substituted for belief; and it also takes on a universality of rights. While in the beginning the motive was aesthetic (explicitly Proustian), and Rushdie insistently spoke of "restoring a past," little by little, in the degree that it ripened and carved out its own niche, his writing became imbued with a new dignity, or even (from another point of view) there became re-established through the exercise of a certain ingenuity what was believed to have been lost: as such all this imposes itself as an act of faith; it provides a new destiny for the identity and it gives direction to a life crowned by posterity. Suddenly, however, it is no longer a question of searching for the "phantom" of authenticity; nor is it any longer a question of aiming for the discovery of meaning, or of trying to look for an ideal reality such as the one Proust was searching for behind all his various "signs." What becomes important is neither the truth of the narrative nor memory in and of itself, as he seemed to have declared. Suddenly the exile is no longer the same grey figure, defined in *alio* or by the base neutrality into which one has invited him to disappear— to be a hanger-on, sustained by a promise and by a cult of the past which calls forth nothing but pious celebrations (as pious as the discourses of the states that have been left behind).

To support a work the exile looks out at an absolute horizon which both requires search and demands movement; he assimilates himself to a new frontier, being "on the air," or alternatively, if one wishes, he brings out into the light of day all the day's clippings as they affect writing, favor a style, or contain a story. There might be clippings with great significance, or orders which affect critical or political functions (whether referring to the past, to God, or to the world around us). Or there might be internal, schizoid-type clippings which induce both fantasizing and encourage a certain kind of style. Or there might be an "ontological rupture" which assumes that "the world is incompatible" and that there is no longer any place for reconciliation, fulfillment, or the re-connecting of the chaotic and discontinuous.

In questioning dogmas, and in linking appearances with the changes that are immanent in them, whatever the culture involved might be, the line of exile writes itself; it incessantly frees itself; it invents; it gets out of itself; it liberates itself from any idea of ever trying to go back. If Rushdie insists on the new, on novelty, this is not so much because he wants to affect a militant modernism (which would be as obligatory for him as political radicalism); it is rather to express the unique position which by definition is his— and also to express some of the tension inherent in occupying that position. He wants the kind of variety or variation that has an affinity to the freedoms which the avant-garde arrogates to itself (and reciprocally the avant-garde wants that same kind of variety or variation too). The exile is precisely the one who, faced with the authority of the Same and the One, declares himself an alien and a stranger everywhere in order to be in a position to respond to separation, to the necessary transformations, and to the passage that is to be realized. "We all cross borders; in one way or another we are all immigrants."

And indeed this latitude is necessary—along with an insatiable taste for story-telling—in order that all the voices contained within

Rushdie might emerge to express themselves. "Myriad voices flow through him," and he lets them pursue him, press against each other, and co-exist side by side in an equality of rights. There are voices of prophets and of seers; there are calls of archangels or, indistinctly, of actors; there is Delhi Slang and Oxonian modulations. There are obnubilations, delusions, and counterfeits; clamors of crowds and of wars; apocalyptical cries raised around a smoldering goat. There is spiritualism, demon worship, possession, and fantasizing. What is heard is a voluble and willingly histrionic kind of banter, which resonates with passion and is expressed in the language of a virtuoso. The entire fictional output of Rushdie can be perceived as a collection of voices which he has called up from nearly everywhere, all in a perspective of enjoyment. Confirming the pluralism of the author, these voices juxtapose themselves with his language of a foreigner; instead of standing behind them like a puppeteer, his voice joins in with them and is heard among them. Far from deploring the dissonance of all the various voices, he collects dissonant voices, that is to say, he is pleased with the different voices thus placed side by side, even though they are unrelated to one another; he cultivates extravagant and grotesque voices for their own sake. He revels in hyperbole and promotes provocation, as if he were the one primarily charged with guarding the whole patchwork vitality; he experiences it as a richness; it is one of the lucky chances of our times. It is as if he is just one more participant in the whole chimerical spectacle of hybridization and riot of color, always wavering between actually speaking or just making noise. To write is to be at a festival, a sonorous carnival; it is to direct a contemporary choir such as characterizes the great metropolitan areas but also "the second world" in the conception of Bakhtine, the world where bodies have retained their gravity, far away from mere shows, semblances, and the hawking of merchandise, and where the people lead the way...It all has its farcical side, its excesses, its formidable state of health and all its ambivalences; and its also points towards a utopian kingdom filled with combinations of all kinds, a kingdom of abundance and of perpetual renaissance.

But these voices are not limited to embodying the very special originalities and singularities of Rushdie; they circulate and—internal demons or echoes of an immense History—they also embroil the consciences of his principal characters. Whether it is Salim, or Shamsha, or Farishta, or Allie, or Aisha, we are always talking about so many split or interlocking subjectivities characterized by so many yawning gaps—by so many split personalities, who allow themselves to be invested by more or less foreign presences. They are "translated" beings, often translated by their misfortune; they are afflicted with madness or prophecy. They are conditioned in various ways by exile, or, more simply, they are marked by their dreams, unless, as actors, they simply happen to be captives of the game. On this edge of the fantastic Rushdie amuses himself playing with various intermediate states (and creatures); he specializes in generic confusions and metamorphoses which confuse identities. Even better, he willingly suggests that all these desubjectivizations take place in moving and sometimes dangerous proximities to one another. (It is well known that prophecy borders on madness, just as it borders on poetry—which disputes with it its own power of enchantment. Prophecy also risks falling back into the political alone; all the pathos of Muhammad resides in a similar teetering on the heights.)

The voices get all their various wires crossed; they pass from one vision into another like so many agitations of possible new identities; on occasion they intersect, enter into a certain resonance, and sometimes even give rise to monstrous mutations. There are in *The Satanic Verses* those who explore all the aspects of emigration; there is a diabolism of exile which can issue in the loss of reason, in perversion, and in death. But does this mean that is where the evil is to be found? The danger would rather seem to consist in the denial of any variety or variations, in the lack of even any possibility of them whether by becoming lost when faced with the horrifying void of the loss of faith (Farishta); or by denying the separation or by trying to force incompatible continuities (Shamsha). In effect, variations, like creation itself, cannot be justified; they rest on sole possibilities or on the power of individuals. Variations are never merely given, they are never simply inscribed as a model to be reproduced or a trace to be reinvested, they can fail, bringing in the wake of their failure negations of self or the kind of diminution of strength and power which is to be found in sadness, resentment, or madness...From this, in *The Satanic Verses*, at the end of the journey, comes the edifying return of Shamsha to his native shores, to the bedside of his dying father.

The Rushdie affair has had the notable effect of breaking the pledge which is constituted by writing as such; it has done this by ignoring the novel and instead, under the cover of a disastrous politicization, restoring the old reactive-type schemes which Rushdie disavows. Behind his name is to be discerned the old opposition between the East and the West. The citizen who should have not only rights but privileges lurks there; "the Muslim apostate" is associated with the name; the suffering man who should retract what he has said is discerned; and, finally, there is the author. Those who have paid any attention at all to the work itself have been all too rare; they would at least have done the author some justice thereby. But this author must surely be taken seriously when he himself defines the affair as a confrontation between those who read and those who do not read; and when he amalgamates today's society of the spectacle with the credulous and fantasized masses, with the intellectuals who remain indifferent, and with tyrants.

Apart from his novel, however, Rushdie has come to signify something else. He has come to be no more than an intermittent rumor, a cause to be made use of, or at best a rather spectral victim with whom one may well sympathize while meanwhile considering him already under judgment. What this means is that, in putting *The Satanic Verses* aside, as those who have condemned him have done, the others, perhaps in spite of themselves (but who nevertheless do know only fragments of the work or who simply may have heard about it) have in effect made themselves the accomplices of all the prejudice against him. In this way he is stripped still more of the infinite power of resistance which a book can have. But there is more yet: for this is a really first-rate writer who has thus been struck and scorned; this a man (as far as that distinction has a meaning) who has been driven into a sterile imprisonment and exile. The spell is already broken, and forever. *The Satanic Verses* are already the prisoners of Rushdie, as he himself is the prisoner of his work; between the novel and the author, as between the author and his readers, there will always be a hovering threat, a noxious gas, a halo of evil omen, and a ring of suspicion—all of which will fatally compromise what should have been the innocence of reading a book. Curiosity may either be motivated to approach the text—or to stay away from it—by a false fame or by all the sinister associations which now surround it. The perception of the book will never be neutral; any study of the text will inevitably be perverted, if only imperceptibly and in a veiled manner.

Even banned, however, this book will remain. (Its humor, density, and extreme sophistication should at least be noted!). A book cannot be killed; it lives and dies on its own. Once the "vases" are "broken," the fragments of life spread throughout the world; voices escape, going their adventurous ways; and there are always encounters, mutations, and festivals of the spirit.

In This Strange Voice in the
Words of the Tribe

by Habib Tengour

I was asked to take a position on the Rushdie affair. My first reaction was not to respond: irritation at an outside solicitation; the din of the media and perverse publishing games, while every day Palestinians, Bosnians, and other people are being massacred. The anonymity of these deaths torments me gravely, not knowing how to testify to their path on this earth.

It is hard to explain, but I won't shy away from the request. I won't step forward under the mask of a literary text. Thus I give Salman Rushdie my support. Through my writing I have already testified on behalf of the writer of *The Satanic Verses*.

In my life—that of numerous others whom destiny made Algerian—torn between the country and wandering and the uncertainties of daily life, where is the protection? Where will the ransom be?

The earth is too vast to settle down. It shrinks from sight when the verb tries to muddle the path.

Question: Is Salman Rushdie English or Muslim?

What does that mean?

Indeed, no one among us ignores the knot of belonging in the depths of our souls. He who unties it exposes himself! Islamic fundamentalism hardly has a sense of humor. Any text that breaks with

Writer, Algeria. Originally written in French.

it is publicly discredited. He who writes it weighs all the risks. Physically leaving the geographical territory is no longer protection. That is definitely the catch. The tribe refuses to let go of one of its own. The latter no longer handles his words, but that doesn't matter. He is in the common imagination.

What can we, what can I do for Salman Rushdie?

Because he publicly returned to God, there is no longer a crime to the group. But who is to evaluate this Muslim position? How to repeal the Ayatollah Khomeini's *fatwa* (it has value only for the imam's partisans)? Can we influence our governments so they intervene with the Iranian authorities?

This seems like quibbling and wooden language, but what to do?

Here, we are a few to try to hold on . . .

To continue to write, with or without support.

What One Faris Chidyaq Said to the Maronite Patriarch in 1855 about Salman Rushdie (Regarding a Question of Censorship)

by Fawaz N. Traboulsi

The story of one of the first martyrs to freedom of thought in contemporary Lebanon deserves to be told. It maintains a bizarre relationship with the theme of this anthology.

We are in the 1820s, on a Mount Lebanon delivered to the arbitrary state of the power of the feudal lords and the church. A large revolt of Maronite peasants had just been crushed by the forces of the Christian Governor, Emir Bashir Chihab, aided by his Druze ally, Sheik Bashir Joumblatt. Elsewhere, the Maronite church was catching up with Rome which had launched its counteroffensive against the ideals of the French Revolution and Protestantism. The Patriarch Houbeiche thus issued two edicts against the "Protestant heresy," forbidding his subjects all commerce with Protestants under pain of excommunication.

There would be more than one excommunication for As'ad Chidyaq, a teacher of Arabic and Syriac supporting the ideas of the Reformation, who didn't deprive himself of propagating them. On the orders of Patriarch Houbeiche, he was imprisoned for six years in the dungeons of the patriarchal seat in Qannoubine in north

Historian, Libya. Originally written in French.

Lebanon, where he died in 1831. The church having been completely mute regarding the fate of its prisoner, Chidyaq's death wasn't confirmed until a year later when an English emissary, on the intervention of the master of Syria, the Egyptian Ibrahim Pacha, obtained permission from Emir Bashir to investigate on site in Qannoubine.

A whole generation of intellectuals was marked by this first martyr to the freedom of speech and thought. And a certain number among them found the courage to express their anger and revolt against this inquisitorial act. A century later, Chidyaq's story still circulates in the villages and hamlets of the mountain. The Lebanese émigré poet Gibran Khalil Gibran, author of *The Prophet*, was undoubtedly inspired by this rebellious character against the arbitrary nature of feudalism and the religious obscurantism in two of his works in Arabic, *Khalil the Apotheist* and *Youhanna the Fool*.

As soon as As'ad's death was confirmed, his younger brother left the country in an exile from which he would never return. Faris Chidyaq (1804–1887), whose whole life was troubled by the tragic fate reserved for his brother, would be one of the great figures of the *Nahdah*, the Arab renaissance of the nineteenth century: a man of letters, grammarian, lexicographer, translator of the Bible, and editor of the first modern newspaper in Arabic. He is primarily known for his masterpiece, *Al-Saq 'ala al-Saq* (*The Leg on the Leg*) written and published in Paris in 1855. This text, subversive for its courageous ideas, satirical character, and long erotic passages, through which Chidyaq reconnects with a long tradition in Arab literature, was published only in clandestine or expurgated editions since it constituted one of the founding texts of modernity in Arabic.

This work, which does include some fiction, is for the most part an autobiographical narrative, articulated around descriptions of cities and countries visited by the author during his long exile, penetrating and critical observations of their morals and customs, and flashbacks of his life and past experiences. They give rise to countless digressions in the style of the Arab storyteller: tales, speeches, "séances of discussions," reflections, conversations, social plans, comic and satirical remarks, poetry, tables of homonyms and synonyms, and so on. The stories of Chidyaq's travels to France and England distinguish themselves from those of other Arab travelers of the period by a sharp consciousness of social phenomena. The author is disappointed to see that the conditions of English and French peasants and workers aren't better than those of his compatriots. His libertarian rebellion and his sharp sense of social justice lead him to the adoption of a radical socialism. Faris calls for the abolition of ecclesiastical and feudal privileges, the separation of church and state, freedom of thought and rationality in religion. Exasperated by their Puritanism, he separated himself from the Evangelists, for whom he had translated the Bible, and he approached an agnostic position. *Al-Saq*, conceived as a homage to two feminine entities—the woman and the Arabic language—and written "as if he himself had been a woman during a period of his life," places its author among the pioneers of feminism in the Arab world. Long before Qasim Amin, he wrote, "There will never be a liberation nor a renaissance of the Orient without a liberation and renaissance of the Oriental woman."

The work of Chidyaq is too rich and too "postmodern" in style to be summed up in a few lines. I will say no more about it. It can be read and appreciated in French thanks to the scholarly and imaginative translation of R. Khawan. This version however lacks some pages in which Chidyaq evokes the tragic story of his brother. This story amounts to eight pages in the original Arabic (the tome is 742 pages in translation). In fact, the question of expurgating the text had already come up on its publication. The patron who had financed its publication had demanded it, but on the author's insistence, these passages were included. The publisher and translator of the French version were not as indulgent. That the same pages that appear in the original Arabic in 1855 were expurgated in Paris in 1991 seems a concerning act of censorship, all the more so since the translator's only explanation is in invoking the fact that these pages do not correspond with the idea of the novel as a literary genre. He says in a note on page 194: "The chapter, in the original text, actually closes with a long appeal by the author, an autobiographical point in which, almost renouncing fiction as a figurehead, the novelist accuses the church of having, in contempt of humane and divine laws, morally tortured his own brother to the point of driving him to the brink of death by an inquisition of another age and an unjust incarceration of six years. He takes advantage of it by enumerating in almost Voltairian fashion thousands of offenses to the religion committed by the very people who pretend to serve it."

The book's jacket informs us that the work is a "veiled autobiography," and we are warned from the first page of the introduction that the hero's name, Faryaq, is simply a contraction of the author's name, Faris Chidyaq; and suddenly the translator wants to convince us (p. 19) that he has transformed the text into a novel, by alleging numerous additions that have nothing to do with autobiography: unpublished material by the author, lexical notes on rare Arabic words, poems, strange stories, myths about jinn and other details. The omission of these passages is perfectly comprehensible: certain among them would be almost impossible to translate. But in any case the text is in no way a novel. The episode concerning As'ad Chidyaq is only one episode among hundreds of others the author reports about his life, his birth, his village, his education, the exile of his father to Damascus and his death, stories of his travels: Cairo (where he marries a Syrian woman from Egypt), Malta, Cambridge (where he translates the Bible and loses a son), London (where he acquires British citizenship), Tunis (where he is invited by Ahmad Pacha, the reforming bey), and Paris. From his time in this capital we learn the name of the doctor who cared for his wife, and those of his associates (his encounter and friendship with the Algerian Emir Abdel Kader, his attempts to meet Lamartine, and so on). All these references which cover dozens, even hundreds of pages are also "autobiographical points" that, not being in accord with the idea of the novel, should have been expurgated.

But it is rather their content that could explain the omission of the eight pages in question. There, the author does not accuse the Maronite church in general; he names two prelates: blaming Bishop

Boulos Masaad, "the maternal cousin of my brother and me," who was the patriarch's secretary at the time of the As'ad affair; he also places the responsibility for his brother's death on the Patriarch Houbeiche. In addition, to illustrate "the thousands of offenses to the religion committed by the very people who pretend to serve it," this impertinent, revolutionary Maronite enumerates a whole lineage of popes and prelates of the Catholic church as promoters of anathema, schemers, blasphemers, hucksters, corrupt, debauching, fornicators, poisoners, and torturers.

Whether or not one agrees with Chidyaq's ideas on religion, whether the information and events he cites regarding the papacy and the Catholic church are true or subject to contention, they are part of the text and deserve to figure in the French translation. Their appearance could certainly have drawn hostile reactions from certain circles, but is that a convincing reason to deprive the readers?

While waiting to be able to read the complete translation of these passages, we can at least cite Chidyaq's ardent appeal for freedom of opinion. Challenging the Maronite Patriarch Houbeiche's right to imprison his brother, he argues that if his brother was accused of having committed a crime, the punishment would be a matter for the Ottoman civil authorities, who should first judge him; on the other hand, if it is a question of a crime of opinion: "Let's suppose that my brother had argued and polemicized about religious affairs and maintained that you were in error, you mustn't kill him for that. You must refute his proofs and arguments with language or written words."

Written 138 years ago, this sentence of the great Chidyaq could today, without changing a word, be thrown in the face of those who pronounced the criminal *fatwa* against Salman Rushdie, as well as those who have supported it, justified it, or accepted it by letting it pass in silence!

I will add in conclusion that in 1861 Faris Chidyaq converted to Islam and took the name Ahmad Faris.